EAST OF SIAM

A chronological list
of Mr. Franck's *travel books*

A Vagabond Journey Around the World
Four Months Afoot in Spain
Tramping Through Mexico, Guatemala
    and Honduras
Zone Policeman 88
Vagabonding Down the Andes
Working North from Patagonia
Vagabonding Through Changing Germany
Roaming Through the West Indies
Glimpses of Japan and Formosa
Wandering in Northern China
Roving Through Southern China
East of Siam (French Indo-China)

There was a young lady of Laos

EAST OF SIAM

Ramblings in the five divisions of French Indo-China

BY

HARRY A. FRANCK

Author of " A Vagabond Journey Around the World," " Roving through
Southern China," " Vagabonding Down the Andes," " Four
Months Afoot in Spain," etc

ILLUSTRATED WITH A HUNDRED OUT-
OF-THE-WAY PHOTOGRAPHS BY THE
AUTHOR AND WITH A MAP SHOW-
ING HIS TRAVELS IN INDO-CHINA

D. APPLETON-CENTURY COMPANY

INCORPORATED

To

THE HOSPITABLE FRENCH COLONIALS

PROLOGUE

THOSE of us who had the good fortune to take part in that great adventure known as the World War can scarcely have failed to notice, among the many kinds of French colonial troops, some little men in khaki and brass-topped mushroom hats, most of them with black teeth. It was not until five years after the Comedy of Versailles that my perpetual wandering over the face of the globe brought me to the land from which they came — Annam, "Kingdom of the Eminent South." There was not only the motive of satisfying, by seeing them at home, the curiosity raised by these little brown men in the French army; as far back as I can remember I had felt inquisitive toward that strangely shaped spot on the map, that slender country which drips like a stalactite of candle-grease down from the southeast corner of China.

Besides, during all my two years of roving about the once Celestial Empire I heard frequently of the wonders of the ruins of Angkor in Cambodia. So one day in early January, a propitious season, I dropped down to Saigon, visited those astounding remnants of the past, and returned overland all the way to Canton. Later, toward the end of April, I brought my family to Hanoï for a month of Parisian change on the way to Yünnanfu, and took advantage of the opportunity to journey through Laos, largest, most interesting, and least known of the five divisions of France's Indo-Chinese empire. So in the end I traveled not merely the length and breadth of Annam but saw all five parts of that dumb-bell-shaped land east of Siam which the French consider their most important colony in the Far East.

So unusual was my luck during those travels that only my overwhelming modesty has kept me from entitling this unpretentious tale of them "Hobnobbing with Kings"; and so very interesting a trip was it to me personally that in the face of my hard-earned knowledge that our ever more herd-minded general public is as fearful of the unknown and the unfamiliar as the most superstitious of wild tribes, and would much rather read of the deeply tourist-trodden streets of Rome and Paris, I have insisted on performing this unassuming task.

Those two well separated months were more than a mere vacation from Chinese travel. To jaunt through French Indo-China is to see a sample of what China itself would probably be under European control, white-man rule — were any nation powerful enough to accomplish that many times larger task — as Formosa suggests what it might be under the Japanese. I hope I have at least made it clear that Indo-China is not in any sense China, but the living line of division between two ancient and very different masses of Oriental civilization, even as its name signifies.

HARRY A. FRANCK.

CONTENTS

ILLUSTRATIONS

ILLUSTRATIONS xiii

ILLUSTRATIONS • XV

ILLUSTRATIONS xvii

EAST OF SIAM

EAST OF SIAM

CHAPTER I

EQUATORWARD

ONE of my jaunts up-country in Kwangtung Province dragged, and I missed the French liner at Hong Kong. Luckily the *Panama Maru,* bound on one of the trips around the world that bring her back to her home berth in Kobe every seven months, also made Saigon her next stop. We sailed early in the afternoon of one of those brilliant days that double the blue intensity of Hong Kong harbor. The Japanese freighter served no free wine with her meals and had none of that interior ornateness that suggests the Paris Opéra gone to sea. But perhaps for that very reason she was more successfully mopped and dusted; and the Nipponese atmosphere aboard was more interesting than the cosmopolitan scent of the fortnightly Messageries steamer to Marseilles. True, she made barely ten knots an hour. But the French could hardly have served better food; the two "boys" were unspoiled, and Captain Ichikawa was a friendly little soul, even inviting me to make free of the chart-room. The quiet, all but noiseless, efficiency of his crew was a startling contrast to the incessantly shrieking chaos of Chinese craft. The three or four first-class cabins opened abruptly upon the dining-room rather than upon the deck; yet even the baby in one of them was Japanese, like everything and everybody on board except myself, and seemed never to cry. A lone Japanese would certainly not have been more courteously treated on an American boat than was the sole non-Nipponese being on this.

It is often said that the Japanese are not individualistic in personality. There were certainly as many types as passengers, however, gathered about our table. The energetic son of Tokyo, now in business in Saïgon, who shared my cabin, was tall and handsome, as agreeable a companion in cramped quarters as any American man of commerce, and he spoke both French and English perfectly. On the other hand the peanut-headed undersized youth across the table looked and acted like the "nut" his cranium suggested. Then there was a medical graduate going out, with the assistance of the mikado's government, to practise upon the Japanese laborers on the coffee plantations of São Paulo—who one evening managed to tell me in near-English that he had read, both in my tongue and his own, all the published plays of Eugene O'Neill. He would give much to see them played, he added, but had never seen a Western drama on the stage. The two women who sometimes graced our board were as different as were the quiet brown and gorgeous-figured red kimonos they respectively wore on such occasions. Even the half-dozen officers rounding out the tri-daily gathering were divided by as distinct lines of demarcation as are their colleagues of any nationality.

Gently we rolled southward, with a drift to the west, over a densely blue tropical sea. It grew too warm, first in our open-on-the-dining-room cabins, then on the deck itself. Summer curtains and awnings appeared; electric fans took up their duties once more, and in one cabin at least spun all the night through. The third morning brought one of those lazy perfect days when loafing in a deck-chair

seems the nearest tangible approach to heaven. We sighted
the coast of Annam that afternoon, hazy, almost mountainous, apparently as treeless as China itself, and had it always
in sight thereafter, a lighthouse winking at us all through
the evening. If possible the weather was even more peer-
less on the fourth day; the sea, flat as a floor, blue as if
saturated with indigo, was covered with light ripples that
made it look like a vast piece of watered silk.

Unfortunately it had not turned tropical quickly enough
to save one of our fellow-passengers. A youngster who
had taken pneumonia during the crossing from Japan to
the coast of China died during the third night. Another
child had gone the same way, two days out of Nagasaki,
and many in the general quarters below the main-deck still
had heavy colds. This boy of three had been the only
son of one of the score of families going out third-class to
Brazil. The funeral, at which the captain personally requested my presence, took place on the fourth evening. Most
of the passengers and such of the crew as could be spared
stood about a kind of altar improvised on the poop. First
the captain, then others stepped up and bowed low before
this, repeating some sort of litany that ended with the
sprinkling of incense. Last of all came the parents, to go
impersonally through the same ceremony. They did not
weep, though their drawn faces showed that they had given
way in private to grief to which it would be bad Japanese
form to yield in public. The Buddhist service was as
simple as it was quiet, wholly un-Chinese, without a sob
or a loud voice, even as the little box wrapped in the flag
of the rising sun floated away astern in the moonlight. It
was as much that atmosphere of the uselessness of giving
way to the inevitable, I think, as the fact that I had left

behind in Canton a three-year-old son of my own, which made me so depressed that I was still pacing the deck at midnight.

By that time we had anchored at the mouth of the Mekong, near a lighthouse. Off again at dawn, I sat, after a last salt bath, wearing the few garments that Japanese custom permits, in a delicious tropical morning breeze as the steamer made its way up a tide-water river with dead-flat banks of low, apparently uninhabited jungle stretching as far away as could be seen in any direction. The stream was as wide as the misnamed Pearl River at Canton, but clean and blue, flecked here and there with a tiny boat top-heavy with its clean-white pointed sail; and it wound so constantly all the fifty miles from the mouth to Saïgon that we headed again and again to every point of the compass. The low jungled banks gave way to brown plains with patches of palms, low thatch houses, and what looked like haystacks scattered far and wide. The inevitable Socony plant appeared, and some distance beyond we ran down at last the flat evasive town, the steeples of which had be-trayed its location, now to port, now to starboard, again over our stern, like the ears of some startled jack-rabbit trying in vain to dodge its pursuers.

There was a reminder of Martinique about the already sweltering city half seen beyond a wharf dotted with white helmets. I had rather expected to be called upon as in-terpreter, but the fat, bored-with-the-tropics French doctor who sweated up the steep gang-plank knew some English, though he spoke it more laboriously than did our captain and several of my fellow-passengers. There was some-thing amusing in seeing these people of two nations which have no overwhelming love for us of the English-speaking races forced to use our tongue in their intercourse. In his perpetually bored way the port doctor was very insistent that every Japanese on board show proof of a recent vaccination, though only my cabin-mate was landing; but when I began to do likewise he waved me politely aside and took my word for it in a way that implied that as a Caucasian I was in a class by myself. An equally courteous, if less bored, official pocketed my passport and gave me the freedom of the half-way station between Hong Kong and Singapore.

Before the dock lay behind me I regretted the habitual lack of foresight that had led me to bring only an extra winter suit instead of half a dozen white ones, and was praising the superior wisdom of the thoughtful wife in Canton who had insisted on my taking along a tropical helmet in January. Luckily other travelers seem to be in the habit of misjudging the winter climate of Saigon, and Chinese tailors at the foot of the principal street are used to correcting such oversights in a hurry. Though it was Sunday they promised me a *complet* or two of duck within two days, at twelve *piastres* each—and while I am on the subject let me mention that the piastre of Indo-China is equal to the "Mex" dollar of Hong Kong and China, averaging a little more than half our own, and not given to fluctuating with the franc.

The Rue Catinat, grilling now beneath the late morning sun, drew me inland. Mingled with its all too plain evidence of propinquity to the equator was that of a considerable relationship to Paris. Between window-displays that might have come almost intact from the Rue de la Paix, black and brown fellows in red fezzes, locally known as Malabars, squatted in booths raised well above the narrow sidewalks—money-changers, sellers of tobacco, and the like.

Here and there a Hindu merchant stared out into the white light of the gently yet perspiringly mounting street. Here Sunday was no British Sabbath. Annamese waiters bustled about the marble tables of hotel cafés well peopled with white men and women instantly recognizable as French. Business as usual seemed to be the motto of all but the most important establishments. Yet even the diaphanously clad Oriental strollers of various origins shuffled along in the narrow streak of shade before one row of shop-fronts.

Saïgon's main street flowed out before long into a sun-stewed square with a cathedral trebly hot in its red brick garb. The view from its tower across the well streeted city, almost forested above the section of wharves and commerce, would have been worth a less perspiring climb. Farther on, the American to whom I had a letter lived in simple bachelor splendor in a low house of thick walls and disproportionately large rooms. Languid with long tropical residence, this former captain in the Philippine constabulary who now represented our great oil corporation seemed to recognize no pastime except the lolling in a reclining-chair with a cold drink within easy reach. I am no suitable companion in the consumption of British whisky—that could be had in this stronghold of its French rivals only by something closely resembling smuggling—and I drifted down toward the port again.

All Saïgon sizzled now in noonday repose. Not merely on Sunday, I later learned, are all offices, all shops except those of the heat-impervious Orientals, closed from eleven until two for the daily siesta. One of the shocks due the rare hurried business man or tourist from the West who drifts into Saïgon is to find it virtually dead daily from the early French lunch-hour until the sun nears the western tree-tops. Here and there an enervated rickshaw-man

dragged his empty vehicle slowly behind him. A few dozing
Hindus, a fez-wearer or two asleep with open eyes on his
haunches among his wares, were visible in the unbroken
rows of shops. Heaps of coolies reposed under the trees
of other streets, under raised porches, their thin legs tangled
together, open-mouthed like dead fish. Otherwise the streets
were empty, not a European was outdoors. All the governing race were asleep in the breeze of electric fans, such
garments as they still wore pasted to their bodies. Had
one of them spied me wandering the streets at this hour
I should no doubt have been taken for mad.

The new-comer soon finds that he too is better for his
siesta, and that there is nothing to be gained in going without
it, for there is little that he can do and no one whom he can
see. No wonder the white residents all seemed tropicalized,
if I may coin a word greatly needed in any attempt to
describe life in Saïgon. Two or three hours of broken
nap, and they must get up again, wearier than ever, spirits
and body alike languid and stiff; for work or its substitute
begins anew. One by one each leaves his house, jumps into
a rickshaw with burning cushions, and goes to shut himself up once more in office or shop. There only the tropically experienced and the well-to-do can manage a comfortable coolness in which those not used to the equator as a close
neighbor can either think or work. The streets begin again
to swarm with *pousse-pousses* — for in spite of the all too
evident fact that it is pulled the French insist on calling
the rickshaw a "push-push," perhaps in memory of the
converted baby-carriage from which this now wide-spread
vehicle was fashioned. Thinner, more washed-out in appearance than more northerly men of their laborious calling, the pullers nevertheless charge madly down upon every
"... .... China. But here they are more

orderly, a trifle cleaner perhaps, with an air of being kept
closely within bounds by foreign rules as well as by the
climate. Less cheery than their Chinese prototypes, they
seem more optimistic. The rickshaw-man of Indo-China
holds out both hands at the end of his run, as if expecting
such a fortune for his services to one of the dominant
race that one hand would not hold it. But his optimism
rarely materializes, and no dispute with one of the race that
rules over his land seems to be worth the effort in such a
climate.

Meanwhile, unable to adapt myself so quickly to the do-
nothing of tropical midday, I had wandered to the end of
the town. It was the same old France, even this far afield—
outwardly imposing buildings generously adorned with
plump naked females in stone, and within, dusty bureaucracy where the buying of a postage-stamp is a transaction,
with much bookkeeping involved. Saïgon is in theory the
capital of all Indo-China, though in practice the governors-
general have all preferred somewhat more northerly Hanoï.
Their palace here, like the cathedral, the Postes et Télégraphes, the Municipal Theater, and all the other examples
of elaborate French architecture misplaced in the tropics,
is set off in its grass-covered square at the end of some
broad avenue. Palatial European residences with an atmosphere of lavishness emphasize the conspicuous scarcity of
native buildings, whether towers, temples, ancient gates or
palaces, or high-class dwellings. For that matter the native
residents seem few, at least until one reaches the outskirts,
though Saïgon was an important center before the French
came.

Farther out are big brick barracks, where young French
soldiers conscious of no color-line mingle freely with colonial troops ranging from black Malgaches to pale-yellow

Annamese. Wide tree-lined roads lead on to the Botanical Gardens, in which men and women Parisian in dress and manners drive or stroll in the semi-coolness of evening; and just across the arroyo bounding it on the farther 'side is the bush—jungle and thatched huts and primitive living, where one glimpses hammocks in hovels of faded thatch on bare ground among banana-plants that carry the mind back to rural tropical South America.

European health used to be so bad in Saïgon that French residents often had the experience of playing baccarat with a friend one evening and accompanying him next morning to Bangkok—not the capital of Siam but the Saïgon cemetery for foreigners, popularly so-called among them from the street that leads to it. The story is still told of a misinformed French journalist in France who was moved to protest at the extravagance of sending all the dead to Siam, "in order not to alarm the population." To-day conditions are better, as healthful as could be expected for wine-drinkers in an equatorial country. But the French seem less at home here than the Annamese in their black two-piece garments, shiny as oil-cloth, their wooden clogs scraping noisily on the cement sidewalks, on the stone-faced roadways beyond, splotched with the red saliva of this race of betel-nut chewers. Their hair, usually in topknots that peer from beneath black band-turbans, the black-enameled teeth they consider so becoming, and the betel-nut that drips blood-red over their lips they have in common with their more wealthy compatriots in coats of transparent black gauze over light-colored gowns.

With sunset comes the great French rite, *l'apéritif*. Men in fresh white and women in their best summer frocks gather on the terrace—in other words most of the public

sidewalk, with slight respect for pedestrians—of the Hôtel
Continental, a scene suggesting the Café de la Paix of Paris
in a tropical setting. The awnings are trussed up, and
the night life, the chief life of Saigon, at least of the visible
variety, grows with the evening. The very common-sense
custom of the European men in going bareheaded after
sunset is a delightful relief from the heavy sweat-begetting
cork helmet. All the Frenchman's comforts of home, from
creamy curaçao of oil-like texture to rich green *absinthe
frappée,* are trotted forth by Annamese "boys" in white
gowns, topped by their inevitable band-turban, jet-black as
the coarse hair most of them wear in a Psyche knot. All
manner of French colonial types join the appetite-seeking
throng—the anemic rounder, the sturdy colonist in his
black shovel-beard, the humped bureaucrat in his pince-nez.
Rare indeed is the man who is not accompanied by at least
one member of the fair sex who could have come from
nowhere but France, garb, manner, and all, in spite of her
pallor and reduced vivacity born of tropical residence.

As a hostelry the Continental was full. But one of the
most agreeable surprises about Indo-China, at least to the
man who comes there from wandering in China itself, is
the number of its hotels with all the comforts of Paris.
They are very French hotels indeed, from the menu to
the thrifty eagle-eyed madame behind the bottle-flanked zinc
counter, even though the midday *déjeuner* cannot of course
be served out on the sidewalk. Rooms may be spacious
or small, but they are always furnished with a big double
bed, symbol of the Frenchman's horror of sleeping alone.
This is unfailingly flanked by the *bidet,* in enameled tin on
loose wooden legs or of the latest bath-tub style. Bath-
tubs themselves are rare, but in a land where perspiration
drips at every crook of a finger the shower-baths, often in

a cement-paved corner of the room itself, are alone worth
the price of admission. All this and more I found at ex-
ceedingly reasonable rates at the Hôtel de la Rotonde, just
across the street from the starting-place of the biweekly
steamer to Pnom Penh.

Autobuses leave Saigon in various directions; toy-like
French automobiles may be had for the hiring. Where
the former, and sometimes the latter, leave off, one may
descend to thatch-topped carts behind humped cattle, or climb
into queer little vehicles something like the jaunting-cars of
Ireland. The well-to-do natives of Cochinchina seem still
to prefer the *malabar*, a horse-drawn box on four wheels, so
named from the Indian immigrants who appear to have
brought it with them. The bus ride to Thudam disclosed
an industrial school where the old Annamese arts that show
signs of dying out, such as inlaying furniture and bric-a-brac
with mother-of-pearl, are being retaught under French
principals. Annamese boys of the working class are recom-
mended to it by the village elders and are paid a bit while
learning. In such matters as these, and the good roads
leading to them, French rule is visibly an advantage. The
rather dusty ride out to the Falls of Trian is also one of
those worth while among the radiating routes covering little
Cochinchina. On almost any of them mangosteen trees
stand forth to make one's mouth water, though it has
never been my luck, thanks to persistent off seasons, to taste
this untransportable vegetable ice-cream, reputed the finest
fruit in captivity.

Smallest and oldest of the five divisions of French Indo-
China, Cochinchina is the only colony among them. The
others are "protectorates," though the difference is hardly
visible to the naked eye. But at least its strictly colonial
status simplifies the task of its governor. He came from

Mauritius and was part negro, according to the official propagandist for more tourists who insisted on taking me to call on him. I should hardly have suspected it in his cool and deeply shaded offices, and certainly not from a later glimpse in more social circles of his beautiful French wife of queenly dignity. A colonial governor ranks high in the matrimonial market of France, whatever his complexion. But if I fancied there was no color prejudice in this motley dependency I was disabused by the secret scorn my companion expressed, as we left the palace, for the African strain in the superior to whom he had been so deferential in official intercourse, though he himself seemed to go out of his way to mention his own Annamese wife and half-caste children. To each nationality its peculiar point of view.

Trains, trolleys, autobuses, automobiles, rickshaws, *malabars,* and boats, not to mention pedestrians, ply constantly between Saigon and Cholon, its rich Chinese suburb. Tiresomely Chinese in many of its details, this wealthy city testifies to French tutelage. Instead of shoulder-wide streets garnished with roaming pigs and untended garbage, there are good pavements, and a modern water-supply in place of the bucket-brigades from river or mud-hole. Still no Elysium, it is immaculate compared to China proper. Here live Chinese who own costly automobiles; here diamonds and other valuable jewelry are widely worn in public; here where it is safe to indulge such inclination under foreign rule, is altered the impression one carries away from the bandit- and soldier-ridden old empire to the north, that the Celestials are the antithesis of the Hindus in this matter of personal adornment. In every shop, whether of a grocer or a seller of porcelains, of medicines or of silks, there is a mighty heaping up of wares, and six clerks where we would have one. Among them an old man fat and cheery of aspect as the Laughing Buddha at the entrance to Chinese temples, naked except for thin cotton trousers and slippers, sits manipulating the balls of his calculating-board. Flat, dry, lacquered ducks, transparent at the edges, hang along cords like bats taking their day's repose. Pigs blown up like their toy counterparts of rubber, lie at their ease, polished and hairless, with outstretched legs, grinning their deathly grin at the passing throng. Now and again a funeral goes by, gaudy and noisy as if the chief actor were among the graves of his ancestors, but more richly ornate and lacking the usual tawdriness, like the town itself compared to old China. But those who have been there then say that the time to see Cholon is during the week of Têt, as the lunar New Year is called in Indo-China, when the canvas and cardboard dragon is promenaded through the streets, opening his enormous maw and twisting his long disgusting body, in which a score of sweating coolies are hidden.

In Indo-China one seldom speaks of going to the grocery; it is rather, "I am going to the Chinaman's." The Annamese, and still more so the other races that make up the native population, are lazy, or at least languid as merchants, and the Chinese get the business and the riches. To speak of retail commerce is to mean the Chinese, and in larger matters they are by no means outsiders. For a hundred and fifty years they have been installed at Cholon, and from there they have spread over all Cochinchina, all Indo-China for that matter. They arrive thin and in rags, and leave, if at all, fat and placid, and as fast as they get rich other gaunt wretches take their places at the foot of the ladder. It is as if they were being perpetually passed through a fattening-machine; and if some of them have no luck, lack sufficient cuteness, there is the recompense of opium to make a plank as comfortable as a rich man's bed.

More or less respected by the people they feed upon, they are discreetly or insolently superior to them, depending on their individual status of the moment. Formerly they made great fortunes quickly in rice. That way is hampered now, because the government sends out rice quotations that reach even the peasants. But still they get rich. So greatly are they the gainers that Indo-China has been called a "Chinese colony administered by Frenchmen." Economically the Celestial is master of the country; his activity, his intelligence in business affairs, his commercial cleverness, his very temperament would make him so, even without the great advantages of a population given to gambling and gifted with a lack of forethought that make for usury at high rates. Thirty-six per cent is legal interest even in the French courts of Indo-China, and the wily Chinese often gets everything merely for lending ten piastres—land, house, furniture, sometimes the whole family as slaves.

A gambling game known as "the thirty-six animals" sweeps through all the villages, especially of Cambodia, like *o bicho* in Brazil. In Cambodia, as in Siam, as in China, slavery has been legally abolished, but it continues to flourish. In the old days the work of the slave for debt covered only the interest; it never paid the principal and set him free. To-day the peasant who borrows in a lean year or after a bad wager may hope that at least his children will get out of the meshes of the spider-faced Chinese lender.

Even from the political point of view the Chinese are a privileged class in Indo-China. Though they have no diplomatic representatives of their own, they virtually have the

Cholon architecture is neither exactly French nor Chinese

A funeral procession in Cholon, Chinese suburb of Saigon

A decreasing form of conveyance in Cochinchina

Unlike China proper, great sections of Indo-China are covered with magnificent virgin jungle-forests

rights of extraterritoriality under the protection of the French. Every Chinese in the colony must belong to a *congrégation,* a kind of association that is responsible to the state for all its members, civilly and pecuniarily. Each man between the ages of eighteen and sixty pays a tax of from 6.60 to 200 piastres, depending on the category to which he belongs. There are six of these categories, with bankers and merchants in the highest class and coolies in the lowest. Though they pay this to the "congregation," it really goes to the government. This is no bright French idea, but was the lot of all Chinese living in Annam long before the French came. Besides this varying head-tax there is a "prestation tax"—whatever that may be—of from two to fifty piastres a year; and any Chinese who wishes to travel beyond the town in which he is registered must pay for a *laisser-passer,* good for two weeks and twice renewable, so that those who are always traveling contribute considerably to the government during the year. Women, children, the sick, and men over sixty pay only a yearly tax of one piastre, and may travel when and where they wish; but even the son of a Chinese by an Annamese woman, and born in the colony, remains a Chinese and must belong to some "congregation."

The Chinese of Cholon and of Indo-China in general rarely speak a word of Annamese or of French and of course no English; nor for that matter do they speak Chinese, for they all come from the southern coastal country where dialects reign. Canton, Amoy, Swatow, and Hainan furnish the chief "congregations." Such intriguing names as Hai Chin and Hung Long Tom are to be seen on their shop signs. Except for the Cantonese, who usually bring wives with them, nearly all these happily expatriated Celestials take temporary native wives, usually Annamese.

But they *never*—the italics are those of a French writer—
leave temporary wife and children behind without assuring
their livelihood. The same cannot be said of the French
in ·Indo-China—nor, the French might retort, of Americans in the Philippines.

If I had come too early to see Cholon in the throes of
the Chinese New Year, at least I was just in time to attend
the most important annual celebration of another alien
group that fattens on the native population. Every January the Chettys, a Hindu caste of bankers and usurers to
be found in all the ports of the Far East, give a great
fête in honor of their protectress, the Goddess Souppramanya. It was the most barbaric spectacle I have ever
seen in many years of globe-trotting. In the evening all
Indians of this class in Saigon, from mere street-booth
money-changers to big bankers, enveloped themselves in
their curtain-like muslin costume, with a spongy towel about
the neck, and formed a procession to their temple in the
Rue Ohier. This Pagode des Chettys—one must get used
to the French way of saying *pagode* for temple and *tour* for
pagoda—is rich and elaborate for its setting, though only
mildly so compared to such structures in India. The contrast between its ornamental tower and the *défense d'afficher*
signs lavished upon its bright pink walls is not likely to
escape even the languid passer-by lolling in his *pousse-
pousse*.

Unlike what would have happened in India, here there
seemed to be no objection to my presence; the worshipers
in fact gave me subtle hints that they were rather pleased
at my attention, though the stern watchman at the door
waved away natives of the colony. There may have been
great inner meaning, plethoras of mysticism quite beyond

my simple ken, in the ensuing ceremony, but to me it
was rather a shock to know that what are popularly accepted as our fellow-Aryans could be so crassly superstitious. Yet such things no doubt are all a matter of
degree and inherited point of view; the unfamiliar always
has a hint of the grotesque, even of the hideous.

Great Hindu bankers naturally wear many diamonds;
otherwise these overfed worshipers were only in white flowing loin-cloths, some with a fold of cheese-cloth over one
shoulder. With three fingers each further prepared himself by smearing on his forehead, his flabby arms, and the
hairy chest that attested his Aryan blood, whitish stuff
mixed by low-caste members of his race from cow-dung
and other ingredients. Hindu musicians supplied an absolutely unbroken caterwauling splendidly in keeping with the
rest of the insane ceremony. One of them in particular
should easily have won the world record for long-winded-
ness. For a full hour, if not indeed much longer, he kept
his cheeks blown out to their capacity without an instant
of interlude, thereby keeping a barbaric kind of fife miaul-
ing without cessation and at the same time beating a drum
incessantly with his fingers.

One by one the fat, bediamonded, all but naked bankers
stood before the opened shrine, itself a vision of untold
riches, sometimes singly, sometimes in small groups, and
with their hands high above their heads shook and twisted
and contorted themselves like madmen suffering the extremes
of torture. The object of these revolting attempts of all
too solid flesh to resemble a snake in the throes of pain
or anger were, as nearly as I could gather, to deceive the
goddess into the belief that the worshipers were acutely
suffering at sight of her divine splendor, or that they were
ready to suffer any agony in her honor. One by one

they threw themselves on the cement pavement laid in small brightly colored squares and writhed and squirmed, twisting their heads fiercely from side to side, rolling over and over, in a way to make mere groveling a pastime, the sweat of torture and of an equatorial climate pouring from their brown bodies until the floor was wet beneath them. The paunchiest creature of them all, his fingers covered with diamonds large enough, in the vernacular of the day, to choke a horse, his dough-like face riddled with the marks of smallpox, doubly repulsive with his great hairy naked paunch, went through contortions nauseating to the hardiest stomach. His voluntary convulsions suggested that he was the chief of the caste, as his diamonds implied that he was the leader in successful usury. If only our bankers and money-lenders had to do some such penance annually instead of merely going to church weekly in a silk hat and a limousine!

At length their divinity, Souppramanya, which like any American worthy of attention looked easily worth the million repute and her incredibly bejeweled appearance credit her with, was taken down from her niche. A dozen men in loin-cloths carried the idol to her silver chariot; two great cream-colored sacred bulls, or, more exactly, steers, wearing fancily embroidered robes over their single humps, were led forth from their sumptuous stables within the temple, and the second phase of the ceremony began. Between two rows of torches, surrounded by oriflammes, sacred parasols in gay colors, and inexhaustible musicians, the extravagant equipage of the goddess set out around the walled inclosure of the altar. Huger than water-buffaloes of the fields, their sleek fawn-colored hides shining, their expression that of their human prototypes haughty with generations of adulation, the sacred cattle trod slowly at the head of the worshipers, their spoiled-aristocrat dignity unruffled by the frequent slipping of their silver shoes on the smooth hard pavement, or at the sometimes painful pulling at the cords attached to their perforated nostrils. Sacred as they were, such coercion by their idolizers was evidently necessary to keep them in order, and this they endured as if even sacred beings were not wholly free from the pull of circumstances. Behind, surrounded by a milling throng of naked smeared Hindu men and boys writhing with religious fervor, came the martyr without whom the ceremony would be in vain. He had prayed and fasted for a week in order to be able to endure his suffering. Lances pricking his feet, an enormous pin thrust through his tongue, he drew a little chariot fastened to him by traces ending in silver hooks that dug deeply into his flesh. His eyes twisted in their orbits, foam driveled from his lips, a figure horrible to behold, urged on by the clamors of the frenzied money-lenders, who now and then still threw themselves in abject contortions on the pavement. The crowd jostled and pitilessly crowded upon a second martyr, who had transformed himself into a pincushion, with needles and pins sticking out of his flesh in every direction. It was an astonishing as well as a revolting spectacle, a vision of fanatical India such as I had never seen in India itself, doubly surprising because of the freedom with which we two white men and a Frenchwoman were allowed to mingle with the worshipers.

Two, three, four times the barbaric procession made the circuit of the temple. A curious noise that seemed to come from within the chariot puzzled me, until I managed to crowd closely enough to discover that the ambulating altar contained a little motor which lighted it with electricity! The gaunt Hindu in charge of this howled and writhed with the others; but in a fold of his loin-cloth bulged two or three electric-light bulbs to replace those that might burn out.

Then quickly the whole performance subsided. The regal-mannered steers were led back to their stalls; the swollen cheeks of the musicians deflated in a final piercing yowl; the goddess was carried back to her permanent throne. In a twinkling the frenzied bankers returned to the placid every-day behavior of their calling, and went to squat on the floor in a raised place too sacred for ordinary beings, where low-caste Indians began to pass trays of food among them. This consisted mainly of cocoanuts cut in two and filled with bananas, red fruits, and several unrecognizable forms of Hindu delicacies. The hairy-paunched favorites of for-tune helped themselves more than generously; the small fry, and the children scattered among them, got only handsful of sticky rice, carelessly tossed to them by the servers.

This spectacle was repeated every evening for ten days. It was very easy to guess what might have befallen those who had dared to wear such diamonds or publicly parade such idols in China, or for that matter in our own expen-sively policed land. Here no fear of robbery seemed to trouble the pious Chettys, most opulent of the thousands of castes of India. All the evening there had hovered near me a man from Pondicherry, that tiny patch of India still ruled by the French. Dressed in the tailored garb of Euro-peans in the tropics, his decidedly Aryan features merely a glossy brown instead of white, speaking perfect French, he seemed far removed from the men of his race who writhed on the floor in their diamonds and loin-cloths. The cere-mony was evidently commonplace to him, for he showed no surprise even at the height of it. His fervor seemed to be political rather than religious, and like many a man of color in the French colonies he was almost boisterously

Francophil. A dozen times during the evening his voice rose high enough above the fanatical tumult to assure me in as many ways of expressing it that India would be the happiest land on earth if only France rather than England held it.

The ease with which I got permission to visit the Saïgon establishment where opium is prepared for sale implied that the French made no secret, whether or not they saw anything wrong in it, of their official sponsoring of this traffic. Opium is a government monopoly in Indo-China, with a similar establishment in Tonkin to the north. In a big airy room of armory-like ceiling, a hundred or more feet long and half as wide, a score of Annamese were at work. What with the heat of caldrons and of the climate, and the sickeningly sweetish smell of the drug, their labor with heavy ladles was no sinecure. In fact the whole personnel works only three hours out of the twenty-four, eighteen hours a week. The poppy-juice comes from India—at the northern establishment especially southwestern China now supplies great quantities, but this is of course not officially admitted—in balls of the size of a cocoanut, or resembling still more closely the Brazil-nut in its native state, for the shell is nearly an inch thick—but made of leaves. These leaves are eventually sold to the natives, who chew them with their betel-nut, no doubt getting some opium-like effect from the soaking of poppy-juice.

The brown jelly-like substance inside is dumped into huge brass pans over fires and ladled constantly as it boils, sweat running literally in streams from the workers. When it has cooled and been well kneaded the resultant dough is placed in other such pans and rubbed down into a concave cake two or three inches thick. This in turn is placed upside down over a very hot charcoal brazier, and every minute or two a workman peels off a skin of the thickness of leather and throws it into still another pan. When all the cake has been skinned away, the leather-like layers in the new pan are treated with water, for they would otherwise be brittle as glass, and are worked again into a very brown dough which gradually swells to fill the pan. Handfuls of specially prepared interior of bamboos, soft and resembling vermicelli, are then thrust into the mass, and brown water runs slowly from these through cloth filters into buckets. Only this liquid is of any value, the residue being thrown away, useless even as fertilizer.

Reduced to a semiliquid form once more, this final product is placed in iron barrels, a single one of which is worth twenty thousand piastres. The stuff may now be sold at any time, though if possible it is allowed to settle six months or more, for like wine and marriage the longer it is kept the better it becomes. Then in the form of a paste closely resembling russet shoe-blacking it is put up in tins of five, ten, twenty-five, fifty, and one hundred grams each. The first retails at barely two piastres, so that every rickshaw-man and errand-boy may afford it; the largest, at twenty-five. The de luxe opium is put up in purple boxes, a special mark on the very best of them indicating that they are reserved for the king of Cambodia. Great quantities of this best purple variety are sent to the old Cambodian sovereign each December, as the Christmas present of the government. His royal colleague, the emperor of Annam, is supplied from the Hanoï establishment. The ordinary tins, with no marks upon them except a cryptic number, are placed in heavy wooden boxes simply marked "Benares"—other code names distinguishing the better grades—and go out in great loads to all parts of the colony. The stuff is

One of Cambodia's soldiers whom the French dress
in khaki

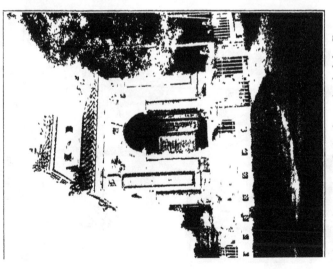

honor of men from Cochinchina who died for France
in the World War

A rickshaw-man of Pnom-penh, capital of Cambodia

A young lady of Pnom-penh with the Cambodian style of ukulele

sold in these tins to any one who can pay for it, in every
little *débit* distinguished by an "O.R," for "Opium Régie"
on signs similar to those indicating authority to retail for
the French tobacco monopoly.   What with government
preparation, license fees, and the like, the drug brings' an
enormous profit to the government; that is, to France.

The official who took it upon himself to get me started
right in my sight-seeing called the opium monopoly "the
shame of Indo-China"; and some other French residents
felt, or professed to feel, the same way about it.   But
even he insisted that if it were not thus openly sold and
regulated the people would smuggle it in; and if it were
prohibited entirely there would be a revolution!   So there
would be, though perhaps not in just the sense the speaker
meant to imply.

We all know that France takes a somewhat different
view of "vices" than do we of the English-speaking races.
The French attitude seems to be, let vice flourish and abound,
that each may learn to save himself from temptation, or
decide for himself how much indulgence he can allow without serious personal harm.   There are hints that this may
perhaps be as effective in the end as our own growing custom
of forcible suppression.   Even in novels based on life in
Indo-China the French attitude toward opium seems to be
about what ours as a nation is toward tobacco.   Many,
some say three fourths, of the eighteen thousand French
in the colony smoke opium, as do most of the various indigenous races, many Chinese, and some Hindu residents.
There are not a few French residents of the better class
who contend that it does no great harm.   Among the
natives, men with the opium habit are treated with indulgence, but the women "never" smoke it; any who did so
would be considered the lowest of human creatures.   On

the whole the Japanese seem to have handled the problem
better in Formosa, for they at least strive to keep their own
people free from the habit, and are systematically reducing
consumption within their own territory, rather than trying
to increase it. The smoking of opium, a Chinese importation, was not a common vice in Indo-China, unless perhaps among the Annamese, before the French came. In
Cambodia and among some of the other gentler races that
make up the protected federation, market-days and big
gatherings are needed to overcome the inertia toward the
habit even to·day. But the government forces it upon the
people for the benefit of the treasury; and the development
of obligatory military service has spread it everywhere.
Lists of villages are sent out by diligent functionaries with
the information that they are not consuming their pro rata
of opium, just as great business houses in other lands protest to their agents that such and such territory should
take more of their goods, and local officials are told to
urge shopkeepers with the "O.R." license to add to their
stocks and push them over the counter.

The opium monopoly in Indo-China is by no means air-
tight. In Laos there are many Miao who grow the poppy
up in their hills far inland, and as they can get little more
than half as much for their product from the French
monopoly officials as from the Chinese constantly engaged
in illicit opium traffic, only a fraction of that grown and
really sold by the Miao is ever reckoned in government reports. The Chinese smugglers have their own *pirogues,*
slender swift boats for the inland rivers, and with these
they are constantly getting opium out of the country, mainly
by way of Siam. Luang Prabang reports only eight hundred thousand piastres' worth of opium a year, yet every

one knows that far more is smuggled out of that kingdom than is sold to the government monopoly, and so easily that customs officers are kept on the Laos-Siam and Laos-China frontiers chiefly for appearance's sake.

CHAPTER II

THE French move freely in and out of Indo-China without passports, but all "foreigners" are tightly bound with red tape. Germans and Russians are not yet admitted at all, and even harmless tourists are treated as suspicious characters. In these days of rapid transmission of information, and its more exciting sister, misinformation, it was something of a surprise to find, five full years after the signing of the Treaty of Versailles, that news had not yet reached the colonial bureaucrats even of this far-flung dependency that the World War was over. Having been officially robbed of my passport upon landing, as happens to all *étrangers,* I could recover it only by appearing next morning at a police office and filling in on both sides a large form designed to bring out in elaborate detail all the past, present, and future history of the signer. One question in particular was puzzling: "Have you ever been in the enemy country?" Since I had been laboring under the impression that France was just then at peace with all the world, I asked the official in charge of my case to elucidate. He seemed to betray a hint of annoyance beneath his perfectly Gallic exterior, and finally explained that the forms were still those used in war days. "The high cost of printing, you know . . ."

One question naturally leads to another: were a few months of helping his countrymen to hold the bridge-heads

28

on the Rhine to be counted against me? But he seemed to be growing suspicious of my straight face, besides, since he was the one functionary in the passport division who flattered himself on speaking some English, his attention was largely taken up with seeing that I did not address him in French, or that I at least should not sully the carefully Anglicized form by answering some of its questions in that tongue. How could that one of his colleagues whose laborious monthly duty it is to translate a dozen or more of these forms for foreigners back into French, as the beginning of a lengthy *dossier* on each such individual admitted to the colony, meet any suspicion that his berth should be abolished, if foreigners were allowed to do their own translating? The expense of putting those forms into English, back in war days, would moreover hardly be justified if they were not used for foreigners as intended; hence nothing more natural than that even those foreigners whose French is far more fluent than their English should be compelled to give their history on these translated forms, even though the official beside me had to help them to turn their French into English.

I had been too long familiar with French bureaucracy to suppose that my passport would be returned at once, merely for a bare hour of filling in a questionnaire. Naturally this had to be taken to men higher up, "for study," before so final an action could be taken. But I could prepare to take the evening steamer to Cambodia "in all tranquillity," the philologist of the passport bureau assured me— in his own tongue now, no doubt because the information was unofficial. My passport would be handed me on the steamer before she sailed, he confided. His manner was such that it was hard to keep from flattering myself that my notoriously honest face had led him to make an admission to me which he would never have dreamed of making to an ordinary traveler.

He had spoken truly too; the passport was returned, even as he had foretold, and the manner of its returning showed how valuable are the services rendered by the swarms of officials who look after such matters. I had strolled across from my hotel to the steamer *Mekong* long enough before to be already deep in deck-chair conversation with the charming young American lady and her merely more elderly chaperon, whom our tropic-emaciated consul had told me to expect among my traveling-companions, when a young man in what looked like a disguised uniform began pacing the deck shouting for "Monsieur Ügh," as nearly as his cross between a grunt and a word can be rendered in English. The fourth or fifth time he disturbed the absorbing pleasure of meeting one's own people, of the preferable sex at that, unexpectedly in a far distant land, I noticed that he waved in one hand an American passport. About the same moment my returning wits confided to me that the noise he was making so incessantly was the Frenchman's most sincere attempt to pronounce the name "Hughes." In a whole-hearted desire to help him out of what was evidently on the verge of becoming a troublesome duty, I rose and asked the shouter's permission to look at the document. It was my own passport. I thanked him cordially for the two forms of relief this discovery brought, and returned to my conversation.

Before long my attention was distracted once more by another stentorian voice, this time calling for "Mademoiselle Ügh!" I offered my services again—and retrieved the passport of the young lady beside me, whose name was no more Hughes than is my own. Barely had she stowed it away in that intricate way ladies have of risking their valuable possessions when a third voice, paging "Madame Ugh!" began to punctuate the summer night. I recognized the man who had despoiled me of my passport before allowing me to land from the *Panama Maru*. It was natural that the same official could not be expected to hand out more than one of the documents that evening, with so few to go round. Besides, this man had hardly had three days in which to recover from the task of receiving me into the country. It caused me no great surprise to find that the paper he now flourished about his head belonged to the elder of the two ladies beside me, though her deceased husband had borne a name not even remotely suggestive of the prolific family Hughes.

Priceless sources of information must the voluminous *dossiers* of visitors to Indo-China be, so carefully compiled by the division of police inspection charged with drawing up and "studying" them. It was not until I had time later to do some studying of my own that I examined my passport, with its square yard or less of stamping and annotation by the French authorities, in an effort to solve the mystery of the name under which we had evidently all three been registered in the annals of Indo-China. Only then did I notice that even more prominent, on the face of the official permissions so generously granted by our Department of State for American citizens to proceed abroad, than the name of the holder, was that of one Charles E. Hughes.

Ah, well, what are colonies and "protectorates" and mandated territory and spheres of influence for if not to provide posts for more officials? The episode might soon have been forgotten in the glories of a tropical night, had not so much surprise been shown by the passport officials and the ship's company that Monsieur and Madame Hughes had booked separate cabins. Our passports were again taken away from us in Pnom Penh, restamped and returned to us there, stamped and registered once more upon our return to Saïgon, and my own was manhandled I know not how many more times in sundry places before my travels in Indo-China were over; but I neglected to obtain exact figures on the increase of the Hughes family before finally leaving France's rich Far-Eastern possession behind. In contrast to all this, I was asked to show my passport once during two years of roving in China, and the asker was quite contented with a visiting card instead.

It was a noisy night about our frail little cabins on the *Mekong,* and dawn found us anchored at Mytho, to which we could easily have taken a train from Saïgon that morning in time to board the craft before she pushed off again. Because the Messageries Fluviales have a monopoly on the rivers of Indo-China against which even the French, of unofficial standing, protest loudly but in vain, travelers pay high for the thirty-six-hour journey from the capital of Cochinchina to that of Cambodia on these rather uncomfortable little river steamers. But again, why trouble with colonies and protectorates if they give no monopolies? For that matter the French steamers between Marseilles and Shanghai charge more for the passage from Hong Kong or Singapore to Saïgon than between those two British ports, where competition reigns.

All day we plowed our way, with frequent stops, up a wide river through a dead-flat palm-tree and banana country. Between halts there was little of interest except our fellow-passengers, and even they were not particularly unique. Eight travelers lolled in the breeze under the tarpaulin above the first-class deck, to which our complexions confined those of us of so-called European race. Besides the young Ameri-

A monument to Sisowath, octogenarian king of Cambodia

A street and pagoda of Pnom-penh, with a bridge railing bearing the cobra-heads that are an ancient Cambodian architectural motif

Saffron-clad priests of Cambodia stand before the doors of pious Buddhists
each morning until alms reward them

Pilgrims to Pnom-penh spend the hot hours in a corner of the great temple
corridor half surrounding the palace grounds of King Sisowath of Cambodia

can lady and her chaperoning compatriot, there was an English couple to whom tropical travel was an ordeal to be
endured only because Angkor is something one must see.
Made miserable by every deviation from the accustomed ways
of their foggy native land, Mr. and Mrs —shall we say
Piffton-Smith? no matter what, so long as we do not forget the hyphen and disgrace them by the mere name of Smith
—suffered acutely from everything: the French food, the
French meal-hours, the French language, the delightful climate, even the friendly little ants in the cabins. What a
pity one cannot find everything just as it is at home when
off on one's travels in quest of the strange and the different!
Only by constant mention of their youthful daughter, Lady
So-and-so, recently married to the far from youthful governor of—er—a British crown colony, could Mrs. Piffton-
Smith endure the martyrdom at all. One must not forget
that daughter any more than the hyphen, though for that
matter there was little danger of doing either; trust Mrs.
Piffton-Smith for that. It was evident that no one in the
family had ever been a Lady before.

But let us be charitable; perhaps it is not merely the women
of foot-bound China who have more cause for complaint
than the favored sex. While we mere men had to use our
oven-like little cabin only as dressing-rooms between a day
of loafing and a night of sleeping on the cot-provided deck,
the ladies were cruelly confined during their nightgowned
hours. Three lively young French officers on a furlough
from their regiments, one of whom spoke excellent English,
completed the cabin passenger list. French soon came to
seem the natural tongue, so that the Piffton-Smiths had new
cause for complaint in being left out of the conversation.
Under the back awning behind the orange-box "staterooms"
was a much larger collection of passengers, untroubled with

cabins, cots, or the fear of creasing their garments. As the day wore on, the human type there gradually changed. The throng grew less Chinese as Annamese travelers wandered ashore at the frequent stopping-places, became more Hindu, more Aryan, the eyes large and straight, with well defined eyebrows, mustaches shading the lips of the men, some with almost Russian beards. Those rare inhabitants of the banks, half seen through the trees and reeds, also took on Aryan features, for all their chocolate color.

Daylight found us at Pnom Penh, capital of the French protectorate of Cambodia. It was a calm, well kept little city, with hardly any of the hubbub of China and none of its filth—at least within sight. The air was less deadening than at Saïgon, less charged with electricity and water-vapor, though still so hot that there was no joy in doing anything equal to the joy of doing nothing. Half a dozen wide streets, much shaded by trees, invited the stroller about a town in many ways quite up-to-date, pleasant as it was with tropical languor. Pnom Penh has been called the Little Bangkok, as Saïgon is the Little Paris. I was at last completely beyond Chinese civilization, though there were some Chinese residents, mainly merchants; most of the commerce of Cambodia is in Celestial hands. White people were not numerous, but there were plenty of other foreigners—black and brown French soldiers from other colonies, representatives of nearly all the lands of the Far East. Yet all other races stood out merely as individuals among the Cambodians, so closely related to the Siamese in clothing, language, the uneven pompadour hair-cuts of the women. With rather stupid faces from the mouths of which dripped betel-nut juice, above perhaps the ugliest female costumes in the world, ending in the inevitable *sampot,* a kind of pants-skirt drawn up between the legs and tucked in behind, they were far from attractive. Gentle effeminate-looking men with long bobbed hair or black tresses wound together in a knot at the back of the neck meandered about between the shafts of rickshaws or toiled slowly about the steamer-landing.

The first men in the flowing saffron robes of Gautama whom I had seen in the two decades since my Siamese journey—though I had seen Buddhist priests and to spare—stood out against the less gaudily garbed laymen. The bonzes are the bosses of the country—always of course after the French. There had been sixty thousand of them in Cambodia the year before, for the Cambodians are very religious. But they pay no taxes, and under the French they are gradually being *supprimés,* so that now they were reduced to 42,250, according to official statistics. Still, these languid beings in bright yellow robes, often set off by red, rose, purple, and other draperies, with shaven heads and Hindu skins, were by no means scarce. Groups of them with their begging-bowls stood before many a shop and house while the sun was still low, sauntering on to make their silent plea to others after a handful of rice or a saucer of cooked fish had been poured into their bowls by the pious inmates.

There was something very French about Pnom Penh, for all its very Oriental aspect. French bread was on sale everywhere; the "Grand Hôtel, N. Manolis, Propriétaire," might, like all the others in Indo-China, have been in Paris—except for the heat—tourist prices and all. Here again were the same marble-topped tables, the same zinc *comptoir* presided over by a sharp-eyed and caustic-minded matron, the same flimsy newspapers in awkward holders, the same letter-paper headed by an advertisement of the Maison Dubonnet. Fortunately we were sailing again that evening and needed its monopolistic accommodations only in the way of food

and drink. Midday, with its lassitude, its invincible som-
nolence, followed so closely upon the déjeuner, however,
that its shelter, and at least the repose offered by its chairs,
with the marble-topped tables serving as props, were essen-
tial. The most ardent sight-seer could hardly have found
pleasure in roaming about Pnom Penh with the unclouded
equatorial sun directly overhead. Dinner in the evening
was to the strains of a native orchestra that might have
done worse, and a veritable stage-lighting effect was produced by the swirling wings of the big electric fans suspended from the ceiling amid clouds of insects.

Pressed by his more belligerent neighbors, Norodom, king
of Cambodia, placed his country under the protection of the
French in 1863, and since then the nominal ruler is merely a
play king. The real boss is the *résident supérieur* sent out
from France. It goes without saying that the royal figurehead is surrounded by all the riches and sumptuous state
which the French and his own doting subjects can supply
him, while the "protector" does all the work. The arrangement seems to be much like that between the couple who
agreed that one should decide all the small questions and
the other all the large, and so far there have been no small
questions in Cambodian affairs. Old pagodas of the Burmese rather than the Chinese style stand forth here and there
in the older part of the capital as a reminder of independent
days when a head fell at the motion of the kingly finger. But
most of Pnom Penh dates from the years of the protectorate.
Little more than half a century has passed since Norodom
confided his country to France, and already much that the
French built in the capital has taken on an air of age, under
the perpetually burning sun and the seasonal rains that
drive vegetation to super-vegetable performance. The beautifully straight streets traced by the French, so out of pro-

portion with the population that passes along them, are
green with grass outside the busiest section. In the far outskirts hover the thatched huts, often on stilts, of the mass
of the population.

The gilded steeples of the throne-room, however, within
the great royal inclosure, infallibly draw the eye that catches
them. This and several others of the palaces are so new
that they were not finished when the World War broke out,
and two of them still had scaffolds about their needle-pointed
spires and along their swift golden roofs. Inside the outer
wall of the inclosure runs a long series of life-sized paintings
from the sacred texts, before which groups of pilgrims bow
down in worship, and squat in contented repose during the
hours of siesta. One of the palaces has a silver floor thirty-
six by a hundred and twenty feet, the solid silver *dalles* half
an inch thick. A gold Buddha, studded with diamonds, that
is said to be worth sixty million piastres is among the many
precious things, as well as much tinsel, inside the plain
bright-yellow walls of the palaces, to which there are no real
barricades. Cases containing jewels of great price in the
Silver Temple are not locked, but are protected merely by
pasted strips of paper, with the name of the guardian written on them. The Cambodians still consider their king so
sacred that they never steal his possessions, and alien thieves
seem never to get this far afield. Of the far-famed Footprint of Buddha within its own special pagoda there is nothing to say except that it is about six feet long, in solid rock,
studded with jewels, with the toes all exactly of the same
length.

Our day in Pnom Penh was well chosen, for in the afternoon the king had a dance performed in the wall-less pavilion
of the palace grounds for the pleasure of visiting French
and British officers. It was a far different dance from those

which kings of Europe give in honor of visitors. While the white strangers in town sat as at a tennis tournament beneath the shade of the pavilion roof in seats provided for those who do not naturally squat, two girls, the youngest hardly in her teens, appeared in the center of the floor. Among his other playthings the octogenarian king chooses annually two hundred and forty girls from the prettiest of the upper class, to be trained to dance before him. But either his eyesight is poor, the choice extremely limited, or he had deliberately set out to insult these guests foisted upon him by the French rulers, for even a popular novelist could not have called this chosen pair beautiful. Flour, or some white powder closely resembling it, covered their faces in ghastly thoroughness, faces in which not the suggestion of an expression seemed to be permitted by the rules of Cambodian dancing, and flour in which streams of sweat cut strange arabesques during the ceremony. On their heads were replicas of the very pointed steeples of the throne-room; costumes gaudy with gold and many colors, quite unlike the every-day dress of Cambodian women, somewhat resembling in fact the garb of a Spanish toreador, covered them from neck to knees. Two big silver anklets clinked above each of their bare feet. It was a costume by no means scanty enough for the climate, and if the truth must be told at all costs there was a conspicuous call for soap and water just where their floured faces joined the gaudily garbed bodies.

Dancing? Yes, perhaps, for want of a word more exactly descriptive. It really was posturing, more or less to the rhythm of an orchestra of native players on strange instruments squatted on the floor at one end of the open pavilion. There was never a quick movement, not a hint of animation in the white faces, though there was considerable expression in the lithe arms and posturing bodies; more, no doubt, than we ignorant Western spectators suspected. But it was impossible to picture the youths in an American dance-hall even suspecting, to say nothing of admitting, that this was dancing. Through it all an old woman tossed from the side-lines, like a football coach, hints to the perspiring and apparently stiffly embarrassed performers. Little by little all the rabble in town sneaked up, noiseless on bare feet, and squatted just within the shade along one side of the pavilion. Cambodia's king, one gathered, was democratic in his attitude. The only element of the population lacking before the ceremony ended were the priests in their yellow robes; like their colleagues of Spain on the day of the bull-fight, they may not morally mingle with the laymen during such ceremonies.

Old King Sisowath himself was not there, except perhaps in spirit. His eighty-four years made him chary of excitement. But before we went off to the later afternoon band concert in a park at the other side of town we had seen his crown, his seven parasols in as many different colors for each day of the week, his two even more gaudy ones for fête days, his two palanquins for state and ordinary occasions, and all those other baubles which the tourist so often mistakes for the rewards of travel. The Cambodian sovereign mounts his throne only once in his life, even so long a life as Sisowath's—at his coronation. On other days he holds audience sitting on a cushion at the foot of it. Yet barefooted servants wandered about dusting and fingering everything, reminding one that even emperors must have charwomen. Crude, violent colors were much in evidence. When the king goes forth in state both he and his chair are so covered with gold and precious stones that the eye quails before him in this equatorial sunlight. Poor old figurehead! Little did Norodom dream to what depths his demand for French protection would so soon sink his successors. Nothing is more symbolical of the real position of old Sisowath than the well known story of how his favorite concubine yielded to the urgings of a young French official on the steamer bringing his Majesty back from Paris a few years ago, and of the king's impotence to punish either of them.

The *Barsac* was somewhat more comfortable than the *Mekong,* though the mother of Lady So-and-so would not admit it. No doubt this was because it confined itself almost entirely to carrying visitors to Angkor rather than making its passengers adjuncts of its freight. A pilot in the headdress of a Chinese nurse-maid, a sailor adorned with a West Indian bandana, short-haired women and all but naked men paddling about in dugout canoes of very fat belly and narrow upturned ends, sometimes with a supercilious drone in a yellow robe among them, mildly enlivened the early hours next morning. The larger boats were pushed along by one oar in the hands of a standing boatman, or boat-woman, as in China, and Venice. Flocks of white birds almost like seagulls skimmed across the yellowish water; all was pleasant as long as we kept moving; only the breezeless halts were painful.

It was in fact a beautiful day's sail up across the Tonlé Sap, the Great Lake formed by the Mekong in high-water time, now nearing its close. This mid-January excursion was indeed probably the last to Angkor for the season, unless later travelers succeeded in making the journey by automobile along the new road soon to be completed. In place of houses on pole legs, twelve or fifteen feet above the ground, there came floating villages, scores of houses tightly bound together. Enormous quantities of fish are taken in the receding waters, and as the lake at its height covers vast areas

Dancers of Cambodian King Sisowath

The throne-room of the king of Cambodia gleams in the tropical sunlight as if covered with polished gold

The populace surrounds the seated musicians at the palace-veranda performances of King Sisowath's flour-faced dancing-girls

the population is reduced to this form of earning a livelihood. The fish heads are boiled for oil, the highly offensive
scent of which now and then reached our nostrils, and the
fish, gutted and salted, are sent to China and Singapore.
Once the sea covered this region, with only an island where
there is now a part of the mainland, so that salt-water fish
are still caught in the lake, and in the flood season fresh-
water fish are taken far out in the ocean.

All day we steamed through a veritable Gatun Lake, now
with jungle and an occasional floating village on one side,
now with a hazy range of hills far off on the left, sometimes
with nothing but the yellowish waters as far as the eye could
see. Occasionally there was not even a junk in sight, no
more trace of man than before his appearance among the
terrestrial fauna; at other times the great expanse, broad as
a sea, was flecked with sail-boats with almost diamond-
shaped sails. But the flooded forest was not dead or dying
as at Gatun, for the waters recede in time each year to save
it from extinction.

We were to have reached Angkor toward the noon following our evening departure from Pnom Penh; but I for one
was glad we spent all the day sailing across the Great Lake,
if only for the sunset. The lake was flat as glass, one side
lost on an ocean-like horizon, the other a low distant endless line of trees. A delicate lilac spread along all the rim
of the sky; then on the western side the limpid air became
pink, and almost suddenly everything was tinged with this
color: the surface of the lake itself, the entire circle of
horizon, every tiniest fleck of cloud in the sky above. Ahead,
a line of beautiful green showed the endlessness of the
drowned forest; on the west, in contrast, there came a quick
heaping up of masses of dark, chaotic, terrifying, gigantic
things which stood upright and seemed to weigh upon the

waters, like fantastic blocks of mountains, standing out as clearly as if their summits were painted along the clear sky, yet looking as if they were preparing for a formidable crumbling away, such as one might fancy the end of the world to be. Gradually, like some mammoth holocaust, the blood-red sun burned its way down into the clouds massed along the western horizon, clouds which outdid themselves in strange shapes, from impossible crags, on which trees seemed to be falling in rapid succession, to snow-clads farther off; and then, after it had been gone entirely for a while and one thought it had disappeared below the edge of the earth, the sun reappeared, a demon face red with rage peering forth as from a cave, from which it advanced down to the very water's edge, spilling blood far out across the lake. Then red chaos, and purple, and lilac, and finally soft mauve night.

Not long afterward we got off into sampans with happy laughing rowers and went away through the inundated forest, among great trees bathing clear to their upper branches, the water under their armpits, or only their heads emerging, like modest women. Higher rose the ever thicker forest close about us; we found ourselves ascending a narrowing stream; and at length, soon after the moon appeared, we bumped against something more or less resembling a pier. It was the end of an excellent road, raised high on an embankment for some distance, and we climbed into—ah, well, it is a small commonplace world at best, this twentieth-century globe, even in its most distant recesses—into what our English friends called motor-cars, though they were those more than familiar things built by an inventive and once eccentric but now widely known ex-Sunday-school teacher of Detroit, and were off for a moonlight ride behind a careful chauffeur who wore no shoes. It was a tepid night, dotted with fireflies, the musical silence forming an undertone to the droning of the cars broken now and again by the soughing of big water-wheels raising water from the small river that turned them. In the palm-tree jungle on either side we made out many little houses on slender legs, the inhabitants of both sexes lolling or strolling in a single piece each of Scotchy plaid wrapped about them like a short skirt.

It was nearly eleven at night when we reached the *sala*, a comfortable spreading bungalow erected by the French for the accommodation of the fussy modern visitors to Angkor. Two decades ago Pierre Loti took all day along that road in a jolting two-wheeled ox-cart, and put up in the stilt-legged shack of Buddhist monks. But we had arrived at a lucky moment, as was evident from the sounds of revelry by night that came to us from beyond the moat just across the road from the *sala*. It was a supernaturally broad moat, looking at least a hundred yards wide in the light of the full moon that drifted lazily across a great building rising to pointed towers that bulked forth out of the night far beyond. An ancient stone causeway across it led to this gigantic structure of Angkor-Vat, before the partly ruined front doorway of which a torch-lighted throng was gathered. Visitors who had come before us, headed by a French novelist and the queenly wife of the governor of Cochinchina, had sent to Siem Réap at the edge of the Great Lake for Cambodian dancers, and with them had come fifty boys bearing torches and most of the native population of the district.

There were a score of girls in the gaudy garments and the steeple-shaped head-dress of the calling, chewing betel-nut, and giggling like a bevy of New York typists as they danced, though the rules call for silence and wholly expressionless faces. Banked behind a dozen seated Europeans in white, and forming a compact circle around them and the dancers, two or three hundred natives of both sexes squatted or stood, many with naked youngsters between their knees. Small boys with blazing torches outlined the inner arc of the circle; the little torch-bearers squatted on the flagstones formed an enchanted circle of flames tapering upward to smoke about the dancers. Some of the spectators had taken places on the steps and the balustrade of the bridge; other half-naked Cambodians, and Annamese with their effeminate knots of hair, gave the gathering a ragged fringe. The ancient temple seemed to have returned to life, the days of very long ago to live again; it was easy to imagine these living dancers the descendants of those carved in stone on the pillars in the background, for all their black teeth and what looked like blood-dripping mouths.

The Annamese spectators were solemn, like men so impressed with their own importance that they dare not break their dignity; the Cambodians were simple happy children, taking the joys of life as they come and giving no more thought to to-morrow than to stone-dead yesterday. The croaking of frogs in the broad shallow moat mingled with that of some loud-voiced species of cricket; birds of the night passed overhead with a startled cry—or was it applause?—at the strange scene below, profaning the great doorway of the dead temple. Beneath the brilliant tropical moon that all but blotted out the Southern Cross well above the horizon, the floured faces of the dancers took on, now a ghastly, now a clownish aspect, as they posed and postured, moving noiselessly in their bare feet slowly to and fro on the century-worn stone pavement. Dressed like the Hindu gods they seemed to be impersonating, they undulated back and forth on the glass-smooth stones, their supple arms waving as if they were mere antennæ without rigidity anywhere, in contrast to their stiffly immovable bodies.

There was a story to be read, evidently, in their deliberate pantomiming, a solemn if not a tragic tale, for all the occasional bursts of embarrassed or prankish giggling, like plantation darkies at a cotton-field celebration. One gathered that a demon with several faces wished to carry off Siva, beautiful lady-love of Rama, and when the two rivals of the ancient legend faced each other with threatening gestures all the childish part of the audience began to shriek, as at the meeting of hero and villain in a Punch-and-Judy show or at the movies. Indeed the spectacle was insured against flagging interest by the behavior of the rapt happy throng in the flickering light before the ancient temple more than by the dancers it encircled. Young and old seemed to follow the story easily; to us Westerners without their background of ancient legends and Oriental symbolism it was merely a picturesque scene, made doubly fantastic by the circle of torches and weird with the thump of tom-toms that lasted deep into the night.

CHAPTER III

SOON after sunrise next morning Fords carried us off to some of the more distant ruins of the ancient city buried in tropical forest. With the heart of the day unbearable in' the sunshine, it is wise as well as customary to get under way early at Angkor, and French breakfasts are brief, if not quite to the point. An excellent road, considering the place and the climate, set off close along the sides of the moat, then shot off at a tangent at the second corner. An abnormally broad moat it still seemed, wide as the Panama Canal even by sunlight; and it was all but covered with water-cress and beautiful white and pink lilies, or their tropical counterparts.

To visit Angkor is no longer a proof of prowess, except of the Ford-endurance needed to make the circuit of ruins covering forty kilometers of throttling forest-jungle. Even as recently as the beginning of the present century visitors had to scramble through the wilderness about Angkor as best they could. To-day there is a network of good roads, French even to their sign-boards, to all the important ruins, with so few ox-carts or other native traffic on them now that they are almost as commonplace as our national high-ways—until suddenly they burst out again upon some other mammoth ruin.

Described by a Chinese traveler two hundred years before America was officially discovered, and many times since,

46

Angkor is still little known to the world at large, though it is perhaps the greatest collection of ruins on earth. Neither Java nor India can show so extensive and so perfectly preserved an architectural ensemble; Machu Picchu, similarly lost in dense tropical forest, though high up among the great ranges of the Andes instead of down at the dead-flat sea-level of Angkor, is a mere village by comparison. Once this Khmer city, buried for centuries and long left to desolation, was one of the splendors of the world. Its monuments still tell the story of the luxury of its royal and military life; its carvings give an inventory of its riches, from jewels to dancing-girls. The least observing must soon realize that this was once the heart of a magnificent kingdom; and what an immense city it was—and is. Angkor-Thom was larger than the Rome of Augustus; the great temple of Angkor-Vat alone has a space four times as large as the Place de la Concorde, which is larger than Columbus Circle.

It seems that about the time of Alexander the Macedonian a people apparently detached many centuries before from the great Aryan race migrated from the direction of India and came to plant itself on the shores of this great river, the lower Mekong. Others say that when India and Burma were being conquered by barbarians at about the time of Christ these Khmer came down from northeast Burma, hillmen with a virility that has since died out, so that they in their turn have now long since been conquered, as they subjugated and mixed with the unspoiled aborigines of this region, "men with little eyes who worshiped serpents." On what queer bases are civilizations built! Just as the old Nile, with its silt alone, caused a marvelous civilization to grow up in its narrow valley, here the Mekong, spreading out its waters year after year, deposited the richness that prepared the

wealthy empire of the Khmer. The city of Angkor-Thom
(Angkor the Great), capital of this empire, reached the
nadir of its glory between the ninth and twelfth centuries
of our era. The Khmer brought with them the gods of
Brahmanism, the beautiful legends of the Ramayana, which
seem to have come to them through the Hindus at about the
time of Christ, and as their opulence grew in this fertile
delta of the Mekong each king vied with his predecessors
in clearing away the forest and in building everywhere
magnificently decorated palaces, and gigantic temples
chiseled with thousands of figures.

Some centuries later—no one knows exactly when, for
the existence of this once important people is largely effaced
from the memory of man—the powerful sovereigns of
Angkor saw arrive from the West missionaries in bright
yellow robes, bearers of a new light at which the Asiatic world
was just then marveling. The savage temples of Brahma
became Buddhist temples; the statues of their altars changed
their attitudes, lowering their eyes and softening their faces
with gentle smiles. The Khmer empire of the Mekong delta
appears to have started on the downward path during our
thirteenth century. The history of its rapid and mysterious
decline has never been fully written, and the invading forest
guards the secret of most of it. There are evidences of a
connection between it and the history of China; for it was
not long after the Tai or Laos race that we commonly call
the Siamese, masters even of Canton until 1053 A.D., were
driven out of what is now southwestern China by a series
of battles along the West River, that the Khmers were in
their turn dispossessed by this hardier though fleeing people.
Time had moved swiftly with them. At least in the art of
their monuments the Khmer were at their height during the
twelfth century, and by the fourteenth they were so weak,

A floating village of Cambodia

At its height the great lake of Cambodia floods whole forests, adding to

Irrigation water-wheels are numerous along the well shaded little river the traveler follows from Siem Reap to Angkor

The steady thumping of a foot-operated rice-huller broke the stillness

perhaps because of the softening influence of tropical living, that they fled before the Siamese and founded a new capital to the southward. The little Cambodia of to-day, conserver of complicated rites the sense of which is almost completely lost, is the last remnant of this once powerful empire of the Khmer, which for more than five hundred years has ebbed away, until it has been all but extinguished under the silence of trees and mosses.

From the end of the fourteenth century Angkor belonged to Siam, which changed its name and set over it a king of its own. Since then the great palaces and temples had been left to time and tropical vegetation, until little more than half a century ago the first European discovered, ruin by ruin, this marvelous city lost in inextricable jungle. This redis-covery is credited to Henri Mouhot, in 1861; but it was not until 1910 that the uncovering of the ruins began. Annam-ese armies had long invaded Cochinchina, then a part of Cambodia, and to save herself from complete destruction the weakened nation became a protectorate of France, barely a year after Mouhot's explorations. Angkor still belonged to Siam; but some wise Frenchman seems to have discovered that it was formerly a part of Cambodia and insisted on a return to the ancient *status quo;* or on applying that doctrine of "self-determination" on which unimperialistic France is so strongly set. At any rate Siam was "induced," by the treaty of 1907, to "give back" to Cambodia all Battambang Province, including the Angkor region. Then communica-tion was opened to the ruins, which had been at the mercy of the elements for nearly a thousand years.

Yet they were not so badly ruined as they might have been. When the Khmer fled before the Siamese of the four-teenth century they could hardly have expected that their architectural marvels would merely be swallowed up by the voracious forest, but rather that they would be destroyed root and branch; and probably for generations they thought this had happened. But even the destroying of such massive works of stone is hard labor in an equatorial land, and the Siamese confined themselves to the destruction of the buildings of a political nature and left untouched the temples and other religious monuments. Buddhism was less respectful, for all its gentleness, and caused many of the Brahman glories to disappear, or replaced them with Buddhist statues and tawdry trappings.

There are monuments vying in size and artistry with the best the ancient world has to offer, scattered through all the forest-jungle over nearly twenty square miles. The French have done a splendid job in uncovering and restoring these marvels of the past. We of the land of boasted efficiency would probably have cleared away and restored too much, for comfort and convenience' sake, and spoiled the effect. In places even the French archæologists have in their professional zeal driven off the forest too ruthlessly, and left some ruins in the sad state of nudity of a stone quarry. But in most cases they have been thoughtful as well as careful. Great green plumes waved high over our heads as we sped along by road or strolled by side-trail to mammoth ruin after ruin. Trees that would be giants beside any of those of northern climes except our redwoods carried without apparent effort mighty loads of vines and parasites that would have stifled the sturdiest elm or oak. All this vegetation gave one the feeling of being so completely surrounded that he might never get out of it again; yet it was not such a forest-riotous wilderness as I had expected, and it was hard to believe that herds of wild elephants were trampling it down only a few miles away. Here and there were expanses of natural half-clearing; white birds in flocks escorted water-buffaloes through swamps that might almost have been passable by Ford.

Yet there was a greater rage for destruction among the plants than had ever been shown by the Siamese. The Prince of Death, Siva of the Brahmans, has given to each beast the special enemy which eats it, to each creature its destroying microbes; and he seems to have foreseen that puny man would try to prolong himself a little by constructing durable things, and imagined a thousand destructive agents to annihilate his efforts. Huge trees which the French call *fromagers*—though I saw no cheese upon them, and our own name of "silk-cotton tree" seems more justified—their trunks as if whitewashed, or spotted with leprosy, or, more exactly still, as if they had been painted in lilac and cream by some fantastic-minded artist, roam the ruins with their buttress roots. Queerly grown in and over the great stone piles like inquisitive serpents, these roots have in some cases wandered thirty yards away in search of sustenance. Laocoön roots lifted great stones in their embrace; one had disdainfully shoved aside a huge pillar and taken on the job of supporting the mass of masonry itself. The banyan, with its aerial roots, does not overthrow the ruins; it gathers them, strains them to its bosom, as it were, so that enormous heaps of rocks that would otherwise long since have fallen apart still maintain the form the Khmer gave them. Trickery rather than force characterizes even the vegetation here in the tropics, though the trees too have learned to fight when necessary. The more brutal *fromager* bursts walls asunder by the slow force of its growing trunk, squeezes ancient buildings to death like the boa-constrictor, swallows them in its great maw. Especially what the French call the "fig-tree of ruins" is irresistible; it reigns as master to-day at Angkor. In the beginning it was

only a little seed, sowed by the wind on a frieze or the top
of a tower. But from there its roots, like steel cables, have
insinuated themselves between the stones, descending by a
sure instinct toward the earth; and having at last reached it,
they have grown quickly from its nourishing soil and become
enormous, disrupting, unbalancing everything, opening thick
walls from top to bottom, sometimes completely destroying
the edifice. Among the palaces, above the temples it has so
patiently disintegrated, it spreads its pale smooth branches
with their serpent spottings, and shades the débris with its
superb broad domes of foliage as with great green parasols.

Here and there along the roads and trails magnificent trees
have been mutilated by man, rare and furtive as he is in
these parts. Deep holes are burned in many a trunk in order
to collect in earthenware pots resin for the making of candles,
as the Landais of France gather pitch from their pine-trees.
Now and then the road is straddled by stone gateways above
which smile huge human faces with long tresses of lianas.
But for all the centuries they have had free play, neither the
slow encroachment of the forest and jungle nor the heavy
dissolving rains have been able to wipe out the impression
of Angkor-Thom as a city of splendid architecture, or the
ironic bonhomie, as Pierre Loti calls it, of these mammoth
stone faces, much more disquieting than the grimaces of the
monsters of China.

Though they were remarkable architects, the Khmer were
rather poor masons. They knew no more of how to build a
vault than by piling up huge stone after stone in horizontal
layers, each reaching a little farther out toward the center.
Their arches are crude, made of immense stones laid one on
top of another, and instead of a keystone they simply placed
a larger stone on top. Their total work is all the more surprising, and its duration that much more marvelous, their

Angkor Vat from its main gateway

A procession of elephants covers the face of one great terrace among the forest-engulfed ruins of Angkor

One can wander for days through the forests of Angkor and constantly come upon new evidences of the mighty architectural genius of the now vanished Khmer

roofs, though they must always have leaked, as they do now, all the more wonderful because the Khmer so little knew how to build them. Some have been shored up by the French; some of them were evidently repillared by the builders themselves. Yet scores still stand, after nearly a thousand years, without any such assistance.

Most of the stones themselves are not so well fitted as at Machu Picchu in the Andes; but the decorations on them outdo anything the ancient civilizations of the Western Hemisphere have to offer. The greatest art of the Khmer was their taste in sculpture, the finish of their execution, their treating of colossal things with the care and delicacy of jewels. Everywhere are figures, bas-reliefs, carvings without end, so delicately chiseled that one might think them lace pasted upon the stone, façades as carefully worked as the most patient embroideries. The stones all have round holes in them, suggesting how they may have been carried to the places they were needed. The reddish, comparatively soft, sandstone or composite of which much of Angkor-Thom was built is common in this part of the world. A French geologist asserts that it is old lava. Yet the task of building such a city even with that was a task indeed in such a climate.

All that first morning, and the next, we kept coming upon new masses of striking architecture in the forest. Now and again the modern road ran beneath towers bearing on each of their four sides mammoth human faces, always alike and said to represent Brahma. Many single faces were carved on eight, ten, a dozen huge stones awkwardly put together. These Cambodian *préasats,* as archæologists call them, whether or not they are adorned with the quadruple face of Brahma, are as characteristic of Khmer art as the palm-tree is of the Cambodian landscape. In one place the road was flanked by a great stone balustrade, a hundred yards long, and by the remnants of what was once another, each in the form of a gigantic cobra with raised head, upheld in the arms of a score of mammoth stone men. The cobra-head motif everywhere suggested a former ardent worship of snakes; human figures with a beak in place of a nose were almost as common. One great wall was covered with a procession of life-size elephants; beyond were walls formed inside and out of thousands of closely set Hindu figures. Here and there were suggestions of the Maya ruins of Central America, but this probably proves merely that minds which have reached a similar development run in similar channels, rather than that tropical people of a millennium ago crossed the great ocean.

The tourist-minded Fords rushed us about all the Saturday and Sunday mornings following our arrival, but left us to our own devices the rest of the four days. The *sala* where they duly deposited us again after each flight outdid the best hotels of Indo-China, except that the roosters housed just behind it might have been spared. But guests of course must have their eggs and their roast chicken, and no Frenchman would be so cruel as to deprive even a hen of its mate. Every living being, European or native, retired immediately after the eleven o'clock *déjeuner* and did not rise again until two or three in the afternoon. To think of doing anything else was all but impossible, to say nothing of actually doing it. Not even the Cambodians, used to this climate at least for centuries, seemed able to endure those burning hours out of doors. For all my tropical experience I soon found that the only way to bear life during that atrocious period was to revert to the reputed costume of Adam before the unfortunate apple episode, turn the electric fan squarely upon my re-

cumbent form inside the mosquito-net, and succumb to the
fond hope of perhaps getting a nap.

Those of us who knew nothing of real hardships also
fancied we suffered one other terrible infliction in that otherwise comfortable bungalow. The French food naturally was
good, with neither wine nor ice lacking, but the principal meal
was made so miserable by swarms of mosquitoes under the
tables that poor Mrs. Piffton-Smith—though of course she
would violently resent the adjective—had to wear even at
dinner the oven-like riding-boots she endured among the ruins
out of an abject fear of "reptiles," though, except for the
stone cobras, the less imaginative of us never saw so much
as a fleeing serpent's tail. If there were duly presented new-
comers at table she mitigated her martyrdom somewhat by
frequent references to her daughter Lady So-and-so, wife of
Lord So-and-so, governor of—and so on. But few travelers
came after us; Mrs. P.-S. naturally knew no French, and
obviously she could not speak to strangers without the formal
introduction that was often lacking; and those of us who
had long since learned that extraordinary daughter by heart
were not, I fear, very sympathetic listeners even to new
anecdotes concerning the Lady of the family. Those of the
women who had no such antidote for those mosquito-tortured
hours wrapped napkins, newspapers, anything at all, about
their legs, and burned under the table joss-sticks enough to
supply a Chinese temple, being unjustly denied the male privilege of relieving their nerves by such remarks as now and
then rose from a man who, driven beyond endurance, tried a
slap or two—and left a splotch of blood on his white trousers.

After my first drenched nap I set out to roam through
Angkor-Vat, most striking of all the ruins scattered over
that twenty square miles of tropical forest. Vat, by the

way, is the Cambodian and Siamese word for temple. Just across the lake-like moat, with its shimmering watery carpet of lilies and water-cress, on the outer shore of which the *sala* sits, the mighty building was heaped into the sky in the center of the only real clearing in the region. From the big stone doorway of long ago through which one emerges upon the great stone bridge and causeway leading to it, the central mass ahead bore a certain resemblance to the Kremlin; yet that is small beside it. The enormous stone slabs of the causeway were worn smooth as polished marble, in places even hollowed out, by the feet of men and women and elephants already dead a thousand years. For the few shod tourists who have followed it during the past decade can scarcely have made more impression on those cyclopean blocks than do the bare feet of pilgrims and of the bonzes in their yellow robes who still patter along it. Strange processions indeed must have trodden this aged causeway, flanked by a massive railing of gigantic stone cobras standing sentinel with raised heads—seven heads each, spread out like fans, the necks swollen as when the deadly snake is ready to strike.

Life had become endurable again, yet the afternoon heat from the stones blazed upon all day by an unclouded equatorial sun was a succession of physical blows as distinct as my heavy Western footsteps along the causeway toward the basilic phantom ahead. Once inside the inner inclosure, this gigantic edifice dominated everything, a more impressive sight, in its way, than the Taj Mahal itself, as beautiful, almost as symmetrical, losing mainly by over-elaboration. Nowhere in the world perhaps has man piled up so many stones as in this mountain-temple. Crushing masses of sculptured rocks, terraces, stone-carved bas-reliefs, stairways leading swiftly upward into towers that seem to scrape the cloud-

less heavens, gave me a feeling akin to depression. At first
sight all one's impressions were jumbled together; disorder
and confusion seemed to emanate from this hill of chiseled
blocks. It is not simple in its lines, like Thebes and Baalbek,
like Machu Picchu and the Taj Mahal, but has the exuber-
ance, the dismaying complications of Hindu art, so that it
is not merely by its enormity that it staggers the beholder.
He who tries to see it all at once suffers the fatigue so common in museums; one must come back often, each time studying a little of it in detail, and then gradually a perfect sym-
metry asserts itself.

Two monsters, darkened by centuries and bearded with
lichen, though under the French they are now shaved from
time to time, guard the front entrance to the temple itself,
like dragons stationed before legendary grottoes. The base
of this mighty pyramid of a structure is more than a kilometer square, and completely about it runs a great gallery that
stretches far to right and to left from the four entrances on
as many sides of the building. Beneath the tropical sky without a fleck of cloud that never for an instant left us during
those four Angkor days the mountain-temple glowed with a
golden-brown radiance, so that the greenish demi-day that
suddenly replaced the glaring sunshine outside gave one the
impression of entering a subterranean passage, though on the
outside there are merely massive pillars. Those galleries surrounding the main structure are nearly three quarters of a
mile in length, and for the entire circuit every inch of the
wall is carved with an endless bas-relief giving the whole
history of the Khmer up to the building of Angkor-Vat, the
whole story of the greatest Hindu legend. For the incredible
chiseled painting along the four outer walls of the temple
has for its inspiration one of the noblest and most ancient
epics conceived by the men of Asia, those Aryan ancestors

of ours—the Ramayana. The uninterrupted bas-relief un-
rolls as long as the legs will carry one, an inextricable series
of battles, warriors gesticulating with fury, combatants by
the thousand, caparisoned elephants, ancient engines of war,
war chariots with wheels strangely up-to-date, interminable
scenes fleeing forever ahead in straight perspective, until
they seem still more infinitely long than they really are.

This wall of endless carvings looks like a single piece for
hundreds of yards. One must look closely to discover the
joints between the enormous stones put together without
cement, yet adjusted with a precision as rigorous as in the
monuments of Egyptian antiquity. I found myself often
comparing with Machu Picchu this gigantic heap of sculptured stones, and at least in this encircling wall of Angkor-
Vat the stone-fitting was equal to that at which the few
visitors to the long lost city of the Andes have marveled.

There are indeed two miles of galleries in the Vat, twenty-
six thousand feet of bas-reliefs chiseled in stone, archæologists tell us. All these pictures were formerly painted or
gilded, but they have been at the mercy of the elements for
nearly a thousand years, and have lost all the brilliancy of
the original colors. Sweating with the eternal humidity of
the tropics, the panoramas have taken on a sad blackish tint,
with, in places, the gleam of wet things. Then, too, up as
high as the puny mankind of to-day can reach, the bas-
reliefs—five meters high on those outer walls—are worn
glass-smooth by the rubbing of secular fingers. In times of
pilgrimage the whole multitude makes it a duty to touch
every figure it can possibly reach. Here and there, in the
parts lighted by the beautiful little windows with thick
carved-stone bars that are among the chief glories of Angkor-
Vat one may still see tracings of the original coloring, on
garments or faces; and sometimes, in the tiaras of queens

or goddesses, a little gold spared by the weather continues to gleam after all these centuries.

In the middle of the face of each quadrilateral a portico opens in this great gallery and gives access to a central court in which the temple itself, properly speaking, rises, a prodigious heap of sculptured sandstone climbing into the blue sky. The grandiose spreading out of the courts of the second story and the formidable upward surge of the central mass all but take the breath away. Such a complication of lines, what a beauty for all the heaviness in the silent ensemble! The infinity of decorations is incredible; the Khmer certainly did not pay their workmen the union wages of to-day; for one thing there would not have been so much care and artistry in the work. The building seems to have been done by Cham and Tai prisoners of war and by regular levies of the Khmer populace itself—much as black Christophe built his citadel in Haiti. Evidently we must have some species of slavery to produce monuments of this kind; "free" workmen cannot furnish the constant enthusiasm and infinite care in details that they require. But in a way those tropical toilers so long since returned to dust had things better than our trade-union bricklayers of to-day, impossible as that may seem. For the story goes that there was one architect for every five hundred builders, and each of the builders had a hundred coolies to keep him supplied with stone! Then artists came to cover every available surface, with the care of painters working on canvas. For the Khmer were of the Hindu point of view, abhorring simplicity and uncovered surfaces.

There are no obscenities among the myriad carvings of Angkor-Vat, even from our Puritan point of view, though somehow one expects them. But the Khmer kings evidently

liked their musical comedies, or at least their ballets, even
as does the tired business man of to-day. For there are
Apsarases carved everywhere, in infinitely repeated groups,
chiseled on every side of every stone pillar, not merely here
at Angkor-Vat but throughout most of the ruins of Angkor-
Thom, forever dancing before their long departed masters.
These perpetually virgin though constantly violated nymphs
of the Hindu paradise, everywhere sculptured in stone, under
the porticos, in the verandas, in the clear-obscure of the galleries, beneath the hard sunshine that falls through crumbling vaults, make the dead walls live. Everywhere they
dance, among the falling lianas, on the bases of temple altars,
their arms supple, their busts stiff and upright, as millen-
niums ago on the shores of the Ganges for the amusement of
Indra, as at Pnom Penh their living descendants dance before
the octogenarian king on the silver pavement of his palace-
temple. The artists of ancient times chiseled and polished as
lovingly as any modern sensuous denizen of the Latin Quarter these dancing virgins—who can say what has become of
the beautiful women from whom these perfect torsos were
copied?—and all these figures in bracelets and rich adornments rather than clothing have been so often caressed in
the course of the bygone centuries that their beautiful bare
throats shine like polished marble. It is the women especially who, during their pilgrimages, touch them passionately,
begging from them the gift of becoming mothers. Unfortunately, like those on the bas-reliefs of Egypt, the feet of
these lovely creatures are badly done, being always drawn
in profile even when the dancer is facing forward, so that
what might seem art to the followers of the reputedly fun-
niest of our "movie artists" merely testifies that the myriad
beautiful stone goddesses of Angkor were the work of a

Unlike the rest of the mighty far-spread ruins, the great green space about
Angkor Vat has never been overrun by the tropical forest

One of the many interior courts of the mammoth temple of Angkor-Vat

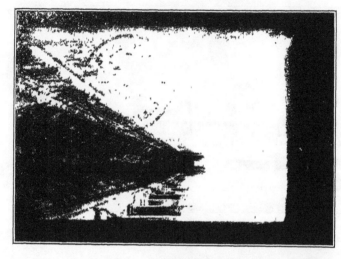

It is fully half a mile around this corridor of Angkor-Vat, and every inch of the stone wall is carved with scenes from Khmer history and Hindu mythology

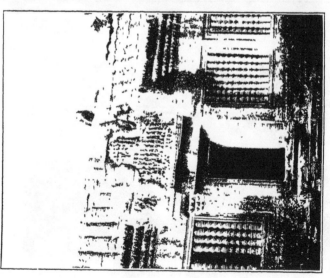

The window-bars, like everything else at Angkor-Vat, are of stone

primitive humanity, still struggling with the difficulties of design.

I raised my eyes to the mass above me, and almost without volition my neck craned to its utmost that I might gaze upon the four giant towers, topped by a central one still larger, in which the temple rises. Nothing lives up there —except flocks of bats—and the stairways of startling height fall under the ardent sun like a cascade of sandstone. The Khmer were no more expert at making stairways than with roofs and arches and the feet of their dancing-girls, and Angkor-Vat has the steepest stairs in the world—even we who so love superlatives will not deny them this. Stairs that are all but sheer walls lead to the lofty heights of this mountain of a temple, stairs so steep that the knee-caps strike on the step above, and so narrow that the foot can only be set down sidewise; and even then there is many a slip, especially in descending. The bygone architects should have been more thoughtful toward dizzy tourists; the Piffton-Smiths never got above the ground floor at all—which was like coming to Rome and going home again without seeing the Colosseum. Even the surest-headed of us clung to the hand-polished old walls in descending, losing our footing often on the worn and sometimes wet steps.

One must climb these cascades of stone, too, between recumbent lions, beasts suggesting Assyrian sacred bulls in stone, cobras spreading out their seven heads like a fan above their angrily swollen necks, as well as between smiling Apsarases, perpetually dancing for their long dead masters. A hard climb, even for me, whose strength lies mainly in legs, and I found myself on the first of three platforms, with a second story, of a height double that of the first, defy-

ing me with still more abrupt stairs, still more closely guarded
by smiles and grimaces in stone. Then when I certainly had
the right to think that at last I had arrived, there suddenly
sprang up before me the third story, of a height double that
of the second! It was like climbing the Andes, like fronting
life and discovering to one's astonishment that what at first
looked like a struggle, perhaps an insurmountable obstacle, is
only the easy preliminary to ever harder and higher tasks
beyond. This progressive doubling of the heights, from
one story to another, was a clever architectural discovery,
enlarging the temple by an illusion from which one cannot
escape. The Khmer were clever architects, as I have said
before; and the memorable stairway that leads to the topmost
platform, with its narrow worn steps on which grass grows
even while the French are striving to keep this most magnificent of the monuments of Angkor clear of it, while pilgrims
and tourists are constantly going up and down them, for their
respective motives, is steep enough to give any one vertigo;
even the sailor we know as Pierre Loti found it so. "One
would say that the temple grows larger, prolongs itself indefinitely, straining itself toward the heavens, so that climbing Angkor-Vat is like those fatiguing nightmares in which
one strives toward a goal that forever flees on ahead. The
gods no doubt wish to make themselves more inaccessible the
more one tries to approach them."

There are four of these stairways, watched over by the
enigmatically smiling Apsarases, one on each side of the
temple. As I mounted, the forest seemed to mount with me,
spreading out on all sides to the horizon, unbroken as the
sea clear to the circle of that horizon. The topmost platform
must be at least a hundred feet above the plain, yet the great
monument seems submerged, drowned in the midst of its
verdure. It is the greatest extent of forest I have ever seen,

except perhaps from the eastern slope of the Andes, where South America falls away into the enormous Amazon basin that stretches to the Atlantic. Formerly, in place of this silent sea of vegetation below, stretched the city of Angkor-Thom, perhaps no more forested then than Peking or a New England city to-day. If one could only push aside the roof of interlacing branches one could still see beneath them the walls, terraces, temples, the long paved avenues flanked by divinities in stone, balustrades, gigantic serpents with raised heads, Brahma-faced towers, all now swallowed up in the jungle. But the forest has become again what it was for incalculable centuries before the beginning of man, so that nothing visible remains of the work of those Hindu-like adventurers who many hundred years ago came here to tempt fate and clear the space of a city of nearly a million inhabitants. It endured only a millennium and a half, that episode of the empire of the Khmer; in other words a very negligible period compared with the longevity of the vegetable kingdom. The scars are reclosed, nothing now appears for all their labors, and the "fig-tree of ruins" spreads everywhere its parasol of green leaves. It is true that in our day other adventurers, from far off to the West, have founded near here the semblance of another empire; but it is small and puny compared to that of the Khmer, not likely to rival it in duration any more than it has in lasting monuments. When these pale-faced conquerors shall have gone their way also, they will merely have cleaned up a little the works of a greater race, and will be remembered only as the charwomen may be in the ruins of our sky-scrapers of to-day, by a charred broom or a broken dust-pan left here and there among the débris.

All afternoon I climbed and loafed about that mighty pile of masonry. In the immense clearing within which the giant

temple sits enthroned, defended by moats and walls, one
had the impression of perfect security, quite unlike the feeling
among the other ruins, for all the nearness and immensity
of the great forest that hangs its black curtain all about it.
Tigers do not cross the great stone bridge, even though the
doors are never closed. The Vat was never finished. When,
at the end of our thirteenth century, the Khmer empire fell,
for no good reason that has ever been discovered, it was
still in process of construction. As this great work of theirs
surpasses any of our own, at least when we consider the
tools they had, it is little short of presumptuous to suppose
that we will endure longer than did that doughty empire of
the tropical forests.

The Chinese scholar who visited this mysterious empire on
the eve of its decline and left the only known documents
on its splendor tells us that the fifth tower of Angkor-Vat,
rising above all the rest and most imposing and complicated
of all, seeming to give the temple a mountain summit when
seen from afar off, but dwarfed by the very size of the
edifice when one is close beneath it, was crowned with a
golden lotus so large that one could see its sacred flowers
gleam in the air from all parts of the city that is to-day
buried in the jungle. Leaning over from the upper platform
at the base of this tower one looks down upon an entrancing
scene below, most of it a hundred feet below. From up
there one sees that what with the tropical sun and rain and
long abandonment each of the superimposed layers of the
temple has become a sort of suspended garden in which
the immense leaves of the banana mingle with white tufts
of the fragrant jasmine. The comfortable French bungalow
across the moat is no larger than a dove-cote. Scattered
about the temple clearing are slender palm-trees up which

Two score stone giants hold the cobra-headed approaches to Brahma-faced Khmer gateways, parcel now by smooth French roads

Three of the many gigantic figures holding the cobra-like approach to a Khmer gateway

Many of the ancient ruins at Angkor are as intricate as they are artistic in at least the Oriental sense of the word

men climb by single bamboo poles tied with vines to the trunk, carrying over their shoulders bamboo buckets that they exchange for others hanging from cut fronds until they are filled with a sap from which is made a brown sugar. Even the almost naked men among the giant leaves of these trees that looked so high from below were far beneath me here. In the forest that surrounds the temple hundreds of parrakeets shrieked; one might think they had come from the four corners of the forest to enliven the solitude of the little stone dancers, who in their turn give the ruins life, and they never leave off chattering until night settles down upon them, as no doubt the dancers themselves chattered when the forest was a park and the ruins a palace.

Under the trees at the edges of the clearing are the shacks of monks where Admiral Viaud, alias Pierre Loti, slept, almost twenty-five years ago now, when he came to Angkor in his two-wheeled cart and went away on an elephant. The frail little houses, to which tiny stairs that are barely ladders lead, are made of wood and mats; some have little festooned windows from which shaven skulls peer now and then, and they stand on poles, well above the ground. All the inhabitants are dressed alike, in bright yellow robes set off by a drapery of orange and other colors that stand out against the old walls, gray with age, sometimes reddish, especially near sunset, as it was now, startling flashes of color against the dense curtain of greenery beneath the clear sky. Too accustomed to Europeans to be curious toward them, they seem to take us as unavoidable nuisances, and when they sing in a low voice and monotonous rhythm they gaze at us without interrupting their tranquil litany. Now some of them are walking abroad, languidly and without haste, their hairless heads shining beneath the low sun. Theirs are curious villages, where there are no women, no animals except

mongrel curs, no tillers of the soil, nothing but these
monotonous singers, yellow of face and dressed in two
brighter tones of the same color. For furniture their simple
dwellings have nothing but an old Buddhist altar, with gods
in faded gold, before which little heaps of ashes testify to
the constant burning of joss-sticks to their tawdry divinities.
About two hundred of these bonzes of Cambodia and Siam
guard the sacred ruins, and nearly that number live here
perpetually, psalming day and night about this pile of titanic
blocks of stone heaped up by their more hardy ancestors, or
by those whom their more hardy ancestors defeated and
drove away.

Sunset, quickly followed by a bright full moon, came, and
the lighting of the immense stage-setting about me dimin-
ished until the forest, already full of shadows under an ashen
sky, in which a yellow phosphorescence mingled with an ever
darker green, died down to a great spread of vacancy without
details or distinctness. In the last light of the day, leaning
over the edge of the uppermost platform, I had seen a procession of multicolored women drawing away along the great
causeway across the moat, a saffron-clad priest with a rolled
parasol across his back leading them. Cruder Buddhas have
here and there replaced broken or fallen Brahman figures
in the great temple, especially within the base of the central
tower in the lofty third story. They are ugly things of
mud and wood compared with the ancient Khmer deities,
and to look upon them gives one the feeling one sometimes
has toward the crude missionaries from our own land who
are trying to replace the more fitting as well as older beliefs
of the East with their own. A quantity of Buddhist idols
of all sizes sit on thrones in this upper story, smiling at
nothing, and pilgrims go about, bowing down before statue
after statue, indifferent, and no doubt unaware, whether they

are praying to Vishnu or to Buddha. Sometimes pilgrims from far-off Burma come in the silence of the night to lay a flower or burn a joss-stick before each of these figures, with a musty smell now, that are crumbling away into the dust from which they, like the rest of us, came. A word from the leader, which one can guess to be some such warning as, "Let us hurry or the hour of the tiger will overtake us," and they make their devotions more hastily, cut even shorter their reverences, and soon their barefoot tread is lost in the drone of a Buddhist service below as they descend the steep stone stairways.

Whatever else one may see at Angkor, one always comes back to the great temple, and that not merely because it is so near the *sala*. I found myself almost unconsciously wandering there in the moonlight every evening after dinner. For one thing it gave a respite from the prattle of tourists, very few of whom ventured into the structure after dark. On the first day I had met two childlike monks in their yellow robes going along the gallery with a broom and a scoop of woven bamboo strips. They were picking up the wherewithal to fertilize some little monastic garden, no doubt for the growing of flowers, since the pious laymen furnish them their food, and the tilling of the soil for useful purposes is not one of the duties of their calling. There is no lack of fertilizer to be had in Angkor-Vat. The pavements that are not open to the sun are everywhere carpeted with the droppings of bats, so thick in many places that one seems to be walking on felt. An almost intolerable odor permeates all the interior, and the squeaking of what the French so fittingly call "bald mice" up under the sharp vaults of the crude massive roofs is always in the ears even of the visitor by day. Then, if one's eyes are sharp, they may make out myriads of the repulsive creatures hanging head down by their claws to the rough stone ceiling, looking during these their sleeping hours like sacks of dark velvet.

By night, clouds, avalanches of these flying rats, aggressive and tireless, greet the intruder. As my steps resounded in the obscure corridors, along which I advanced feeling my way foot by foot, for all the brilliant moonlight outside, sharp little cries multiplied to a concert, as of thousands of angry rats above my head. The horrible odor seemed to increase as one after another of the sleeping creatures unfolded its hairless membranes and joined in the general movement. It is always half-night up there under the vaults and roofs, and perhaps they do not sleep too soundly, or know the hour exactly, even by day; with the night the least intrusion turns chamber after chamber into swirls of the squeaking creatures. They descended to touch my hair; the wind of their wings was like the breeze of electric fans running riot in the darkness, cold in the tepid night as the breath of death. They swirled about me in swarms on their silent wings, uttering their angry little cries, as if banding together to repel an invader. One might have fancied them the unappeased spirits of the Khmer gods of long ago, or the unsaved souls of those who built the mountain-temple, resenting the profaning of the sacred edifice in the solemn hours of the night by the crude, heavily shod being of the modern world. If I stood perfectly still for some time, the chorus decreased, died down, disappeared, as if they had all gone back to sleep again. But with the first step forward they detached themselves once more, one after another, and soon the same noisome gyrations of unseen squeaking things was all about me again. My flesh crept at the damp contact of their wings, at the very thought of their touching me, and for once I was almost afraid of the dark, a feeling I had not known since early childhood. I kept myself with difficulty from fleeing headlong out into the moonlight.

No longer paled by the excess of sun, the bas-relief of the gallery, the figures on the terraces, the dancing Apsarases everywhere took on a nebulous clarity that in a way made them all the more beautiful. The moon shone in silver streams through the carved stone bars of the narrow windows; out in the courtyards the massive block of Angkor-Vat with its five towers seemed more gigantic than ever, too enormous to be merely the work of pygmy mankind. The more than steep stairways had about them something so uncanny that it took more exertion of the will than of the thighs to climb them; I had the feeling of entering a mammoth burial-vault from which there would never again be any escape. As if fearful of having to accuse myself of cowardice I climbed the first story, doubly high to the second, forced myself up to the third. A light like a fallen star twinkled at the top of the highest stairway, at the door of the sanctuary beneath the central tower. It was the votive-lamp of the Chettys, the Hindu money-lenders of Cholon and Saïgon, who offer this eternal flame to the abandoned gods. Then suddenly the squeak of swirling bats became more than my nerves could bear, and I retreated, slowly only because of the indignity of frankly running away, and the likelihood of tobogganing down those long cascades of narrow slippery steps at a false movement made in haste.

On Monday I set off on foot to Bayon at the crack of dawn, knowing how painful walking becomes soon after the sun rises above the tree-tops. The Elephant Terrace and Bayon, with some of the striking old ruins in their vicinity, about which I spent the morning, I had already

hastily seen as we were Fording bungalow-ward on the first
morning in order not to delay Mrs. Piffton-Smith's luncheon
and nap. Now, alone and at leisure, I found them second
only to Angkor-Vat. Bayon, impressive as a cathedral, is
the oldest sanctuary of Angkor-Thom, two centuries older
than the great temple in which the genius of the Khmer
terminated. In its day it had half a hundred towers, each
and every one of them bearing on all its four sides the face
of Brahma, the highest rising nearly fifty meters above the
plain. Now many have fallen, been destroyed, or been removed by the French to save the others; and still there are
so many of them that one feels the futility of trying to get
out of sight of their myriad-faced god. Those enigmatical
faces of Brahma, or Siva, some of them two men in height,
crowned by diadems in stone, gaze so multitudinously down
from even what remains of the pyramidal mass that one has
a feeling of self-consciousness as when one is the focus of
the eyes of a living multitude. Those visages with the
enigmatical smile, the half-closed eyelids, the great flat noses,
all with the selfsame expression of ironic pity, are not merely
on every face of every tower; they gaze even from worn
stones, no larger than a fist, picked up in the underbrush.

Toward the end of the ninth century, four hundred years
before the decline of the Khmer, Bayon, ruder and even
more enormous than Angkor-Vat, was in its glory. The
fifty towers of different sizes formed several stories, and
the topmost could be seen from any part of the now abandoned city. To-day most of it has to be reconstructed by
the imagination, including the vast cleared space that made
it possible to see the crushing stature of the ensemble. In
fancy one can rebuild the successive terraces, the great stairways, the sumptuous avenues which led to it, bordered by
so many columns, balustrades, divinities, rampant-headed

cobras, and monsters, now crumbled away in the grass. But even the faces of Brahma that remain gazing to the four cardinal points of the compass seem to affirm, to force upon the beholder, the omnipresence of the god of Angkor.

A shower-bath, lunch, and a nap, and I was off again, for a three-hour elephant ride. There are two of these great beasts attached to the *sala,* but like the goat-cart at the zoo they are now rather curiosities than useful means of transportation. Akin to all holders of sinecures, they stood before the door lazily swinging their trunks and watching with cunning little eyes the Fords that have taken nearly all their work away from them. The American ladies mounted one of them, Mr. Piffton-Smith and I the other. The mother of Lady So-and-so would not risk her precious life in such an adventure, and how her husband persuaded her to let him undergo this terrifying experience is a domestic secret to which I have no key.

I shall forevermore think of the elephant as a synonym for caution, for slowness and docility too, for that matter. The *cornacs,* as the French call what we know as mahouts, drove these pacific monsters more easily than we do a horse, nay, as easily as one can drive an automobile, except that nothing would induce them to move faster than two miles an hour. Like domesticated man, there was nothing whatever wild about them, and with every step up the only hillock in all the region the prudent beasts felt every stone before trusting their weight to it, until they seemed to personify the precautious mother of a Lady whom we had left behind. Little by little we dominated the immense sea of absolutely flat forest. Here where once there were innumerable palaces gleaming in the sunshine, little more was visible above the endless spread of vegetation than the block of Bayon and the five towers of Angkor-Vat. The view across the vast forest-jungle left even that great temple like a needle lost in a haystack, so tiny was it in its immense setting in the midst of what looked like an endless and a trackless wilderness.

So terrifying was this experience of rising a hundred feet or two above sea-level on these cautious monsters that poor Mr. P.-S. had to be helped down at the summit like an infant, and only the impossibility of covering on foot the mile or two back to the *sala* induced him to mount again. Cambodian workmen, under orders of the French, still toil in several of the ruins, and here they laughed and shouted as they threw blocks of stone down the slope with insulting words. Then we went slowly, more than slowly, back, and across the mammoth bridge over the moat for a circuit of Angkor-Vat. It was as if, knowing they could not compete in speed with the Fords that have replaced their fellows, the beasts had no intention of trying; or it may be that there is an elephant union. That would even better account for their skill in wasting time at every movement, at every moment, making their journey the shortest possible within the three hours allotted us. The foundation of Angkor-Vat and the bridge leading to it are raised two or three meters above the ground, to facilitate mounting and dismounting from the elephants that were once the only beasts of burden in this region. But there was no time to dismount and mount now; the hour of the tiger would indeed have come before the lethargic animals took up their funereal march again. As we crept slowly round the temple, the elephants tore large branches from some of the tropical trees high above our heads, and munched them as languidly as a plumber eating his lunch on some one else's time. Men in breech-clouts were still walking up the frail palm-trees with bamboo buckets in which to gather their sugary sap; the bonzes were chanting their monotonous litanies from their stilt-legged huts; and

This palace-temple of Bayon once had more than fifty towers or pinnacles, and on all four sides of every one of them appeared the face of Brahma or Siva

Dancing-girls of the Hindu type cavort on all four sides of the great stone pillars of many an Angkor ruin

Cambodian coolies toil among those ruins of Angkor which the French
consider worth preserving or restoring

Weeks at Angkor would not exhaust the interest even of the casual
visitor, to say nothing of the archæologist

then the sun disappeared swiftly in the sea of jungle and gave us that brief fleeting twilight of the tropics.

On Tuesday morning I mounted a tiny horse and rode away alone through the woods, the delightful freshness of an early tropical morning all about me. A light two-wheeled cart was also to be had, but I preferred the miniature sample of the equine world—until the blazing of the sun began in earnest. Though there are on the whole few feathered crea-tures in the forest that has swallowed up Angkor-Thom, as if even they were afraid of the denseness of the jungle, the singing of birds and insects made a mild ceaseless music. Sometimes it sounded as if a bird was whispering a cordial invitation to me from the bush—or was it merely whistling to keep up its courage? There was such a wall of verdure on either side that, like will-o'-the-wisps, they were never really visible. Monkeys dashed from branch to branch, scores of monkeys, though not one had we seen during the official trips by Ford. Evidently they keep out of the way of tourists, perhaps because they cannot endure their inane chatter. But now they played by the dozen about the ruins, as freely as if they recognized in me a close relative, and indulged in a pantomime, worthy of any stage, that was plainly an imitation of the workmen among the remains of Angkor-Thom. A Cambodian legend assures us that monkeys formerly talked like men, until the men made slaves of them and forced them to work. The monkeys did not like this, and as they are timid but intelligent they simply ceased to talk like us and pretended not to understand, so that from that time forth they have lived in peace, gathering nothing except for their dinners, and gamboling among the trees to their hearts' content. The thin Cambodian coolies who toil for the French about the ruins have not been so clever.

CHAPTER IV

THE CAMBODIANS AT HOME

THE efficient French manager of the *sala* at Angkor, and those few of my fellow-guests who saw me set out on foot for Siem Réap that Sunday afternoon, gave me credit for being at least half mad. I have often suspected as much myself. The native town was nearly five miles away along that almost excellent French road by which we had come from the edge of the flooded forest on the evening of our arrival, and obviously it would be at least as great a distance back to the *sala* again. But it was a delightful walk, even while the sun was pouring its rays like a molten flood of gold down into the roadway, and with every step forward its aim became less exact, so that the infinitesimal streak of shade along one dense forest wall gradually grew to be worth attention.

There were road-signs as in France, now and then an ox-cart with two wheels drawn by as many oxen. On the whole, though, the road was deserted, and for a long distance there was nothing but the Chinese wall of unbroken forest close on either side, with frequent visions of lianas in blossom, and in the streak of sky above, occasional flashes of strange tropical birds. Then there came scattered villages, water-buffaloes at pasture, more bourgeois birds sitting serenely on the spines of the beasts as on a telegraph-wire, naked children who live in the water, their gleaming skins mirroring the sun like the scales of a fish. At length, some little dis-

tance from the ruins of the ancient city, there began an almost
endless succession of thatched huts back among the trees,
stilted villages, so to speak, for every one of them was raised
head-high above the ground on more or less haphazard posts
that had once been the trunks of small trees. None of these
simple homes had a clearing about it. The inhabitants had
wisely cut away only enough of the underbrush to give themselves room to move and to plant a little, and they lived completely in the shade of the great forest about and high above
them. Steps were cut in the earth bank of the little river that
more or less followed the road, down to the water's edge and
what seemed to be fish-traps. There were also some simple
but ingenious nets, and strangely shaped boats, the smaller
ones paddled, the larger poled. A quiet Sunday-afternoon
languor that was probably perpetual rather than only weekly
hung over everything. The leisurely splashing of water called
attention every little way to a large wheel, made of now age-
blackened bamboo, that forced the river to lift itself by the
scoopful into the little gardens beyond the houses. The
slow regular thump of a wooden pestle worked by foot-power
betrayed here and there woods-dwellers caught in the act of
having to hull rice for their evening meal, in the hollowed
upright section of log that serves them as mortar. Otherwise, there was only the forest and its natural noises.

Siem Réap, of which I had once before had a fleeting
moonlight glimpse, was almost a city, in the Cambodian sense.
For the Cambodians are not a townspeople, but prefer the
woods, which, with a bit of tilled soil, gives them all they
need. The place was entirely Siamese, its little houses all
perched on piles and its temple decorated with golden horns;
and even these were tucked back into the forest that crowded
the wider place in the road closely on either side. Evidently
the inhabitants sleep on the open-work bamboo-splint floor

of their porches, as some of them were already, or still, doing now, with the sun barely touching the tree-tops. It was not always easy to tell the sexes apart at a glance, for girls and younger women cut their hair in the ugly Siamese pompadour fashion, slightly longer than that of the men. Grandmothers, old men, and priests dispensed with theirs entirely, having more or less recently shaven skulls. Both sexes wore like a short skirt a mere piece of cloth wrapped about the hips and thighs, a costume so simple that most Cambodian girls never learn to sew. Some of the younger women, especially if they were far from the family clearing, had a cloth thrown carelessly over their breasts; but about the house and in its immediate vicinity they had nothing above the waist to hamper them from working, or from suckling one of their interminable infants, carried on the hip, Hindu fashion. There seemed to be much bathing and washing of clothes, such as they were, reminding one of Ceylon. Bougainvillea hung in purple masses about the wooden house of the French *résident* and some of the other better buildings. Police in half or full khaki uniforms, topped by a kind of tam-o'-shanter, seemed out of place in this languid Eden.

The Cambodians are a slow and quiet race compared with the Chinese, even with the Annamese, so gentle that even the shoulder-poles of their oxen are seldom weighted down with heavy loads. The Tai, as the race to which they belong is better known, are about equal in civilization, under equal circumstances, to the Chinese, according to those who know them well, except that the Tai are superior in personal cleanliness and the lack of monkey-like curiosity, and the Chinese in foresight and industry. Here there was none of the crowding of staring or chattering throngs about the foreigner, so common an experience in China. The Cambodians seemed to have a greater sense of personal dignity. As a people they appeared a little surly toward the French, therefore toward white men in general, though this may only have been bashfulness. Physically the individual type is more sturdy, and observers agree that they are much more reserved in their personal habits, than the surrounding peoples. In situations where the Annamese squirms and howls the Cambodian shows neither fear nor excitement. Simple timid souls, however, manly and infantile at the same time, they are too naïve to be any match for the world of to-day. Though they are physically stronger, laborious in their leisurely way, intelligent, and not easily swayed from their purposes or beliefs, they will let a puny Annamese chastise them without any attempt at retaliation, because they are afraid of the tricks this more sophisticated fellow might play upon them if they dared to resist. For though the Annamese really look down upon, even hate, the French, they are regarded by the other races comprising Indo-China as the special pets of the foreign rulers. Being nearer in their own sophistication to the modern wisdom, or trickery, of the Westerner, they know much better how to turn the presence of the French to their own good than do these isolated woodsmen of Cambodia, a prey to all sorts of rascalities. The spirit of tolerance, renunciation, non-resistance, of this timid forest-dweller who ornaments his body with symbolic tattooings is so great as to make what in the Chinese seems to be that quality appear none at all.

So while Cambodia is rich, the Cambodian is poor. "Wealthy as Cambodia" was for centuries a byword among the Chinese. The yearly flooding of the Mekong, the Nile of Indo-China, annually brings down a new covering of rich soil for all the delta. Yet even the hasty traveler notes the

far greater prosperity of less fertile Cochinchina. There is
only thatch in Cambodia; in Cochinchina, inhabited by all
the races of Indo-China, including the Cambodians, there
are tiled wooden houses, always a sign of prosperity, for the
fear of fires causes any race to get beyond the thatch stage
as soon as possible. Not merely the Chinese, with their
special privileges, but the Annamese, so easily outdone by
the Celestials in commerce, become in their turn the harsh
commercial exploiters of their simpler neighbors, not only
the Cambodians but the Moi, the Muong, and the Laosians.
Even the recently arranged export of Cambodian cattle to
Manila has proved of no real help to the people themselves,
for they are often cheated out of their working cattle by the
tricky Chinese or Annamese traders.

The Cambodian is exclusively an agriculturist. Even
though he makes his own tools, carts, and houses, that is
merely an adaptation to his isolated life. In whatever he
does he works with the spirit of the genuine artist, which
means that he gives too little attention to getting all possible
material benefit from his labor. Thus during the past several centuries this little people—they are barely a million
and a half—has been terrorized, vanquished, despoiled,
forced to fly, in the dry season, before the Siamese, at the
mercy, in the wet, of the Annamese flotillas. The first were
looking for slaves, and deported people en masse to culti-
vate their lands of the Menam; the second came killing the
people off and driving them out in order to take their lands
for themselves.

To come through the forests and see so low a type of
humanity, at least in so far as ambition and the ability to
build lasting things go, and then suddenly see the towers of
Angkor-Vat, through the half-cleared vista of the old cart

road, is to refuse to believe that the ancestors of these built that. It shakes one's belief in the equality of man; for surely without masters of higher type than these hut-dwellers of to-day this people could never have produced such things. But no, one reflects, peoples, like individuals, have their day, their prime, their productive years. They develop for centuries, then at a certain level accomplish rapidly for a time, then sink into old age. All our own real progress has been during the past few hundred years; we may soon cease to be productive, perhaps not even remain static, like the Chinese, but drift back down-stream, like these simple gentle Cambodians. Possibly some of their once great creative ability might be revived; more likely not. Besides, it is better to let others have the next chance, just as we each give way in turn to the rising generation, than to try to resuscitate what is past, as we sometimes try with the individual. For it is impossible to backwater in life.

Though they have lived more or less intermingled for centuries, there has been little racial intermixture of the Cambodians and the Annamese. They are too nearly like oil and water, the real dividing-line between the Chinese and the Hindu world which makes the name "Indo-China" so fitting. It is only recently that Cambodian girls have not been forbidden to marry foreigners, and there are far fewer *mariages à terme* with the French, and the resultant half-castes, than in Annam. Yet it is said that the Cambodian, interbred with some other race having more aggression in its fiber, makes an excellent human specimen. There is little repulsion between the Tonkinese and the Cambodians, for those two groups are historically little acquainted. But the two discordant races are so different

that to train a French official in Annam, or even in Cochinchina, and then send him to Cambodia, is almost as bad
as to send one from Algeria to Madagascar.

Whereas the Annamese language is a singsong of many
tones, like the Chinese, and they use, or did at least until the
French came, Chinese characters for their writing—so that
Japanese and Annamese, Korean and Chinese, could all read,
though not speak, together—the Cambodian tongue is in one
tone, like our own, and their writing is similar to that
of Siam and India Cambodian music seems such to Western ears. Their freedom from the cacophonic hullabaloo
of the rest of the Far East gives the traveler ground for
hoping that here at last he is running into our own Aryan
influences again The Cambodians accompany themselves
on a kind of guitar, and are the only people in Indo-China
who have so far been taught to play band music well.

The favorite game of Cambodian boys is to keep a ball
made of bamboo splints in the air as long as possible, kicking, striking, butting it with any part of the body except
the hands—real football, which of course ours is not. Their
dances, of immemorial tradition, are a kind of drama of
pantomine ballet, perpetuating the old Hindu epics, given
only by troupes of imperial dancers from the royal harem.
The people themselves do no dancing.

Once from the north, influenced by the more mystic
Buddhism of Tibet, with Sanskrit as the language, the Cambodians are now of the Ceylon or southern Buddhist school,
the language of which is Pali. The Annamese, on the other
hand, inherited the harsher northern Buddhism by way of
Mongolia and China. Thus the clergy, as disdained in
Annam as in China, has great prestige in Cambodia. The
monks are very simple, and in their piety at least are
worthy the profound respect with which they are surrounded.

A rural Cambodian family at home

Though they live only on what they can beg, they are not hermits and anchorets, as in the Chinese atmosphere of Annam, but live the monkish life in common in the numerous temples of the country, quite independent of one another. Priests become laymen, and vice versa, very easily; all Cambodians are in fact expected to don the yellow robe at least once in their lives. Most of them being country people, the monks do not find it repugnant to engage in manual labor. There are many woodsmen, brick-makers, even clock-menders and other industrious "artists" among them. Personally I saw none of this, but only meditation and begging; and I am quite ready to admit that I am hopelessly prejudiced toward those who withdraw from their share of the world's work and troubles the world over. During the three months of the rainy season the monks of Cambodia practise "the retreat" and refrain from all pilgrimages; the rest of the year they go and come almost at will. Their five commandments are: thou shalt not kill, steal, lie, drink intoxicating beverages, or take the woman of another—which is not, be it noted, celibacy in the Christian sense. It is said that at least they never drink strong liquor, and so careful are they to avoid killing that they have a special word ("Bahboh!") and gesture to drive off the militant mosquito without injuring it.

There have long been *salas,* or public houses maintained by the government for travelers, along the principal roads of Cambodia, for the same reason that there are *dak-bungalows* in India. They do not want strangers in their houses, which are semi-sacred; and from that to the Hindu belief in caste pollution by so much as an alien shadow is no great step. Suicide, as common among the Annamese as with the Chinese, is rare among the Cambodians, not because they are greater cowards or more generally happy, but because

of their fear of vile reincarnations. They burn their dead,
like the Hindus and the real Buddhists farther west; the
Annamese practise the loathsome Chinese and Western custom of burying their corpses and keeping them as long as
possible.

The Cambodians have a feudal Hindu civilization, entirely
distinct from the mandarinic, communal, oligarchical civilization of the Annamese and Chinese. In theory all land
belongs to the king, and any that lies uncultivated for three
years may be demanded by some one else as a concession. Only the produce is taxed, the assessments being
gathered by royal delegates quite independent of the provin-
cial authorities. In reality the French have not greatly
changed the ancient order of things during their sixty years
as the "protectors" of Cambodia. They have improved the
ways of communication, beautified the old royal city of
Pnom Penh. They have done much against smallpox:
formerly those who had never had this disease were considered "not yet born to existence." They were exempt
from taxes; a girl could not marry, a boy could not claim
the rights and duties of an adult, until a pock-marked face
could be presented as a certificate of maturity. The French
have given the country peace, external peace, that is; old
residents say there is piracy in the provinces as usual, even
more of it the past twenty years than a century ago. The
French are impotent to stop criminal violence against the
natives, and the local authorities have every interest in
coming to an understanding with the robbers instead of
fighting them. The Chinese merchants of Cambodia pay
pirate insurance.

The French have kept the old forms of kingly rule; and
"beneath an appearance of order there still reigns the old
anarchy," said a French doctor long resident there. Under

cover of the French the ancient injustices of despotic Oriental rule have been perpetuated and modernized. It is
next to impossible for an ordinary Cambodian with just
cause for complaint to get satisfaction. The mass of the
people dare not tell the wrongs done them, even were there
some one both willing and able to listen to them, because
of the fear of reprisals. In a forested Oriental country
very few would risk giving testimony, even if it were not
the Hindu-Buddhist temperament not to complain; for
vengeance is easy. Native functionaries stick together; they
are closely related to the ministers of Pnom Penh. Even
if a case is taken directly to the French *résident,* about all
he can do is refer the matter to the governor of the province involved, "for information." There are many clandes-
tine tariffs for legally gratuitous formalities. By law reg-
istry of birth is free; in practice it costs all that those
concerned can be made to pay. There is a tax on fur-
naces used in the production of fish-oil; but because the
same Cambodian word also means a little portable stove
made of glazed earth, on which all Cambodia once did its
cooking, tax-gatherers have laid by great personal fortunes,
and most of the people have gone back to the three sticks
stuck in the earth used by their ancestors to hold their
rice-pots over a fagot fire.

It is the old story of a very alien race unable to help,
whatever its good will, except in superficial things that are
easily understood, because it cannot get down into the
deeper facts. In the French courts the interpreter reigns
as absolute master, and erects a stone wall between the best
judge and the parties before him. Even the making of
good roads has augmented rather than decreased the help-
lessness of the people, for now French officials, often
changed, dash to and fro between their posts, whereas in

the days of slow native travel they got perforce some clear idea of the needs of the people. The French of course see to it that their rule is treated with full honors, whatever the results of it. There is a costly series of splendid fêtes at Pnom Penh in honor of each new *résident supérieur,* which contrasts sadly with the poverty-stricken people whom he comes in theory to help, and who must pay for all such festivities. The fact is that he rarely comes for any such purpose, but to follow his career with the least possible trouble and the greatest possible advancement. But in the eyes of the Cambodians the French are merely a passing phase, as the Siamese and their other conquerors were before them, and they endure this brief affliction as true fatalists do any other misfortune.

The minister of the palace is the real power in Cambodia. A former interpreter—all who knew a little French when the French took upon themselves the "protection" of Cambodia naturally got in on the ground floor—imposed first upon Norodom as secretary-general of the Council of Ministers, is now a kind of political comprador. An intelligent hard worker, supple, well informed, speaking French fluently now, he has made himself indispensable to the superficial and unstable French administrators and is richer than old King Sisowath himself. Naturally he drew a marvelous personal advantage out of a situation that he was no doubt stupefied to find falling into his hands, and with an almost Chinese point of view toward political matters he tends to perpetuate himself, every day perfecting his double game between the king and the French *résident,* peopling posts with his relatives and retainers, keeping his political fences in order. It is the story of the rise of Charlemagne's forebears all over again, in an Oriental setting. Some *résidents* have tried to outwit this now richest and most powerful

man in the kingdom, but he always comes out best. He
is the real master; the other ministers, the crown prince,
even the octogenarian king himself tremble before him, mute
and resigned.

   To this have the descendants of the mighty Khmer sunk
in the millennium since they were forced to abandon Angkor-
Thom. Yet after all the Cambodians are the only people in
the peninsula who have left enduring works of their intellectual past. Their great art, in which the grandiose perfection of the ensemble is combined with the most delicate
finesse of detail, is their certificate as one of the great races
of mankind.

CHAPTER V

ON a blazing Sunday late in January I was off at six
on a little train that carried me, not uncomfortably,
from daylight until dark, through a jungle country of few
villages and no towns. Bienhoa, half an hour from the
Cochinchina capital, has rubber plantations of some extent,
the well spaced trees still small but already adorned with
sap-gathering tin cans. Beyond, jungle and forest soon
began again, endless jungle-forest, so that there are countless acres available for rubber, and before the century is
over this form of exploitation will no doubt have reached
vast proportions. The wilderness, broken only by little clear-
ings for occasional stations, was so dry in this hot prelude
to the rainy season that it had almost the autumn colors of
the north. Most of the land was deadly flat, but there were
low hills now and then, densely wooded and brushed, especially after little Cochinchina lay behind us and we entered the great coastal strip known as Annam.

For all the wilderness, a splendid road, with huge native
trees well spaced on either side of it, followed the railway.
Train and highway used the same bridges, which custom I
found to be common throughout Indo-China. A horn manipulated by a loin-clothed coolie at either end warns the automobile driver whether or not it is best for him to proceed.
For the bridges are only wide enough for one train or one
vehicle at a time, and though the trains of Indo-China are

not large, nothing short of a motor truck could dispute the right of way with them with any great prospect of success. There are of course no unprotected grade-crossings even in this faintly inhabited region, where an automobile a day is an event, and where there are few ox-carts and fewer pedestrians. As in France, the bridge and gate men govern themselves by the time-table rather than by the facts, though here it is a languid Annamese coolie instead of an old woman or a crippled war-relic who holds up traffic so much longer than necessary.

The government owned and operated railways of Indo-China, destined some day to be joined together in one system, are not yet continuous. The eight hundred miles just then in running order were broken up into three isolated jumps along the coast, not to mention the line from Hanoi up into China that has been leased for a term of years to private interests. All are of meter gauge, burn wood, and make very good speed, considering their difficulties, as was proved by this day's feat of covering the more than 260 miles between Saïgon and Nhatrang—longest of the three sections, even without counting the branch from the Cochinchina capital to Mytho—in the twelve hours between equatorial dawn and darkness.

The French have evolved a curious type of train to fit the peculiar division of humanity in their Far-Eastern possession. The last car is divided into first-, second-, and third-class compartments. First-class accommodation consists of two crosswise seats facing each other in the center of the coach, and the second, with twice that capacity, differs mainly in the color of the leather upholstery. Third class, occupying half the car, has bare wooden seats of American arrangement. The rest of the train, unless it includes also a few freight-cars, is made up of fourth-class box-cars innocent of springs and with four rudimentary benches fore and aft the full length of them. Officials armed with government *réquisitions,* or passes, usually monopolize the first class, and even with their boxes and bags rarely fill it. Europeans with purchased tickets, an occasional Eurasian, and now and then a wealthy native, go second-class. Well-to-do natives, and the poorer French residents, endure the hard seats of the rest of the car, and only in the more populous regions do they fill them all. There are no color-lines, except that Caucasians are not allowed to travel fourth-class. This rendezvous of the Oriental masses is often packed to rush-hour proportions, and is so free from cramping rules that even rickshaws may be dragged in as baggage.

The half-dozen of these springless box-cars for every first-second-and-third-class coach is symbolical of the proportionate division of classes in the population of Indo-China. To the simple countryman who occupies the rough *wagons* making up the bulk of the train, even the third-class compartment represents such luxury that he comes to gaze in awe and what may be envy at the *richard* who can afford to ride there. Yet even in the deeply upholstered center of the last car, fares are not so high as on our own railways. There are no sleeping-cars, for the simple reason that the trains of Indo-China do not venture forth at night. The back end of the last fourth-class car is commonly taken up with a makeshift buffet-kitchen, in which the privileged occupants of the rear coach may partake of not particularly Parisian food, salted with such a jolting as may or may not be an aid to digestion.

All through the hotter hours the train twisted and squirmed its way among jungle-clad hillocks, the shades drawn, electric fans whirling. Farther north were sandy half-arid patches; then, two hundred miles or more above Saïgon, hills appeared and grew to be almost mountains, fairly well wooded and thick with underbrush. At length the forest gave way to scattered-bush land, resembling parts of Texas, untilled, perhaps because it is too arid for cultivation. There were almost no inhabitants, at least in sight. Here and there huddled half a dozen miserable time-blackened and dilapidated huts made of palm-leaves; now and then a garden-patch with a plastered house of dull-red tile roof, and outhouses suggesting plentiful servants, testified to the presence of some isolated French official or railway man. Perhaps there are towns along the edge of the sea not far away, since fishing and farming are the principal Annamese occupations.

From Phanrang near the sea a branch railway that degenerates into a motor-bus carries passengers with time to spare up to the plateau of Langbian. For high up in the distant mountains to the left toward which the sun was descending is Dalat, an expensive hotel and hill-station which the European residents of southern Indo-China call their Darjeeling. All this mountainous region back of the narrow strip of rice-growing coast-land is inhabited by Moï, "savages" who wear breech-clouts and look at life accordingly. There are several undomesticated tribes scattered throughout Indo-China, some of them dangerous even to the white man who claims to rule over it. Many parts of the hinterland are unexplored by the self-styled rulers, and portions of it are impossible without a wild-man guide, who may not consent to lend his assistance. Queer claims are those of the Caucasian and Japanese races of ruling over this or that country when they only control the modernized edges of it.

These Moï in their loin-cloths, most savage of the wild

tribes of Indo-China and looking not unlike our Indians, hold some clusters of mountains where it is still not entirely safe to go. Some have renegade Annamese leaders; one tribe lives in trees, in which it builds little houses, out of wholesome respect for tigers. The visitor to the Moï is expected to announce his arrival and friendly intentions by beating on a drum set up at the entrance to every village, as we knock at a door. If his visit is agreeable, a man bearing rice comes out to escort him, and if he is prepared to give salt in return, he is made welcome. Though they have little or no intercourse with the rest of the world, the Moï suffered greatly from the recent epidemic of "flu," and fevers and smallpox have often ravaged them. The average Moï woman has ten children, of whom only one or two reaches maturity. Thus the estimated three hundred thousand Moï are constantly decreasing. It is curious how many savage tribes have less success in raising their young than do most wild animals. Perhaps it is nature's way of keeping down an intermediate creation.

The Moï language, with no tones in the Chinese sense, sounds almost European. At the age of puberty boys and girls alike undergo the formality of having their teeth filed down to the gums. With some kind relative sitting on the chest of the sufferer, lying on his back with his head between the legs of a primitive vise, and with a wooden bit forced into his mouth, a medicine-man breaks off the teeth with stones and hacks and chips them away. It is their idea of making themselves beautiful, and the boy or girl who has not undergone this punishment is not considered marriageable or otherwise of adult status. After a day of this frightful work the operator leaves his victim covered with blood, his gums in ribbons, his lips like hashed beef-

steak, and incapable for a fortnight of eating anything but
liquids. Nor is this all, for the patient is then given a
stone with which to continue the beautifying process himself, when he has a moment to spare, until not a sign of
tooth remains above the level of the gums. Among some
of the tribes the lower teeth are given a saw shape, so that
the open mouth suggests that of an aged shark that has
lost its upper plate.

Dalat is the chief hunting-ground for tigers in Indo-China.
So well are these hunts organized by the French that the
brave hunter bags his beast as safely as royalty does.
There is a French colonial official whose chief duty it is
to oblige those who wish to boast that they have killed a
tiger. One orders a tiger by telegraph—tiger *à la carte,* so
to speak; the official sends out coolies to lay a bait that
has reached just the right degree of olfactory attraction
to the great cats, and in due season the bold hunter lays
one low without the slightest risk. Thus Indo-China is full
of successful tiger-hunters, without a scar to show for it.
The Annamese down on the coastal plain live in such dread
of the tiger that they never mention their greatest four-
footed enemy except by the respectful title of Ong Kop
(Lord Tiger), and in the woods your coolie will make a
clawing sign rather than speak openly of the fearsome beast.
Children have been carried off by tigers within a mile or
two of the Annamese capital. Yet the Moï hunt them
with primitive weapons that are hardly more effective than
a sharpened pole. "Moï," by the way, is simply the Annamese pronunciation of the Chinese character "man," meaning barbarian, a term much used by these two races to
designate the despised peoples who have not the honor of
being of the same blood as they.

Heavy clouds, and one gust of rain, as from the swiftly passing nozzle of a celestial hose, swept over the train late in the afternoon, though in Saigon rain is unknown at that season. Near Tourcham real mountain ranges climbed down to the edge of the plain and crowded the railway so close to the sea that we caught several glimpses of it, and of waterways beautiful at high tide. The name of this all but isolated station is taken from the great Cham tower that stands on a hillock near it. The Cham were an ancient people, of Hindu civilization also, who occupied this coastal strip many centuries ago, long before the Khmer swept down into the peninsula, and they left behind them gray stone towers that stand forth weirdly in the wilderness of to-day. Mammoth rocks heaped themselves up into half-jungled hills as we raced onward between low mountains— the coastal group on one hand and the forerunners of the great Annamese chain inland on the other. Toward sunset the arid landscape grew green again, some paddy-fields and scattered villages appeared; then the region as far as the eye could see turned frankly to rice culture, though with cattle grazing now in long brown stubble. But this fertility did not last, even where there was evidence of plenty of rain recently; in its place came bush, primitive unpeopled jungle, trees in white flower shrouded with vines, kapok trees shedding their vegetable cotton, flatlands, or at most low hills. Patches of Indian corn and tobacco flashed by, clusters of miserable wattled mud huts with old straw or palm-leaf roofs that looked like beggars' caps, but there were no people at all compared to almost any part of China.

Nhatrang had a booming beach and a constant sea-breeze, and seemed spacious and pleasant, a trifle cooler than Saïgon. But this I take partly on faith, for I never saw it by day-

light. Thick tropical night had fallen when the train came
to the end of its rails, and almost before I knew it I had
been whisked into the stopping-place provided for Europeans. This was a cross between a government *sala* and a
public inn, exactly what a French establishment in the
tropics run by a slippered Alsatian who had completely
forgotten his native land, except for its German accent,
would naturally be. It seemed that I, the only European
to whom Nhatrang was to play host that night, had broken
a fixed rule of travel in these parts. Of two Annamese
youths who had boarded the train some miles away to
drum up passengers for two rival motor-buses, I had come
to terms with the least respectable, whereas all Europeans
hitherto had patronized the official mail-bus belonging to
vested interests. But the terms were favorable accordingly,
and as between outsiders and vested interests my sympa-
thies are inclined to radicalism.

I was called at three, and we were off again in the
bootleg autobus that had clinched our agreement by carrying me from station to inn the evening before. It was
still dark when we crossed a broad estuary or river by a
bac and struck off into what seemed to be mountains. A
bac, as all diligent students of French know, is a ferry,
but the genus that abounds in Indo-China is worthy a
name of its own. How many times during my gasoline-
propelled travels throughout the colony my eyes fell upon
that capital T on its back like a helpless turtle, which meant
one more river to cross by the precarious Annamese method,
I refuse even to try to guess. As a special concession I
might admit that there are at least a thousand bridges in
Indo-China that have never been built, some of which I
fear never will be. One is rolling serenely along a smooth
French highway, swathed in that delight which comes from

swift comfortable motion, so long as it is uninterrupted,
when "Brrgrrum!"—another sign-board with the over-
turned T. The vehicle slithers down a steep and probably
slimy bank, all but sinks a collection of ancient planks
criminally put together, and stops just in time to keep from
sliding off the farther end of them. If it is daytime, two
or three or half a dozen Annamese of either sex and any
age have been aroused from their siesta by the overworked
horn and the compact of automobile and their disjointed
sleeping place, which they begin forthwith to pole or gon-
dolier across the fluid interruption to traffic. If it is night,
profanity and slapping on the part of the chauffeur and his
assistants may also be necessary to metamorphose the several
huddled sacks about the intrepid raft into living beings and
to move them to indulge in similar exertions. Sometimes,
if the expanse of water is not too great, there is a rope
or chain from shore to shore. The boatmen use chain-handles
weighted at the end with a block of wood by means of
which they wrap themselves easily about the transfluvial
cable as it is dragged up from the slimy bottom. But
whatever the method of propulsion, the craft is sure to run
aground or meet some other form of delaying mishap before the crossing is completed, and to creak and groan
and rend itself in a way to assure the inexperienced that
his trip is about to end at the bottom of that particular
strip of water. Nothing is more adaptable than the human
spirit, however, and within a week a *bac* meant no more
to me than entering the ring does to a bull-fighter.

I traveled first class, at two thirds what the same privilege would have cost me in the regular conveyance of the
poste coloniale. That is, I sat wedged into a corner of
the front seat with the driver. His assistant, having yielded
his usual place to me for whatever reward may have been

promised him by his chief, rode for two days on the running-board, one bare foot hooked over the front door or one skinny hand clutching a support of the baggage-laden roof. It was a place convenient for his duties anyway, for these consisted in catching sight of the next kilometer-post in order to compute the fare of each new passenger, clambering along the side of the car like a chipmunk on a wall to collect it, slapping or booting with a bare toe pedestrians who did not speedily give the vehicle the widest possible berth, and watering the radiator wherever time and water were to be had, as if it were some jungle beast perpetually dying of tropical thirst. Behind me rode an average of fourteen Annamese, with a few babies usually thrown in. These second-class passengers enjoyed the privilege of being less likely than I to catapult through the wind-shield at one of the sudden stops that were always imminent; but no doubt the honor of my position, and the lesser likelihood of being sprayed with betel-juice by some garrulous fellow-passenger, made my double fare worth while.

The chauffeur, like his understudy, was dressed in tropical French fashion, as was proper to his honorable calling, a soft felt hat crushed down over his head, his shirt-collar wide open, after the latest fashion of European beaches. Once he abandons the comfortable and pleasing garb of his own people, the Annamese jumps to the most ultra-modern mode of his rulers. Until I had met others of his clan who seemed to have learned the chauffeur trade in a tailor-shop, I considered this driver the last word in perpetual homicidal intention; looking back upon him from the vantage-ground of uninjured escape from Indo-China, I grant him perfection among Annamese wielders of the steering-wheel. For one thing he wore shoes, which is by no means common among his brake- and clutch-stepping compatriots, and the little French he tortured when there was no visible way out of it was at times within reach of an attentive understanding, in itself a rare virtue. His chief amusement was the crushing of dogs, those thin yellow dogs that are almost as numerous in Annamese villages as children and pigs. It was a kindness to the gaunt curs perhaps, but I never reached the point of taking great pleasure in seeing one of them disappear beneath us with one short helpless yelp. When he could not find enough of these pitiful animals within reach, he brushed against frightened *nha-qués*, the leisurely peasants of Annam, in order to see how far they could remove themselves in a single jump. Not a few of them made the records of mere athletes seem the performances of babes in arms.

To be the driver of an automobile is to the Annamese more than a trade, it is a title. The first chauffeur of the *Résidence Supérieure* at the capital of Annam wears the dragon decoration of his emperor, and other chauffeurs passing through Hué go to his garage to kowtow before him. The ease with which Orientals adapt themselves to our inventions is one of the wonders of the East. One would suppose that a people quite incapable of understanding, much less inventing, such a mechanical contrivance as the automobile would stand in awe of it, and of those who had contrived it. Not at all; on the contrary they take it as calmly as they do the growths of nature, as they do the miracles with which they credit their demons and invisible spirits, showing the same rage or surprise if it does not respond to their senseless chastisement as at their gaunt sore-backed domestic animals refusing to work under their heartless lashings.

Thanks perhaps to French discipline, or because the Annamese are by nature a more quiet leisurely race, my com-

Motor-buses link together the railways of Indo-China, crossing broad sandy river-banks on strips of woven bamboo splints

In Annam prisoners working in the streets wear a light remnant of the old neck-torturing Chinese *cangue*

An Annamese summoning a ferry from across one of the many rivers which still offer no bridges to automobiles

In the "Marble Mountains" are many grottoes, some of them elaborately fitted up as temples

panion on the front seat was not so wild as the average
Chinese chauffeur. Yet on the whole it was no great
pleasure to ride beside this solemn little brown man in his
misplaced near-European clothes. Though it was always
passable, the road was in places atrociously surfaced, for
all the road-gangs along the way. Especially among the
mountains that often came down to the edge of the sea
it is no joke even for such famous road-builders as the
French to keep up a highway in a land of tropical rainy
seasons. An autobus of the same bootleg line, lying upside down in a creek where a bridge had broken down a
week before under its thundering impact, did not give me
that reassurance of complete safety at his high speed which
the fellow himself seemed to have. It was bad enough to
see one of the mangy yellow mongrels that slink about
every Annamese hut disappear under our wheels every hour
or two. I could comfort myself that these at least should
be glad to be so suddenly put out of their lifelong misery.
But in the course of the morning the nerveless Asiatic
at the wheel succeeded in running over a handsome foreign
hunting-dog loping along beside its shotgun-armed French
master on a bicycle. Perhaps he did not deliberately overtake the animal—unsuspecting, because of the kindly European atmosphere it lived in, any such treachery as the
orphaned mongrels of Annam are constantly on the look-
out for—but he could at any rate easily have avoided it.
The Annamese passengers, gazing back at the writhing corpse
in the dust as we sped away, seemed to look upon
such incidents as one of the pleasures of travel, due them
in consideration of the high fare on these strange foreign
vehicles. One had the feeling that they grinned and chattered and nudged one another not so much because of a
certain more or less natural antipathy toward the race to

which this particular dog was attached as out of sheer
Oriental joy at beholding suffering. On the tanned mask
of the driver's face there was just the hint of two con-
flicting emotions; one the satisfaction of having added another dog, better than the average, to his score; the other
a possibility of vengeance on the part of the Frenchman
kneeling in the dust beside his dying pet, that transferred
itself into a more deafening roar and breakneck speed than
ever.

That autobus trip from Nhatrang to Tourane was through
much prettier scenery than the one by train the day before. For one thing the highway runs much closer to the
coast than does the railway. Outcroppings of the great Annamese chain came down to the edge of the China Sea
every little while, especially during the first day's stage from
Nhatrang to Quinhon, and our road wound and twisted,
buckled and climbed, over high rocky spurs, along the sheer
edge of breath-taking slopes, up and down between sea-level
and several thousand feet above it, often with hair-pin
turns high up along precipitous cliffs on the very edge of
the densely blue ocean. It opened many magnificent vistas,
of weird indentations, bold headlands, charming little beaches,
now and again an unbelievably blue bay thickly speckled
with the sails of tiny boats dancing in the whitecaps as
to Pan's pipes, yet seeming to have no fear. They were
mere cockle-shells, these sea-going canoes of the Annamese
fishermen, made of bamboo splints tightly woven together
and covered with pitch. Scores of them, baking bottom up
in the sun on raised frameworks and gleaming under a
new coating as with varnish, lay along the road through
Annam. Sometimes the road itself was made of bamboo
splints, woven together into great mat-like strips six feet

or more wide and in some places half a mile long. These carried the heavy autobus across deep sand, at either end of leaky *bacs,* in which it would otherwise have floundered almost as quickly as in the water itself.

Deeply green wet jungle surrounded us much of the time, cactus stretching out spiny arms toward us. Blinding white salt marshes contrasted with a road in places so red that the saliva of a nation of betel-chewers did not spot it. Striking peaks of the coastal group alternated with tame stretches of dusty highway down at sea-level, gusts of rain from mountains of black clouds with blazing tropical sunshine. Wherever mountains and foothills receded enough to leave a suggestion of plain, however narrow, rice-fields filled every level space. The young rice of the first crop of the year was deeply flooded now, peasants plowing thigh-deep in it behind ponderous water-buffaloes that seemed to be in their element wading in slime. Some men and more women were clawing in the mud up to their biceps; others paddled about the fields in the light canoes of woven bamboo. Stones were so rare in some sections of this ancient route that the well-sweeps used for irrigation were weighted at the short end with balls of mud and straw. Along the road there was no more suggestion of fences than in China itself, but the smaller foot-hills were here and there cut up into green fields by thin lines of greener bushes.

With an hour's hot halt for refreshments for man, woman, and gasoline-consuming beast at a village boasting a tolerable Annamese imitation of a French restaurant, we rode on through scorching midday into the slightly cooler afternoon, ending the first day's stage with sunshine enough left to photograph pretty Quinhon. In the last few miles big rice-plains had opened out; we had bisected a scattered town of some size; files of coolies had increased until the road became an almost continual procession of them. Quinhon is beautifully situated on a spit of sand and earth projected out into a bay surrounded by mountainous shores. Thus there are both mountains and sea on all sides of it, except where the road enters the one long street of the native town, merging beyond into shaded drives and foreign houses in garden-groves, none of them a hundred yards from either beach. The French suppress somewhat more successfully than the English-speaking races the tendency to insist on erecting in the tropics dwellings exactly like those at home, and the houses they build in Indo-China are not entirely unfitted to the climate.

The ruling race monopolizes this tongue of sandy land running out into the densely blue, very deep harbor surrounded by high hills, where one small ocean steamer, flying the British flag, now rode at anchor. The native town is little more than two unbroken lines of shops, and between them and the French residences stood a whitewashed market building of modern lines, even at this late hour half filled and all but surrounded by squatting women in the woven palm-leaf hats of parasol shape that are the most prominent feature of every Annamese market. They sold all manner of native foodstuffs, fish from the sea, long rolls of dark-brown sugar wrapped in leaves, arec-nuts and the betel-leaves and lime that go with them, recalling the Indian women of the Andes selling cocoa-leaves and similar ingredients of an analogous mild vice. Though French paper piastres, fractional silver, and big copper sous are the ordinary Indo-Chinese medium of exchange, in the markets the masses still use *sapèques,* as the French call Chinese "cash."

It was at Quinhon that I saw for the first time in Indo-

China, though by no means the last, prisoners wearing the *cangue* once so common and now so rare in China Instead of the great planks of Manchu—and Puritan—days, however, these contrivances about offending necks were a very light frame of wood, as if the French, though unable to do away entirely with an old Annamese custom left over from the centuries of Chinese rule, had insisted on softening this form of punishment. Native justice prescribes leg-irons too, and sentences men to hard labor even for not paying taxes, but French rule seems to temper Asiatic cruelty by wrapping bands of cloth about the ankles so that irons shall not chafe the skin. Most of the convicts also had an iron band about the waist, and this was connected with the leg-irons by two chains that clanked constantly with the prisoner's short steps. Yet the fellows could even climb cocoanut-trees in these, and they did not seem to have any difficulty in getting permission from the soldier guards to step into a shop and buy cigarettes or the makings of the betel-nut cuds with which the black teeth of both prisoners and guards driveled. The men who thus dropped behind soon caught up again with their fellows, pushing and pulling two-wheeled carts of sanitary purposes and drawing loads of broken stone.

For all its French colony, the people here gaped at a foreigner almost as much as in China—though perhaps it was merely because I was out in the sun and on foot at such an hour. They gathered to watch me write wherever I drew out my note-book and gaped open-mouthed at my antics with the camera that few of them seemed to recognize, but with more respect, or fear, than Chinese crowds show under similar circumstances, remaining quietly at some distance, like well trained children. Frenchmen, even women and children, began to appear when the sun neared the horizon, strolling under the trees and along the edges of the blue bay out on their breeze-cooled sandspit. At the more or less French hotel where Europeans passing through Quinhon spend the night I was joined that evening by the only man of my own tongue I met between Saigon and Tourane. He was thin and lanky with long tropical living, but filled with Scotch humor, and announced himself the chief engineer of the steamer in the harbor. He did not seem to believe my tale that I had come all the way from Saigon by land, much less that I hoped to go clear on into China without taking to the sea, though he had sailed into this and all the other little ports along the coast of Annam half his life, during which his chief pleasures were a meal and a "berth" ashore now and then.

CHAPTER VI

THROUGH ANNAM TO ITS CAPITAL

WE were off again by the same conveyance at four next morning. Long before daylight the road was alive with files of coolies, two loads bouncing at the ends of each shoulder-pole, the same familiar lines of jogging carriers as in China, with the difference that here there were as many women as men, for the bound foot is one advantage of Chinese civilization that was never adopted in Annam. All up and down the long slender kingdom of the Eminent South endless miles of coolies of both sexes come trotting to market to sell to one another. Always they jog in Indian files, even on the wide modern roads, unable to cast off centuries of training along the narrow trails of old Annam. All wore palm-leaf hats; some carried parasols also, even before daylight, perhaps as a protection against the setting moon. With the first rays of sun, flung horizontally across the already tepid world, double lines of pole-bearers stretched ahead and behind, on both sides of the road, as far as the eye could see, the women carrying with a floating motion, many of the men not carrying at all. New lines, cut out in fresco against the brightening horizon, came jogging in along the dikes of the paddy-fields. As both sexes dressed and carried alike, and the men wore their long hair in Psyche knots, it was not easy to distinguish man from woman until we were close upon them, sometimes not even then. Evidently the

Chinese found this annoying, for when they conquered Annam, centuries ago, they ordered the women to wear short garments with wide sleeves. China's power over the kingdom of the south virtually ended during the Ming dynasty, however, and the Manchus did not succeed in introducing the queue.

The country was now perhaps a bit less mountainous than the day before, the strip of plain wider, certainly more densely populated, and all its products were bound marketward. Here and there in the files a mother carried a child at one end of her pole and a small pig at the other. The hasty glimpse as we dashed past was not enough to decide whether the youngster or the pig had been brought along as a counterweight. Like their near relatives in China, the pigs of Annam refuse to walk to market. Coolies carry them in baskets—"like foreigners in chairs"—or merely with a band from their jouncing poles about their bellies, which would seem to the disinterested observer to be more painful than walking. Who would be so bold, however, as to claim to grasp the point of view of a pig?

Often that morning the road ahead looked like a flowing river of coolies, parasol-hats and jogging poles forming a kind of scum on the surface. We dashed through this endless stream like a steamer through a narrow waterway, our incessant horn always clearing a passage just soon enough to escape doing the ceaseless multitude of dodging pedestrians bodily injury, the chauffeur's assistant striking a resounding thwack, with a whip that he seemed to carry for no other purpose, on every palm-leaf hat he could by any stretching reach. We dashed as peremptorily through markets squatting along and, so rare is wheeled traffic, even in the road at the frequent villages, markets noisy with bartering, gatherings that recalled Haiti in other ways

When it rains in Annam, as it does on every provocation, a simple straw raincoat covers either sex among the masses

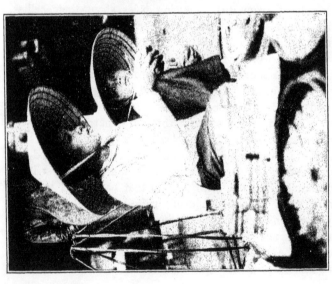

An Annamese girl, chaperoned by her small brother, sells her wares in the market-place of Hué

Like the southern Chinese the Annamese are expert boatmen because they learn their calling long before they reach the dignity of clothing

Swinging in the village squares is a favorite diversion of the Annamese populace during the lunar New Year's season

than the pell-mell with which they scattered as we rode down upon them without so much as slackening speed. Annamese markets are always a broad vista of whitish palm-leaf hats, so that they look like an individually roofed congregation. There were hat factories beside the road where more of this ubiquitous head-gear was being fashioned, of other materials as well as palm-leaves, it seemed, for the brass top of one soldier's hat came off in my presence and disclosed the filling to be the apartments-to-let columns of a New York newspaper, yellow with several years of tropical service. In certain movements and when the wind is blowing the Annamese must keep his mouth open to hold his hat on, by tautening the ribbon under his chin. Wanderlust in Annam takes the form of going to market, especially among the women and girls. They like the sense of freedom it gives them, the company, the gossip, above all the bargaining, at which the women of Annam are past mistresses. In the afternoon we met these same files of women, or at least their exact counterparts, jogging homeward as heavily laden as they came, for they often buy as much as they sell.

In this section, all through southern Annam in fact, every one not in mourning wore black. Compared with those of Cambodia and of some other parts of Indo-China, the women were almost prudish in their dress. Like the men they wore thin cotton pantaloons as voluminous as those of the modern college youth, and a jacket barely disclosing the neck, and more often than not all this was covered with a flowing cotton coat reaching almost to the ankles. Rarely was a breast revealed even during the frequent nursing of children that in many cases should long since have outgrown that form of nourishment. True, in the hottest hours of the sea-level day many of the women, especially

the older and less attractive ones, wore in their own villages nothing between hat and pantaloons except a diamond-
shaped breast-protector, tied on with cross-strings across
the back, outdoing from the rear the most extreme of
Western evening-gowns. But on the road and in the market even the flowing coats seemed almost *de rigueur.*

Among the coolie class these overcoats of both sexes were
of thin cotton. The better-to-do men in the towns and in
the autobus wore jet-black ones, thin as gauze, transparent
as mosquito-netting, with flowered designs of the same hue
woven in them, like the pattern in lace, and fastened together down the side with little gold buttons. Beneath
this the well dressed man wore a white jacket-shirt and
very loose cotton trousers, and thrust bare feet into black
slippers or wooden clogs. A black cloth carelessly wound
about the head distinguished most coolies, but all men above
that class wore that most unique item of the Annamese
costume, a black band-turban permanently arranged in many
little folds, rising in stairway fashion up the forehead
and descending in the same manner at the back. This mere
head-band, without top, is worn indoors and out, even, one
suspects, during sleep. In place of the male turban the
women wrap black cloth about the long single thick braid
of their generally luxuriant hair, and wind this about the
head. Out in the sun the palm-leaf hat sits on top of
turban or its feminine counterpart. At least along this
main route of French railway and autobus highway both
men and women of the well-to-do class wore gold and other
valuable ornaments openly. Long necklaces of grains of
gold of the size of peas are the favorite adornment of the
women who can afford them; there were bracelets, sometimes several on one arm, earrings usually of gold, and
miscellaneous jewelry to suit the individual taste or purse.

Rice lands stretch for many miles north of Quinhon, some so broad that they looked like great inundated wheat-fields. In other places the hills closed in like interested spectators, but still left room for a broad strip of cultivation. Sunk to the knees in this slime, pantaloons rolled to the tops of their thighs, men and women clawed about the roots of the young rice. Here a laborer up to his—or her—middle in mud and water toiled feverishly to stanch an overflowing pond by slapping hasty handfuls of oozy black mud on a broken dike. On another such division between the paddy-fields two Annamese of indeterminate sex were alternately pulling and letting loose in rhythmic cadence the two ends of a cord bearing in its middle a pail made of straw, the simplest Oriental form of lifting water from an overflooded field into a thirsty one above. Farther on, a coolie condemned to hard labor to earn his rice, turned with his bare feet a primitive wheel that set in motion an endless chain of simple buckets. To protect himself from the sun he held in one hand an open umbrella, and no doubt dreamed himself a mandarin. Right, left, sometimes everywhere as far as the eye could see, were rice-fields, mirroring the sun so brightly that the eye quailed before them. Yet there was little color to make gay this landscape of the plains; it is green or nothing, except for the bluish tinge of masses of the Japanese lotus or hyacinth. The Annamese planted this in a few selected spots to celebrate the victory of the yellow race over the white at Tsushima; and now, as if to punish them for their seditious thoughts, it has spread far and wide, invading their ponds and rice-fields, obstructing their watercourses. To-day the peasants of Annam spend much of their time laboriously digging out and carrying away this prolific and troublesome plant, good for nothing, not even as fertilizer.

In so narrow and intensively cultivated a land it is a great problem even to find space on which to throw the stuff, yet their food is just so much decreased until they can rid themselves of this disastrous invasion of flowers.

A few red humped cattle lolled under wayside trees, or grazed on dikes where they were mirrored in the flooded fields, as were the mountains in the background and the huts in cocoanut-groves against the more or less distant foot-hills. Clusters of water-buffaloes on vacation lay immersed to their nostrils in mud-holes or swung their mammoth horns with an inhospitable air along the mud ridges between the paddy-fields, or fed on the edges of the uncultivated hillocks in which the great mountain range always bulking clearly or hazily to the west gave up its contest with the sea. A pair of birds stood blithely on the backs of some of the amphibians; on others a boy, at times even a girl, lay at full length, head pillowed on rump or withers. Among the trees especially these ponderous beasts resembled, exactly as to color, that other survivor of the dinosaurian age, the elephant. Some of them were of that dull creamy hue of the sacred "white" elephants of Siam and vicinity. For a semi-albino buffalo is common in Indo-China, its eyes red, a rough red skin showing through scarce whitish hairs, as if it were half roasted in the Annamese sun—perhaps it is only because it is not rare enough that this abnormal beast is not also regarded as sacred.

A whole population was toiling in the rice-fields, or trotting elastically along the dikes, two pole-balanced loads bouncing from every shoulder. The rural Annamese are not lazy; on the contrary they are very hard workers, though they have some of the natural indolence of the tropics. Agriculture is laborious under the best of conditions, to say nothing of those of the Orient; with his seldom lacking flock of voracious children the *nha-qué,* the peasant of Annam, can rarely rest. Small, but of great endurance, the countrymen of the Eminent South are forever on the run, like ants in haste to provide themselves against a drouth or a famine. Both sexes can trot indefinitely under great loads; even a six-year-old boy can propel a sampan, though he may not yet have reached the dignity of clothing.

Rice is by far the principal product of Annam, fish or fruit being a slow second. Thanks to its rice, Annam is rich; all Indo-China is rich, else why this Western form of "protection"? Low as they seem to us from the land of exorbitance, prices are high compared to China. There were a few beggars, now and then one obviously leprous, yet few indeed measured by the rows of them along any important Chinese route. A visiting French novelist, angry at the exchange between its real currency and his poor paper francs, entitled one of his chapters on Annam, "Under the Sign of the Piastre." There are so many piastres in Indo-China that the Chinese and the Chettys, the "usuricultors" who lend to the unforesighted peasant at highwayman rates of interest, and even French officialdom and monopolists, cannot take them all; there remain some for the *nha-qué,* the toiling peasant who earns them all by the sweat of his brown back—and those of his women-folk.

Since almost all the Annamese are agriculturists, there is no aristocracy between the emperor and his mandarins and the *nha-qué,* little exploiting of any other than the agricultural resources of the country. Whatever wealth it has comes from the soil, almost entirely from these flooded rice-fields mirroring the ever near-by chain of mountains that shuts off this laborious people close on the west. For the real Annam is only this very narrow strip of fertile lowlands on the eastern slope of the Siamese peninsula. Like the Nile in Egypt, this main highway, close as it is to the sea, takes in all the narrow country. The Annamese chain crowds the toiling peasant so close to the sea in many places that he is often driven into it as a fisherman to escape starvation. He cultivates only the valleys, both because he knows little else than rice and because the Moï, the barbarians of various tribes, make it uncomfortable for him back in the hills. Yet narrow as their country is, of the eighteen or twenty million people in French Indo-China two thirds are Annamese. For as if to make up for its slenderness, that strip of flatland between the mountains and the sea is incredibly fertile, so fertile that its overcrowded toilers trouble themselves far less with fertilizing than do the Chinese.

Bamboo of all sizes, palms ranging from mere fans to great masses of leaves, magnificent trees, some of them bearing the jackfruit on their trunks, cocoanut-palms hugging the coast-line, banana-plants all but hiding thatched huts, above all the straight and slender arec-palm up which climbs the clinging betel-vine, broke the monotony of the rice-fields. There were miles of hedges gay with what looked like a small pink rose, and large flowers made up of many tiny ones, care-free, unconstrained bushes, not the domesticated hedge-rows of England. In places a shock of colors like an explosion emphasized the landscape. Then, after so long a stretch of rice-fields that they grew wearisome, we went high up over a spur from which spread out another great vista, more than half of it the dense, very green tops of cocoanut-palms. Beyond came miles of wastelands, with sand white as snow piled up over sterile hillocks.

There were hundreds of graves among these barren sands, strewn as closely together as are the green unmarked grave-mounds that emerge everywhere from the rice-fields, where agriculture gnaws at them year after year, century after century, yet never destroys them. Though January was not yet done, and the lunar New Year was still a week off, preparations had almost everywhere been completed for that important date. Here and there a man was still touching up his family graves, giving them a new top of sand or earth, weeding and clearing them of all vegetation, before the Annamese New Year should overtake him and bring reproach from the spirits of his ancestors. But most of this work had already been done, so that the rounded knolls, such as stretch in hundreds of millions from northern Korea to southern Annam, were bare and smooth now, all showing some sign of recent care. Here in the waste-lands the graves looked like sand-mounds left by playing children; farther on came queer coffin-shaped ones of cement or baked mud, just as if a coffin above the ground had merely been plastered over.

The Annamese live and keep shop on a wooden platform a couple of feet above the earth floor; and generally mere boards laid on two sawhorses, covered with a thin reed mat, serve them as beds. Rarely has a native house more comfort than that. As all houses should be redecorated at New Year's, there is a great market then for new reed, grass, or fiber mats, and whole processions of them were coming in from the country districts on the shoulder-poles of men and wives. Some were plain, some had simple designs, some had streaks of color running through them, and I saw many rich with red and purple and lush-green hues that no doubt would grace the hard couch of the wealthy. To the Annamese the mat is the symbol of the

bed, of the couple, the household; and believing as firmly
as the French that it is not well for man to sleep alone,
they always sell these mats in pairs. If a family buys only
one mat at New Year's renewing-time, say the wiseacres,
some member of it is sure to die within the year. From
the moment that two persons are gathered together they
should buy two mats, and as there is very little single
blessedness in Annam, merchants do not wish at any price
to divide a pair and run the risk of never selling the odd
one. Bachelors and old maids, one gathers, are as badly
off at New Year's time as a one-legged man in a shoe-store—
and it serves them right, any native of early-marrying
Annam would no doubt answer, were his attention called
to one of those rare and unnatural beings.

Every little while during that all-day journey from
Quinhon to Tourane gusts of rain sprang up, between
stretches of blazing sunshine, and then men, women, and
children, every one of the outdoor class, slipped on palm-
leaf rain-coats that were shaped like opera-capes, or like
barrels with one stave removed so that the wearers could
get into them, and which they turned in any direction against
the slant of the rain. Scores of boys in these leaf rain-
coats sat their water-buffaloes or their red humped cattle
and let it drizzle. A real shower brought out so many rain-
coats that the whole landscape—people and houses, buffaloes
and hillsides—were covered with palm-leaves.

In the slimy pond at the entrance to every village the
inhabitants were washing their rice, their clothing, their
water-buffaloes, their night-buckets, themselves, everything
that is dirty, and dipping from the same spot water for
their kettles. They live with their cattle, their sway-back
pigs, their chickens, ducks, and orphaned curs; at noon-time
everybody in the villages, even the yellow mongrels, the

black pigs, the wilt-tailed fowls, slip into the *cai-nha,* or thatched hut, for the siesta; and by night there is a similar congregating. Yet they are not so filthy as the Chinese; all things are relative. It behooves a more southern people, eager to live out its allotted span, to show less innocence of the meaning of cleanliness than do the incredible Celestials.

Once that day we met an elephant. He was being slowly driven along by a nonchalant coolie dozing astride his neck, grazing as he went. Somehow an elephant strolling down a modern highway, marked with kilometer-posts and traveled by autobuses, daintily picking a bit of weed or a tuft of grass here and there, and attracting no more attention than a cow or a water-buffalo, was more impressive than one all dolled up in a circus-parade.

When it was not clambering over a spur of the ever jostling mountain chain to the west, this road through Annam was always the same—a dike between two rice-fields, dusty or muddy in the country, filled with people, pigs, and dogs in the towns and villages. Then suddenly, frequently, inevitably, another *bac,* an ancient floating contrivance that leaks and creaks with age, which Annamese push across some river or inlet of the sea with poles that seem too heavy for their meager arms. Sometimes the commander of the *bac* is a woman, strongest of all the crew, not only in will-power but in muscle. Once in a while we crossed a woven-bamboo bridge that gave with a groan under our cruel weight and regained its shape as an invalid knocked down regains his feet. But the short rivers of narrow Annam are often so wide and so erratic that they discourage the building of bridges. For the stream rises or falls, according to the season, disappears, comes back in a

towering rage; and red with anger some morning it carries
away not only bridges, where any exist, but dikes, roads,
villages, the very railways, anything that dares to loiter in
its imperious path.   Then, too, Indo-China has terrific
typhoons, which tear down her forests, to say nothing of
destroying roads and bridges and the other puny works of
the French usurpers.

The French do their best to keep the highways of Indo-
China up to their own far-famed standard, especially this
ancient route through Annam that is still sometimes known,
in memory of the days when Chinese officials went over it
in chairs, as the Mandarin Road—though now it is Route
Coloniale No. 1.   A French *ingénieur de routes* lives in
every stretch of a hundred kilometers or so; there was
much road-mending all along that two-day autobus journey.
An army of *congaïes,* the supple young women of Annam,
trotting like black ants along the dikes, carried stones, mud,
and other materials in little baskets at the ends of their
shoulder-poles; at frequent intervals we dashed past long
heaps of broken stone; men and women, boys and girls,
the two sexes working and looking incredibly alike, and
showing no sign that they recognized any difference in sex,
toiled to keep the road passable.

The roads of Indo-China, even this principal highway of
Annam, are constructed for one vehicle at a time, as are
the *bacs* and the narrow cement bridges across the slighter
streams that were constantly breaking through from the
mountains on this journey up the eastern coast of the
China Sea.   There was little reason for them to be wider,
for few automobiles take advantage of the Frenchman's
expensive road-building, though there were then more than
four thousand motor-cars in Indo-China, and any one who
has recently traveled in continental eastern Asia knows that

means a great many. We passed a private car or two during the day, the south-bound autobus of our own line, and the rival mail-carrying government buses, the one bound in our direction constantly racing past us or being in turn left to swallow our dust or wallow in our mud. A few big clumsy carts drawn by water-buffaloes brought rice to market; further than that there were almost no other vehicles, except rickshaws. No wonder road-filling markets and startled villagers, to say nothing of pigs, curs, urchins, and chickens, were not prepared for us when we roared down upon them out of the south and on like an avalanche into the north. Nearly all the carts of Indo-China are drawn by man-power; even massive machinery is hauled by human muscle, though there are a few stout little horses. A hammock slung on two poles, with a woven-reed or split-bamboo cover over it, were the only survivals of the sedan-chairs once so numerous along the Mandarin Road. To-day you can scour all Indo-China, from Bac-Lieu to Laokay, and never meet, at least on a main road, a single palanquin, nowhere find a chair porter, once so numerous, but only a thin line of autobuses and automobiles, and many rickshaws.

We met rickshaws everywhere, plying even between towns far apart in the well inhabited sections of this Shoestring Country. Red rickshaws rattling with the iron-tired wheels of our buggy of a generation ago, nearly all carried two passengers, and freight or baggage enough to sink an ox-cart. Yet the little runner, seldom as large as either passenger, trotted mile after mile across the country, rarely falling into a walk. Even in hard-working China two adults are hardly ever seen riding in the same rickshaw, but in Annam it is so common as to be almost the rule. It is of course nice and cozy, romantic and unoriental, to see a man riding along with his wife half in his lap—granting that it always is his wife; certainly it is some one's wife, for nothing is so rare in Annam as old maids. Sometimes there is a half-grown child also, for good measure, giving the skinny puller the task of dragging three persons and all their movable belongings along mile after mile of highway, until you wonder whether even the dull-witted human horses themselves do not realize that it might have been better for them if the French had never come to build roads capable of two-wheeled vehicles.

Tourane, where the autobus ended its northward task some time before sunset on the second day out of Nhatrang, is a "foreign concession." One suspects that the "protected" emperor of Annam lost little time in conceding this much to the French when they expressed a desire for a *pied à terre* in Annam, with a status similar to those they hold in Shanghai and Tientsin. As a matter of fact Tourane, the best harbor in Annam, was given to the French, along with the islands of Poulo Condore and Touron off the coast of Cochinchina, in return for their help to Gia-long in consolidating the claims of the present dynasty at the beginning of the nineteenth century. Tourane bulks larger on the map than on the spot. It suggests a real-estate boom in some aristocratic old hamlet that died out long before the "plotting" by its optimistic sponsors reached its justification. In area it vindicates its conspicuousness on paper; on the spot it is even more roomy than the average town of Annam under the French, straining itself to cover as great a space as possible, like some of our largest American cities, like a squatter who fears that anything he may not claim will be taken away from him. Grass-bordered roads rather than streets, broad rural highways among widely scattered French tropical residences in spacious yards, each with the atmosphere of a private park, the necessary official buildings of a French headquarters, shops and market-place enough to supply the wants of the residents, and the Hôtel Morin, half grocery and half *pension,* for the acommodation of transient foreigners, just about complete the inventory. Scattered at the end of a short wide river where it empties into an excellent blue harbor in which ocean steamers can anchor close to the town, it is no city at all compared even with obscure Faifo a few miles south; but as a residence of foreigners it takes on a false importance.

By the same token it has some of the comforts of home, or at least their tropical counterparts. The expenditure of two piastres a month brings daily to those householders capable of appreciating such luxuries two large bottles of sterilized water from the French government hospital. Ice, without which the French refuse to live for a day in their Far-Eastern empire, is brought every morning from Hué, sixty-five miles away. I was reminded by contrast of the endless individual tasks of boiling all water that passes the lips of any but the most foolish foreigners in China, and that four fifths of the foreign residents there know ice only from homeland memories, while thousands of them never enjoy the luxury of a really cold drink from the time they leave their transpacific steamer until they embark for home again. Wherever half a dozen Frenchmen are gathered together in Indo-China there is an ice-making machine, or at least some means of getting a daily supply from some more fortunate group. The most constant cry in any French hotel dining-room in the colony is *"Nuoc-da!"* Natives who have become sophisticated in such matters have much sport in startling the Moï and other wild tribes back of the sea-level strip with the "water-stone" produced by their French masters. A piece of it passed from palm to palm until it disappears like a few drops of perspiration produces more astonishment among the hills than does an automobile or airplane. It is pure magic to the naïve wearers of the loin-cloth, and by such things have the people of the West won their prestige among them.

Until I reached Tourane I had not seen a Christian missionary in Indo-China—that is, not a Protestant missionary; the French do not admit that their own priests are missionaries in a land over which their own flag waves. Glad as the traveler always is to meet his own people in very foreign parts, I had been half conscious of a feeling of relief at the scarcity of avowed soul-savers, compared to the swarms of them in China itself. This paucity of workers in the spiritual vineyard of a race in some ways more Christ-like than we is not an indication that Protestant missions have wilfully overlooked Indo-China but that the French do not fervently welcome them there. In all the colony-protectorate there are only a few proselyters from the English-speaking world, and they are confined to three or four stations. In activity as well as in territory they are forced to be very circumspect, and thereby hangs the sad tale they have to tell the traveler who will listen.

They came first in 1911, a bit of pollen wafted southward from the great mission-field of China. At first they were allowed comparative freedom, or at least were graciously ignored. Then came the World War, and in due time the discovery that the United States might not after all join the Allies. Neutrals were rated little better than enemies in this far-flung slice of the French empire. All American missionaries in the possession were ordered to leave. The Canadians might remain, since they were allies; but as they were merely individual workers in what was virtually an American mission-field, they had little choice but to leave also. When the war was long enough over for its bitternesses to have become somewhat diluted, the missionaries were allowed to return, but only to find their goings and doings more hampered than ever. They were almost freely admitted to Cochinchina, because it is rated a colony, in which the laws and customs of France apply in most matters. They were allowed in Tourane, because it is a "foreign concession." But the rest of Indo-China being merely under the "protection" of France, missionary work there is a different matter. The authorities had discovered that the treaty of 1877 between the emperor of Annam and the Western world, by which Christian missionaries were granted the right freely to propagate their doctrines in the emperor's realm, applied only to the Catholics, "because they are the only Christians within the meaning of the text." Moreover the startling fact was unearthed that "the emperor and his ministers are against the teaching of the Protestant doctrines to their people"—as if the poor little puppet on the throne of Annam would dare to be against anything unless his French guardians suggested it. Similar difficulties developed against admitting missionaries to Tonkin, Cambodia, and Laos, and to-day the saving of souls in the Protestant fashion is not a flourishing enterprise in that part of the peninsula east of Siam.

On the other hand the Annamese are converted to Catholicism by whole villages, particularly after some priestly assistance in the courts, a communal loan, or some other legitimate Catholic form of propaganda. One great inducement is that the converts are allowed to retain their ancestor worship, under a slightly different guise. But then, the Protestant missionaries permit their rare converts to keep all the wives of whom they are possessed at conversion, so long as they do not add to them afterward. "What," the missionaries quite properly ask, "could be done with cast-off wives if their converted husbands found Christianity a means of getting rid of their support?"

In Tourane there was a Protestant church—though the French deny such false places of worship any other name than *temple*—and a school. But those great educational and medical institutions so common in China with its thousands of missionaries of who knows how many sects are not a feature of the Indo-China landscape. The French have many hospitals, but they are government- rather than priest-operated. They have found it uphill work to encourage the Annamese to go to them, and only of very late years have they attracted any great percentage of the population, though clinical service is free and even in-patients pay very little—lying-in cases, for instance, are charged about a piastre a fortnight, just enough to pay for native food. But when the French doctors go to call on patients outside the hospitals they ask fees of five piastres a visit of French and Annamese alike. Naturally an Annamese earning ten piastres a month cannot call in the doctor often, so they fall back upon their own medicine-men. *"Mais quoi donc!"* cry the French; "A doctor must have his pay like any one else, *n'est-ce pas?"* True enough no doubt, though after two years of associating with the foreign missionary doctors of China, whose fees amount almost to nothing—unless the patients are non-missionary foreign residents—one begins to dream of some more ideal method in matters of health than the competition of the market-place.

I coaxed one of the few Americans engaged in saving souls in Tourane to take a needed holiday and visit the "Marble Mountains" with me. These farthest-south outrunners of the great rock hills that become so numerous and so fantastically individual in form farther north, dotting by thousands the Bay of Along and stretching far on down the West River in the Chinese province of Kwangsi, seem wholly out of place here protruding from the flat sandy coast-land. It is as if the gods, carrying these absurd heaps of molten rock from their equatorial melting-place to their allotted destination, had dropped a few of them unnoticed on the way. Across the river, by native boat, we walked for hours along the beach toward them, close as they look to the town. The sea, stretching away to the eastward like a sheet of molten steel, rolled great breakers in at our feet. Had they swept over us we should probably have been less drenched than we were with perspiration from that endless plodding through the sand.

The incandescent sun stood sheer overhead by the time we reached that misplaced cluster of savage heaps of rock. Jagged mountain peaks jutting out of the sand like islands from the sea, the "Marble Mountains" of Tourane, taking their name from the marble-like rock of which they are formed, rise in thousands of pinnacles, nearly all of them sharp as needles, the peaks themselves pointed as the head of a Roman spear. Nature evidently did not intend man to explore these isolated crags standing out so sharply against the white sand all about them. For not only are the myriad rocks themselves needle-pointed, but all the vegetation that steals its scanty nourishment among them bristles with thorns. No four-footed animal has ever been known to venture up them; and only hardy climbers of the two-legged species, with the price of a new pair of shoes available, are wise to attempt the ascent, slight as is the elevation. From the summit of the highest, once the climber can find standing-space for both feet, spreads a brilliant scene of beach and sea, of rice-green plain backed by the endless Annamese range not far inland, and, dim in the offing, the hogback island which the government rents to a syndicate of Cantonese who gather there the ingredients of bird's-nest soup.

We fell upon our wilted lunch at a temple cut into the lower slope of one of the "mountains," a temple quite like those of China, even to the languid attitude of the priests. Then we explored grotto after grotto, deliciously cool after our infernal climb. In the largest of them the Annamese have set up other Chinese-style temples, for the attracting of pilgrims. Half-naked families peered forth from little huts nearly buried in the sand as we skirted the bristling waterless heaps on our way to the river, down which native boatmen sculled us back to the town.

The mission stands so convenient to the railway station in the outskirts of the widely scattered concession as to suggest that the workers in this difficult bit of the Lord's vineyard wish to be prepared at any moment to abandon their task at the behest of their powerful rivals. The train that picks up there the broken end of what in a few years will be a continuous railroad the whole length of Indo-China strains its way for more than two hours toward Hué, the Annamese capital. First there is a desert of brush and sand from mountains to the sea, its blue bays dotted by so many sails that one's sympathy is rather with the hunted fish than with the crowded people who must have them or starve. Huge fish-nets on poles, pulled from the shore, leave the denizens of the deep little chance for safety except by taking to the far high seas. Then for twenty miles the railway crawls along the face of a cliff, not a hundred feet above chaotic heaps of rocks boiling in the surf of a vast stretch of blue ocean, burrowing its way through many tunnels. At length both rocks and sea disappear, some densely jungled hillsides succumb in time to a plain, now planted with rice, now covered with low brush, single weather-faded thatched huts or clusters of them scattered across it, and with the sudden tropical twilight passengers blend into the chaos of rickshaw-men of the capital of Annam.

CHAPTER VII

MAROONED IN HUÉ

THE river at Hué runs parallel to the sea, some twenty miles inland, and there is a screen of mountains to the south, the direction from which evil spirits come in Annam—just as the north, the reservoir of bitter cold and conquering Tartar tribes, is the quarter from which they are to be guarded against at Peking. There are also two islands near-by, known respectively as the White Tiger and the Blue Dragon. Hence it is not strange that the royal geomancers of several generations ago considered this the proper place to establish a new capital.

It is a very roomy town, like all those of any size and importance in Annam, probably not so much from Annamese custom as from French influence. On the foreign side of the river, where the traveler is set down, are all those things properly pertaining to the French superlords. From the railway station a wide grass-sided boulevard along the river-bank passes in its mile or more of existence a rather imposing school, hospital, barracks, and government buildings, many comfortable French residences, the *cercle* where the ruling race gathers of an otherwise empty evening over its coffee and wine, its dominoes and cards, and brings the traveler at length to another grocery-hotel named for the tropically energetic Morin brothers. Just beyond, only across the street from the French windows of the room assigned me, stands the palatial residence and offices of the *résident supérieur,* real ruler of Annam.

The whole machinery of the actual government of the "protected" kingdom is confined to this side of the river, the south side, direction of evil influences. Probably the river was kept between the real and the puppet rulers purposely; the French have as good reason as the emperor of Annam to keep up the fiction of his sacredness and unapproachability. Yet space is still so plentiful in this French section of Hué that almost any official—and there are virtually no other European residents—has his own garden and greensward among trees, large enough to be called, with a little stretching of the southern Gallic imagination, a private park. In any habitable direction these shade away into thatched huts that may be tailor-shops and the like as well as native residences. Up a creek tributary of the river bulks forth on its knoll the tropical-weather-worn old cathedral, under a nap of fine vegetation, a contrast to the low insignificant buildings of the missionaries of Tourane. Not the least conspicuous thing on the French side of the river is the Monument aux Morts, in Annamese style, the names of the French heroes who went home from Annam to die in the World War facing the boulevard, where the passer-by can scarcely overlook them, those of the Annamese who made the great sacrifice for the "mother-land" around on the side facing the river. Of course he who takes the trouble to go behind the monument can read those also; possibly the emperor can even make them out with a powerful field-glass from the flagpole of his citadel, if he ever climbs so high; or it may be that the placid river is more in keeping with their memory than the road with its broken stream of Oriental and Western traffic.

I found the weather in Hué quite different from that of Saïgon. When rain falls in Cochinchina it is dry in Annam, and vice versa, thanks to a high range between them. Ever

since I had left Canton the weather had been bright and
equatorial in temperature, but as I came northward the
humidity had steadily increased in density, and now the
rainy season this so plainly augured overtook me in earnest.
For the first time since leaving Hong Kong I was comfortably cool, though white was still my favorite garb.
It did not seem to be so with the French of Hué, however,
perhaps because of some connection between that color and
the sacredness of the emperor. There was an attention to
dress worthy of descendants of Beau Brummel and his
spouse, if he had one; but white suits for men were
rather looked down upon, and of course to so much as
step out of a bedroom without a coat on was almost as
incredible a breach of civilization as in Brazil itself. A
thick Scotch mist reigned all my first, and what I had
planned to be my only, day in the capital; and that evening
at the very height of the motion-picture tale on the wall
of the outdoor covered sitting-space in the grocery-hotel
courtyard tropical rains began to fall in earnest. Hardly
did it let up again as long as I remained in Hué—except
for the all-important day that justified my stay, during which
the weather behaved à *merveille*. It poured without cessation, confining me to my hotel room, making even a dash
across the courtyard to the other parts of the establishment a shower-bath with mud foundation, forcing me to
put off my visit to the real Hué across the river, the "citadel" with its palaces, bringing forth again the cloth suit
for which I had so roundly berated myself at Saïgon, and
leaving me none too warm at that. Everything took quickly
to mildewing, and in less than forty-eight hours pocketbooks
and the extra shoes of those who owned them were covered with a delicate vegetation. Soon stories began to come
in of dikes giving way, of thousands of coolies being rushed

to save this or that town, built several meters below the river, so that a broken embankment would mean disaster.

Nowhere could the rainy season have overtaken me with less cause for resentment, however, for I had to tarry several days in Hué rain or shine. I did not know this when I arrived, but found it out next morning, when I went to present to the "résuper" the letter of introduction I had won from some other official along the line. The real ruler of Annam, less telegraphically known as the *résident supérieur,* received me in his palatial dwelling and bureau a few steps beyond the grocery-hotel with a perfect Gallic mixture of courtesy and that something which leaves one no chance to presume upon one's fancied importance. Yet the writer of that letter must have been either an important personage or the "résuper's" boon companion in school-boy days, for it certainly could not have been my own virtues that won me the precious privilege the superior resident of Annam offered.

In the course of our official platitudes he mentioned that the ceremony of the lunar New Year greeting of his loyal subjects to the emperor of Annam across the river would take place the following Tuesday morning. It was then Friday, and by Tuesday I had hoped to be leaving Hanoï for the Chinese border. But the most important personage of Annam went on to mention that, while only French officials were ordinarily admitted—which I found later not to be sternly true—he thereby invited me to remain for this crowning feature of the Annamese *Têt.* This very special favor, I gathered from his meticulous deportment, was not so much in my own honor as to that of the then still gratefully remembered country to which I belong.

Expert as I was in my academic days at ministering to the gastronomic demands of my fellow-students, I have never

been a good waiter. For some inexplicable reason the loss
of time brings me more bitterness than the loss of money,
though of the first I have habitually far more to spare than
of the second. Certainly I did not care to squander wan-
tonly in Hué the better part of a week that I had planned
to spend in hurrying back to my family in Canton, with
whom communication had been rare and precarious. Yet I
felt it a duty to my curiosity, if not to my country, to attend one royal levee before the time comes to settle down
to a respectable life of immobility. There are few such
ceremonies left in the world, and still fewer of them are
open to Europeans—as the East insists on considering Americans. I murmured a polite acceptance.

But life is an incessant series of ups and downs in this
vale of tears. The next words of the ruler of Annam
turned my satisfaction into disappointment. When I—
or it may have been the "résuper" himself—brought up
the obviously important question of court costume, he remarked, "Of course you have with you your frock-coat
and *chapeau de forme?*"—in other words the ceremonial
head-gear of politicians and other successful exploiters of
the general public. Or if not, it seemed, I could get along
with *le smoking*—which as a Frenchman he of course pronounced "smocking." Now *le smoking* ordinarily means
our more modest form of dinner garb, disrespectfully known
as "soup and fish," and not only that part of my wardrobe,
but the even more absurd long-tailed livery of night life, I
had left at Canton. The motive for this dreadful oversight
had seemed sufficient in the days when it occurred. I did not
care to have the Chinese bandits I was almost sure to meet
on my way home have just cause for wreaking Bolshevik
vengeance upon me by catching me in possession of such un-
sightly things, or give them the false impression that I was

worth holding for ransom, or, more likely still, endure
the painful experience of seeing one of them bedeck himself
in that unseemly garb. I could of course not weep openly
in so official a predicament, but it looked indeed as if for my
carelessness in packing, my failure to remember the oft-
learned lesson that the equatorial regions of the earth by
no means forgo the perspiring amenities of social intercourse,
I was to miss something which very few of my countrymen
have seen. True, the "résuper" murmured something to the
effect that some way would be found to *me tirer d'affaire*,
but I took this to be merely a kind way of softening my
unavoidable disappointment, and having received official permission to visit the palaces across the river under less interesting circumstances I took my leave.

I had barely broken my first French roll and tasted my
wine at the eleven o'clock *déjeuner* when one of the black-
turbaned "boys" in snowy white laid before me the card
of the "Chef de Sûreté d'Annam." Misfortunes certainly
come in clusters. The chief of the security of Annam,
police-head extraordinary of the land, suggested trouble,
with emphasis on such persons as spies and unwanted
visitors; hence it was with something akin to trepidation
that I hurried out to the grocery division of the hotel and
presented myself before him. Perhaps I had somewhere
neglected to have something done again to my passport, and
was to be ordered out of the country, which would not
greatly matter, now that I had lost the privilege of hob-
nobbing with the emperor, except that they might send me
back the way I had come, or perhaps from Tourane as the
most convenient port, and spoil my plan of going all the
way from Angkor to Canton by land.

I found the bearer of the dreaded title an upstanding,

opened keg of olives. The *résident supérieur*, he remarked, after the customary words of greeting, had sent him to see me. So I was in for it, even as I had feared! But to my astonishment and growing relief the chief of Annam's security showed no signs of official wrath. Conversation ran along in a perfectly neutral manner until my fellow-guests in the dining-room must have been nearing the sad French substitutes for apple-pie. Then at length, in a very tactful way—which was fortunate, since I am nothing if not sensitive—the guardian of the security of Annam introduced the apparently irrelevant and immaterial theme that he and I were of about the same build; to which, so long as he did not also charge me with rivaling him in manly beauty, I acquiesced. In short, he interrupted himself in the midst of some genial story based on the natural spiritual affinity between republican France and my own Republican land to say that he had come at the suggestion of his superior to offer me clothing for the coming ceremony. He would be glad to assemble the requisite outfit from his own wardrobe; he had already done as much, some years before, for another *journaliste* from my country—what a barbarian and unprovided nation he must have thought us!

We began forthwith to take stock. For a moment it seemed that I would after all need only to wear his trousers, for the conference disclosed that in Annam *le smoking* means black pantaloons topped by a white tuxedo coat giving up its duties abruptly at the waist, what is quite fittingly known in the dancing circles of the Far East as a "monkey jacket." Nay, even a full-length white coat would do, and that I had. I was even the possessor of black trousers— if ever the baggage I had checked at Saïgon should catch up with me. But further discussion brought to light the annoying fact that those straying trousers had a faint stripe

in them, and that would never do; it would be almost equivalent to *lèse-majesté*. Then that white coat—did it have one
button or two? Two, as far as I recalled. "Sapristi!" The
chief of the security of Annam threw up his arms in a gesture
of dismay. A coat with two buttons would be worse than
no coat at all in Annamese court circles, I gathered from his
excited demeanor. Also I should have to have a vest,—
beg pardon, purists of the editorial function, I mean a
w's'c't—and that curse in any climate, let alone in the tropics,
a stiff collar. All these things the chief expressed his delight
to be able to furnish, and the day seemed to have been saved
—until he glanced down at my feet. They were incased in
brown shoes. Moreover, though I am not perpetually conscious of that fact, they must be large feet, compared at least
with those even of athletic Frenchmen of my own build,
for the chief not only disclaimed any ability to provide me
with shoes of such a size from his own wardrobe, but doubted
the possibility of finding a pair as large as that in all Hué.
Plainly I have overlooked the opportunity of becoming a
great popular comedian and riding in my own limousine.
But surely Buddha would provide, in so small, or even large,
a matter as that, and I planned to settle down in Hué for five
days rather than wend my way homeward bitter with
disappointment.

Once I had reconciled myself to losing several days, Hué
was by no means the worst place on earth in which to pass
the time. My hotel room was more home-like than those
for which we pay several times as much in our own beloved
land; food, wine, and ice were in keeping with French standards, and if the evening movies in the hotel courtyard were
not worth going to the Orient to see, the types of French

the numerous crosses between those two races. Then too
the rain did now and then slacken, though so weary did the
senses become of hearing it pour on the graveled road outside that it never seemed to do so. One briefly clear evening
I took a walk in Hué itself, the walled but very much
Frenchified imperial residence across the river from the
newer foreign section. The river is so wide that seven big
incongruous steel arches are needed to lift the modern bridge
over it, and the town beyond proved to be extensive, though
from the farther bank it looked merely like a façade of shops
backed by forest. A whole village of queer boats, most of
which spend their lives in bringing produce to the big half-
covered market-place on the northern bank, were anchored
about that end of the bridge. At first there seemed to be
no great population. But gradually this impression gave
way, as the town, orderly with wide right-angled streets,
stretched leisurely on and on out various directions, long after
one expected it to succumb to jungle or fields, until I began
to wonder if there could be as much city scattered among the
trees here as in the forest of Angkor-Thom.

Whatever the French have left of shops and native handi-
crafts is outside the wall and moat of the imperial residence.
Once, they say, these were labyrinths of narrow dirty streets;
now they are neither labyrinthine nor unclean, and much of
the picturesqueness one expects is lacking. In the wide-open
shops that lined the principal extramural streets one saw
Madrasis in little red fezzes, most of them with black-toothed
Annamese wives, and children with the luminous eyes of
the Hindu. But there seemed to be few Chinese merchants.
The Annamese themselves evidently kept shop here more
than is normal, perhaps because the capital with its swarms
of loafing functionaries had impressed them with the ease
of this sedentary occupation. Between the river and the

mountains that shield the capital from evil southern influences there are many waterways, and sampans and humped bridges were frequent. But on the whole the charm of the Orient had been cleaned and modernized away.

Much of the old atmosphere remained, however, within the *citadelle* which the native city partly surrounded. In Annam towns of any importance are encircled by ramparts and are known as citadels. Once, and in some cases still, the rather roomy residences of native officials, the citadels of Annam have little in common with the walled cities of China, teeming with jostling humanity. The crenelated walls of Hué inclose a space a mile or more square, but it is a newer, lower, much less imposing wall than the ancient ones surrounding Peking and most Chinese cities. A moat stagnant with water-lilies and other broad-leafed vegetation protects the wall, and short stone bridges older in appearance than they probably are in years give entrance to it in three or four places through Chinese-style gates. Inside is an astonishing spaciousness, trees and greensward and shaded boulevard-wide streets, a veritable park scattered with dwellings, as if nothing were so plentiful as space. With overcrowded China always in mind, I was constantly astonished at the roominess of Annamese cities. Within the citadel, Hué is a city of gardens, less a capital than a great inhabited park, more an Oriental Versailles than a Paris, not so much a center of hard official duties as a perpetual summer residence of Eastern potentates. As those on this side of the river really have very little to do with governing, the atmosphere is in keeping with the facts, and the ostensible rulers of Annam can spend their time growing flowers and parading their singing-birds.

Never, surely, was another walled city so bucolic as this residence of the sacred emperor of Annam. Quiet and calm

reigned everywhere along its wide roadway under trees that
joined together overhead into an almost concealing forest.
Lotus ponds, as covered as the moat with flowers and big
green leaves, lay here and there through the half-forest;
many of the houses—most of them, I was to learn later, the
homes of mandarins—were set in roomy gardens surrounded
by low walls with imposing gateways. With its broad river
and its canals, bordered with water-palms, its flower-decked
bungalows, its wide silent roadways, the chimeric roofs of
its palaces, the splendid circle of its forest, its quiet and
cleanliness, Hué was indeed a great contrast to China. One
day when for a little while the weather was clear—no,
not that, for the humidity was thick as cream, but at least
the sun was doing its best to shine through it—I evaded
the royal guards and mounted the iron ladder of the Eiffel
Tower of a flagpole, which stands at the front of the citadel.
From it the royal palaces stretched away among the trees one
after another in a straight line, impressive by their colors,
perhaps by their architecture, but never by their height, as
if their builders scorned to take advantage of that cheapest
means of exciting admiration. From this elevation little else
than the palaces and the tree-tops are visible, but down beneath the foliage the stroller will find many humble huts
made of poles and thatch, not only within the citadel but
only a short walk from the palaces of the sacred Annamese
emperor. Yet about some of these simple, but probably on
the whole as comfortable, homes of the ordinary mass of his
loyal subjects, there were some fine clipped hedges, as if
these faded-thatch hovels were merely a means of disguising
wealth still naturally modest from centuries of envious
mandarins. Rich and poor have the same little squared garden, the same dwarf trees growing in pots of baked earth,
the same water-jars sweating in the sun.

He who is privileged to visit the home of a mandarin
enters the principal room directly from the garden, without
steps, and finds it furnished with a big bed of naked wood,
with no other bed-furnishings than a porcelain pillow and
a reed mat. Besides that there is a round table with stools,
and the altar of the ancestors. This now sometimes bears a
photograph of the deceased in the place of the ancient tablet
—the one evidence of progress, and an unpleasant one, for
it is far more agreeable to picture a bygone member of the
human race from no other data than his posthumous name
in Chinese characters on an upright stick than to behold
him photographically in all the moles and wrinkles he left
behind him in the grave.

All this I did not of course see in one day; the rain was
too incessant for that. Long as I remained I could not have
seen it all if I had not defied the rain, helped thereto by
the attitude of the natives toward it. A rainy day does not
keep the Annamese indoors; like the inhabitants of most
southern countries where deluges fall for days at a time,
they make the most of it. I had only to glance out my hotel
window to see scores of both sexes, bare to the knees, even
to the loins, all ages wearing their mushroom hats and the
palm-leaf rain-coats that turn so easily this way or that,
according to the slant of the storm. On they went, carrying
their shoulder-pole loads or doing whatever else the pursuit
of their rice required of them, quite as if the sun were
shining. It is so hot when it does that in some ways a rainy
day is a more pleasant time to work; and what is mud when
you can wash one foot with the other at any water-hole?
Thus Hué on those wet days was a vista of broad graveled
streets, lined by trees and grass and spaciousness, and dotted
with human figures dressed only in palm-leaves, so far as the

eye could see, like some strange Eden that defied any but
the most practised eye to tell the sexes apart.

As there seemed to be no prospect of the rain halting, I
dived into a rickshaw one afternoon and went to visit the
palaces across the river. It was as well that I had brought
along my special permit from the "résuper," for soldiers in
the now familiar Annamese uniform of khaki rompers and
blouse below a mushroom, brass-topped hat and above bare
feet—here however with imperial yellow rather than the
ordinary red wrap-leggings—expect a permit from Europeans, though coolies of both sexes were going freely in and
out. A fine pretense this that the French are merely protectors; and incidentally it keeps other Western nations from
finding out too much of what goes on in the privacy of the
emperor's own department of the governing of Annam.
There is nothing very exciting about his palaces. So low
that they are not seen at any distance, they are few and unimposing compared to the Forbidden City of Peking. Yet
small as they are beside their Chinese counterparts, like the
same thing not too exactly done in miniature, they are in
general artistic and in some ways perhaps superior to their
more pretentious Chinese models. One's impression of them
and of the dynasty they represent improved with seeing.

Workmen on a bamboo scaffolding were repainting the
exterior of the main audience-chamber, and Saturday afternoon being pay-day, even as in other lands, a group of mandarins with ladylike hands, on some of which cat-claw finger-
nails still remained, sat at a table keeping books in French
style and paying out French paper piastres to the men and
women as they filed past. Building after building, Chinese
wood-and-paper buildings under top-heavy tile roofs, all of
imperial yellow, stretched lengthwise one behind another,
like squads of soldiers with a passageway through the middle

Overlooking, from his flagpole, the palaces of the emperor of Annam

China itself cannot outdo the old bronze urns before the main palace of
the Annamese emperor

The throne-room of the emperor of Annam, on the afternoon before the New Year's ceremony

of them, as do those of a Chinese yamen, back to the main
and finally the more private edifices. All these were inclosed within a walled compound. Under the incessant rain
the polished tiles of the courtyards between them resembled
great lakes of uncertain depth, in which all the surroundings
were mirrored as in a broad horizontal pier-glass. The old
bronze lanterns before the palace verandas, exactly full of
rain-water, were as beautiful, as graceful, as any I had seen
in China; and being carefully preserved in this still imperial
land, they showed their fine points to better advantage. They
are hardly the favorite lanterns of his Majesty, however,
who is more French than Chinese in his tastes and thirsts.

The gaudy audience-chamber was on the whole more conspicuous than lovely. The real throne-room, on the other
hand, was a gorgeous place well worth seeing, in spite of a
goodly supply of those chandeliers which seem to be Europe's
chief contribution to the splendor of Oriental kings. From
a vast expanse of varicolored tiles gleaming as if they were
made of glass, rose a forest of red pillars with imperial yellow five-clawed dragons climbing them. Decorations of
every conceivable Chinese form and color, but with red in
the ascendancy, added to the rich yet not chaotic ensemble.
There were many fine vases, quite evidently Chinese, though
the "guide" who saw to it that I chipped off no souvenirs
and slipped nothing into my pockets called some of them
French and contended that many of the others were made
by the Annamese themselves, in earlier days, before those
of his countrymen capable of such things had all died off.
But they looked to me so much like Kingtehchen ware, the
best of Kingtehchen at that, that for once I might have been
tempted into a wager if one had been offered.

Naturally there was the throne, and all the other things
that go with emperors' throne-rooms, but all those I was to

see better during the ceremony that was keeping me in Hué. Suffice it to say that the throne-room of Annam was the most gorgeous place I had seen in many a moon, on the whole artistically pleasing, and—that the rank and file of Americans may understand just what I am trying to say —worth several million piastres, or about half as many dollars.

Beyond came more long tile-covered rooms, shed-like in shape, in which were many spirit-tablets and tables covered with porcelain fruits. There were even some small baskets of real fruit, perhaps because it was now New Year time, when the spirits of the departed cannot be deceived with pretended food, and when their descendants are surest to remember them. All these things and many more stood in imposing array before the six shrines of the present dynasty. I fear, however, that with my incorrigibly plebeian mind and tastes I found most interesting of all the flocks of ordinary coolies with dusters and brooms, who roamed about all the buildings among these king's playthings and slept on mat-covered boards beside them.

The story of the emperors of Annam, since Gia-long asked through the bishop of Adran for the assistance of the French against his dynastic rivals at the end of the eighteenth century, is not an entirely happy one. Some of them have even lost their jobs entirely for not behaving themselves, or for disobeying the French. There was Thanh-thai, for instance, deposed in 1907. He had been cutting up—among other things one of his concubines, merely to try his hand at surgery. So the French, not realizing perhaps that such things happen even in Philadelphia, nay, in Paris itself, sent him into exile and called in a doctor to help pick out one of his many sons to take his place. The eldest they passed over as a plain idiot, and chose a boy in prison, who howled because he thought he was being led forth to have his head lopped off. By the time they had washed and dressed him in the imperial robes, however, and seated him on the throne with the jade scepter in his childish hand, he had reverted to type and was an emperor both in appearance and demeanor, scorning already the common people among his kowtowing subjects. But in 1916, coincident with a certain busyness of the French at home, an independence movement broke out under this youthful king, which the French naturally insist was engineered by the Germans. The scheme was to have servants poison all the foreigners in the colony some evening, but some one "squealed." So Jy-su, born in 1902, was also exiled to Réunion, a French island off the east coast of Africa, which he still graces with his surgical father and one favorite wife. There they are both very happy, according to the French colonials, who regard Réunion as a second Garden of Eden, and where the ex-Sons of Heaven "have all the women they want"—a French as well as a Mohammedan notion of paradise.

All this gave the then reigning emperor, Khai-dinh, his chance. This French-ruled king of Annam, a rather distant relative of the man and boy he succeeded, came to the throne in 1916, when he was nearly thirty-five. He must have been troubled with something akin to vertigo by his accession, for until then, though he had been a kind of prince, he had enjoyed by no means the income or the importance of a railway station-master. If I have inadvertently called him king I apologize; his official title is Koang-de, Son of Heaven, written with the same characters as those for the Chinese Hoang-ti, son of a similar celestial realm. In fact the emperors of Annam claim descent from an imperial family of China, which had descendants to spare. Khai-dinh

visited France in state in 1922, influenced perhaps by an
American president, for that was the first case of an emperor
of Annam leaving Annamese soil. It was even more important for him to go, however, for in the Indo-Chinese pagoda
on the outskirts of the Bois de Vincennes he performed a
ceremony to release from the necessity of wandering perpetually through eternity the shades of thousands of Annamese who had fallen in the World War, unsaved either
because they had not been able to comply with the final rites
of their religion or because their bodies had not been recovered. He also placed in a French school his son and heir
—the only one, I believe, for all the wives Khai-dinh
maintained.

Khai-dinh was nearing forty when I graced Hué with my
impatient presence, and was already anemic with tuberculosis.
The other day he died, and twelve-year-old Vinh-thuy, the
crown prince, ascended the throne under the name of Bao-dai
(Greatness Sustained). But he returned at once to France
to continue his studies, and Frenchmen will tell you that
Annam is now governed by a Conseil de Régence, presided
over by the mandarin Ton-that-tan. For in theory the emperor governs. In Cochinchina, which is admittedly a colony,
a French lieutenant governor is the supreme functionary,
but in the four protectorates the native sovereigns are still
nominally the heads of the governments. Annam and Tonkin
are under the Annamese emperor; Cambodia and a part of
Laos still have kings. The native laws apply, unless a foreigner is involved, when the Code Napoléon is used. The
protectorates maintain almost intact the laws and administra-
tive machinery of the days when they were independent of
French authority. The native sovereign appoints all officials,
but the French *résident supérieur* can reject any candidate;

the native rulers dare not ignore his smallest suggestion, and the lesser *résidents* keep a sharp eye on native functionaries in the provinces. New laws may be of either French or native initiative, but both sides must agree, which of course means that the French have the final word. All royal ordinances are drawn up, not only the French but the native texts, in the *Résidences Supérieures*. In Annam the old Chinese system of choosing officials and mandarins from among those who have shown the greatest proficiency in scholarship still more or less prevails, rather than the Irish system of our Western world

One wonders what the thoughts of Bao-dai will be when he comes back really to take his father's place. Educated in French schools, Parisian during all his formative years, he will suddenly be plunged into this old-world atmosphere, to the customs, the ideas, the ideals, even the spirit of which he will surely have become a stranger. Will he regret the ardent life of the Occident he will have left behind, or will the old soul of the palace of his ancestors penetrate and possess him, and insensibly make him an Oriental potentate?

I softened my enforced stay in Hué by also three times visiting the imperial burial-places some ten miles from the citadel, on the French side of the river. The low rolling hillocks close about the Annamese capital are covered with graves of the rank and file by the many thousands. Nearly all these mere mounds of earth were cleared and rounded off now for the New Year, the few still covered with grass and weeds suggesting very unfilial descendants or, more likely still, a line died out. As many Annamese as possible have themselves buried near the tombs of their sacred emperors, as the Hindu who can manage it has his body burned on the bank of the Ganges at Benares. The French are gradually restricting the grave-lands, but they must move slowly in a matter so important to an ancestor-worshiping race.

All important Annamese make preparation during their life-time for their burial, some building their own tombs, where they often come to sit in meditation. While he is still on the throne each emperor has a geomancer, or a consultation of geomancers no doubt, choose the site for his last resting-place, always in the shelter of a natural screen, a butte or hillock that will protect the dead from the evil spirits that are forever flying about through the air. In such a garden several buildings are constructed, their number and arrangement fixed by ancient custom, superstition, and rites. There is an inclosure for the material remains, a pavilion for the memory, a temple for the soul; our miserable way of putting all these together, so that we cannot commune with the memory of the deceased without seeming to smell his bones, is not the Annamese way. Thus things were conceived by the sages who erected beyond the gates of Peking the mausoleums of the Ming, and the Annamese sovereigns have since changed nothing of what they got from their Chinese masters.

The royal tomb is the last residence of the sovereign, and in some ways the most sumptuous, as befits a palace of eternal repose. He may come back in spirit at any moment; therefore his loyal people are always prepared to receive him. Here is his great wooden bed, with its mat and cushions and porcelain pillow, not only for himself but for his favorite wife. Here is the tea, the rice, the *nhoc-nam*, or salty sauce in which the Annamese dip their food on the way to the mouth, cups of *chumchum*, or rice whisky, the arec-nuts, betel-leaves, and the little pot of lime that goes with them for his favorite minor vice, even cigarettes, everything he will need when he arrives. All these provisions are renewed every morning of the year, generation after generation, so that he will find nothing stale on the day when he finally comes. He will find again, arranged under glass, his royal playthings, the trinkets and gew-gaws, the jade shrubs, the precious crystals, the coffers inlaid with mother-of-pearl, the weapons he loved, even those great Sèvres vases which the ambassadors of a more respectful France sent him as New Year's presents; more things perhaps than the living emperor has now in his living palace. Perhaps the worst punishment of Thanh-thai and his son, deposed in 1907 and 1916, respectively, is that they cannot have their tombs here among those of their ancestors—unless the French relent after they are dead, which for politic reasons of influence on imperial conduct in the future they probably will not do. That Khai-dinh succeeded in dying on the job was probably the most successful accomplishment of his life.

Nothing in Indo-China has the charm of these old royal tombs; in them lives intact the melancholy beauty of old Annam. One can walk or rickshaw all afternoon about them, and never tire of seeing them. Perhaps the tomb of Tu-duc is the most striking; another can be reached only by boat. That of Gia-long, epic sovereign of Annam, founder of this dynasty and of Annam's present subordination to the French, is not the most elaborate. He was so very busy getting back his kingdom that perhaps he did not have time to prepare properly his last place of repose, for with the aid of the French he chased out his usurpers and grouped under the rule of his jade scepter all the land of Annam, being the first native son to govern as master from the frontiers of China to the banks of the Mekong. Even the tomb of Tu-duc is unimposing compared to those of the Ming emperors of China. But they all have a setting in solitude among unexploited

forests, and are kept in a state of cleanliness and repair rare
in the great land to the north. Weather-blackened structures
in a hot, rainy, and often humid climate, though originally
reddish, blue, green, multicolored, some overgrown with a
fine vegetation, these Annamese temples of the dead do not
impose upon the heavens like those of China. They blend
themselves harmoniously into their densely green surroundings, the fleeing lines of their low walls barely cut out against
the sky. As in the palaces of the living, it is not in the elevation of verticals that their builders looked for beauty, but
in the prolonging of unreflected lines, in the grace of colon-
nades, terraces, superimposed roofs nonchalantly stretching
to the horizon. Nothing dominates except two slender
grayish pillars lost in the verdure before each tomb, the
symbolic camel's-hair brushes of the man of letters. In the
large court of honor stone mandarins mount perpetual guard,
in a row on each side of the entranceway, their saddled horses
and their little elephants beside them, all dull and weather-
tarnished and sometimes crumbling away.

But the stone mandarins, the horses, elephants, and
mythological monsters guarding the royal tombs of Annam
are only pathetic little things compared to those of China.
Once I stood a living caretaker in the place of a missing stone
one, and only by looking closely at the picture can one distinguish him from those of stone or plaster, whereas in China
my head hardly reached to the knees of many an imperial
guardian, and the horses, elephants, and camels of the Ming
tombs are fully life-size. Nor are the materials so rich in
these tombs. The dragons that unroll their coils on the roofs
of glazed sun-polished tiles show signs of crumbling away;
the bricks tend to disintegrate into the earth from which they
came. Some of the most effective of these royal Annamese
tombs are covered with pictures of scenes and people made

entirely of broken crockery, pieces of porcelain cups, plates, bowls of Chinese design, and of many colors set in cement, much as the Annamese inlay their furniture with mother-of-pearl. Even fragments of broken bottles—nothing is so plentiful as bottles in French-ruled Indo-China—have been used in this way. These monuments recall the rags torn up and sewed together into the saffron robe of the Buddhist priest, because poverty is blessed. Yet even in this decoration the resting-places of the royal Annamese dead are beautiful.

In the woods, as we were driving homeward from the tombs—my first visit having been by automobile—we met a boy carrying on his head bananas and some other fruit, his grandfather kneeling beside him at the edge of the road and burning incense in a bush. The chief of Annam's security stopped his car. He was, I may have neglected to mention, in some ways an unusual Frenchman. Big and handsome, a soldier at Peking in the Boxer days, he spoke excellent Annamese and still knew some Chinese, and his interest in the natives was more than official and perfunctory —so much so in fact that one got a hint now and then that he sometimes felt the recent loss of his bachelor privileges, for all his enthusiasm as a new benedict. He spoke to the pair, and in the tone of an interested friend rather than of a martinet official. The result was a naïve frankness instead of a taciturn imitation of stupidity. It seemed that the son of the one and father of the other had "taken the sickness" while gathering wood, and they had come to implore the spirits of the forest to pardon him any harm he may have done them. They had come twice before, and now the father and son was so much better that they were sure their amends had been accepted, but they were performing the effective rites once more, in order to be on the safe side.

Though it is getting ahead of my story, such as it is, I came out to the tombs again on the afternoon of *Têt* and found every one very busy about the royal mausoleums. The soldier-like caretakers whose permanent duties are there had freshly washed the very red coats they wear over the usual black Annamese garments. Men in these bright red tunics, some holding imperial yellow umbrellas over the trays covered with red cloth borne by others, were bringing the dead kings their New Year's food. Mandarins, some of them evidently descendants of the emperors, came and donned transparent deep-blue cloaks over their black gowns, much decorated with French orders and the ivory plaques that denote the mandarin's estate, and kowtowed inside and outside the tombs. Some of these ceremonies were elaborate, that at the tomb of Thieu-tri, which I chanced upon at the right moment, including a procession and incense-burning rites in the courtyard, with yellow and faded white parasols very much in evidence. Old women in purple, green, and other conspicuous head-bands and cloaks crowded the interior, where a high mandarin was master of ceremonies There seemed to be no great objection to the presence of a European inside, except during the actual interior ceremony of greeting to the royal spirits, when the mandarin opposed my entrance in a resolute manner rare, especially toward the ruling race, among this easy-going people. Though I was the only foreigner nearer the tombs than the capital itself, I was no doubt perfectly safe from physical interference even had I persisted in entering, and perfect Oriental courtesy was shown me; but once again I sensed the probability that the Annamese do not love the French, from whom of course few of them distinguish the rest of us of the white race.

CHAPTER VIII

AN IMPERIAL HAPPY NEW YEAR

I WAS called at six on the eventful morning, and as soon afterward as was consistent with that meticulous personal attention befitting an imperial audience I was whisked away to the palaces in the automobile of my sartorial benefactor. Those who have suffered similar experiences need not be told the feeling of interloper, of usurper, with which I wore my borrowed plumage, though to the naked uncritical eye I must have showed little of this, for the bemedaled stiff-necked officials deep in the seat beside me showed no signs of finding me incongruous. All had gone easily, except in the matter of disguising my feet. Look as I would, not only in the merchandising part of the hotel but among all the native shops, there was not another pair of shoes in Hué that could be stretched over those extraordinary extremities. In my desperation I had turned my brown ones over to the head "boy" with orders to blacken them every half-hour during the intervening days, and nights, orders emphasized by promises of great reward and by threats of corresponding punishment. It had not therefore been merely the rain that confined me to my chamber. When the crucial moment came success seemed to have crowned my persistence. The shoes were not only black, they had a hint of luster. If only the false color did not rub off before the show was over! It did, as a matter of fact, but not so completely, I flatter myself, as to call widespread attention to the deception.

147

The ceremony was set for eight sharp. I suppose it might have been at Peking Manchu hours, and all over before daylight, but for the bed-loving French. A score of Frenchmen were already herded inside the door by which we entered the imperial courtyard, a side door, by the way, a detail not without its significance. Another dozen or two dripped from other automobiles not long behind us. The French officials had come in their best uniforms and their most numerous medals; some of the men in civilian dress wore gold medallions about their necks. All were not equally resplendent in the requisite court dress. Visitors must be *en tenue,* but that, it became at once evident, did not mean that one must strive for the elegance of a Beau Brummel. Some of the costumes had all too plainly been shaken free of their moth-balls too late to be pressed; others had arrived in the colony when the Franco-Prussian War was still a burning question. The group was sternly confined, however, in one respect: only the reputedly more manly sex was present, in any form, capacity, race, color, or condition of servitude. No woman, the sponsor for Annam's security himself assured me, has ever seen this imperial New Year's ceremony. Only persons in good standing, which in Annam does not include females, may by any hook or crook be admitted. Once two Frenchwomen had sneaked in by some still mysterious deception, and it had been the painful duty of the chivalrous chief of the security of Annam personally to drag them out of their hiding-place and chase them outside the grounds. Surely, whispered the incorrigibly skeptical spirit within me, there must be peep-holes known to the more enterprising of the emperor's wives; but on second thought I decided that their superstitions probably accomplish what the sternest husbandly admonitions might not.

We had been greeted one by one at the side door to the

The waterfront of Hué, capital of Annam, offers a contrast between its native craft and the French bridge

Once a visitor surreptitiously snapped this glimpse of the mandarins of Annam kowtowing before their emperor on New Year's Day

The scores of homes of mandarins within the "citadel" of Hué were all richly decorated for the lunar New Year

Inside the "citadel" and near the sumptuous palaces of the emperor of Annam are the perhaps more comfortable homes of his humble subjects

courtyard by two mandarins in the flowery costumes of old
Chinese times, topped by the same stepping-block head-
dress with absurd side-pieces to be seen on statues at the
Ming tombs of China. Inside, scores of other mandarins in
the same garb flocked together. All wore black knee-boots,
ancient robes of varying colors, silks decorated according to
rank—but you can see it all in old Chinese paintings or on
the Chinese stage. Like so many things which last longest
where they have been introduced with the most difficulty,
the costumes and manners of Ming days remain officially
correct in Annam centuries after they have been abandoned
in China. Not merely do back-waters show the greatest
stagnation, but the Manchus never conquered Annam, though
they now and then got tribute from it. It was just as well
that photography was forbidden; the absence of the colors
in the developed films would have made them too bitterly
disappointing. If there was any color in the spectrum missing in the gathering, or in the building and its decorations,
I do not know its name. All the prism seemed to have been
invited to the ceremony; and as if to supply any tone that
had inadvertently been omitted, and to cause my gorge to
rise with wrath after all the trouble I had taken to live up
to the sartorial rules, who should come slinking in at the
last moment, with the air of a cat returning to the comforts
of an old-maid home after a night of dissipation on the
housetops, but a Frenchman—though in his conspicuousness
he looked more like a Swede or a Hollander—wearing the
loudest check suit in the Ghettos of Christendom and carrying
a camera! It is true that this last was promptly taken away
from him. The French exploit their own colonies even in
photographic matters, and this ceremony had been officially
filmed some years before. Yet he not only was admitted
to the courtyard but was allowed to sneak under cover of us

respectable members of his race into the palace itself; and so help me if he didn't even have on tan shoes! All through the ceremony he stood forth from our courtly throng of Westerners like a splotch of red ink on a white suit, though he made every effort except the two obvious ones to be inconspicuous. Political or social pull are powerful institutions, and audacity is not confined to American reporters.

The great audience-chamber in which the New Year's ceremony is usually held having been covered with a network of bamboo scaffolding for more than a year, his Majesty awaited us in the somewhat smaller but more sumptuous throne-room. The little "résuper," in a uniform worthy of the admiral of the European fleet, had arrived with some of his staff last of all, as befitted his standing; and, piloted by the receiving mandarins, we had filed in by twos behind him and lined up on the right side of the richly decorated chamber —on the left or heart side of the emperor, be it noted, which is the place of honor in the Orient. Dazzled by the forest of pillars climbed by yellow dragons, I was at the very foot of the throne before I saw that the emperor was already there. He stood so still, and his garb and the racial and sickly yellow of his face blended so harmoniously into the ensemble of the imperial decorations, that even then I was not sure for a moment that I was not looking at a lay figure in his place. Yet he was not inconspicuously dressed. Again I plead my incompetence in the matter of inventories, but some of his garb could not have escaped the most unobservant eye. He wore an imperial robe of such richness of embroidery and decorations that even a woman, had her sex permitted her to behold it, nay, were she, by profession, both a dressmaker and the concocter of social columns, could not adequately have described it. Whether or not some of the imperial wives had put in a safety-pin here and there at the last moment I have no means of knowing, but the wearer himself could not have adjusted it to such a nicety without expert assistance of one sex or another. He stood in the embrace of a chair that the lineal descendant of St. Peter himself might have envied, two golden dogs half hiding his feet, which were incased in high boots of the Ming period and turned out at right angles, as if he were in imminent fear of tottering. They were so exactly such boots as those of his predecessors in a glass case near-by that they might indeed have been borrowed from it. On his imperial head sat an indescribably magnificent openwork crown of gold and precious stones, beneath which, later developments disclosed, he wore the ordinary black band-turban of the Annamese male. Many jewels gleamed from various parts of his person; on three fingers of his left hand he wore clusters of enormous diamonds, and as he constantly held that hand over the other, these stones drew the eyes like a flash-light in a darkened theater. In his clasped hands he held before his face an ivory wand containing a mirror, just such as are to be seen in old Chinese statues and paintings, and which has something to do with the holder's unworthiness to look upon the spirits of his ancestors, if I have not bungled my theogony. His almost golden-yellow face was somewhat chinless, his form slight, even under the imperial robes, his general appearance so effeminate that he suggested Mei Lan-fang, China's most famous actor, aged by a decade or so and with the slight changes between Chinese and Annamese features, playing one of his inimitable female rôles.

Evidently this chief ceremony of the ordinary Annamese year is one of the rough spots in the kingly career, for everything pointed to the suspicion that the emperor did not enjoy it. His face remained as motionless throughout the throne-room service as if it had been made of wax, but his body shifted nervously on his legs, as though the ancient boots were too tight for him, or the right angle at which etiquette required his feet to be set made standing difficult; and his little eyes roved constantly from side to side, especially toward the Europeans, until at times he suggested a trick poodle constantly in fear of doing something that would bring a whipping after the performance from the trainer who could only stand blandly by while it was going on. Though it was not unpleasantly warm so early in the morning, he wiped his face every few seconds with a folded snow-white handkerchief. Two men in musical-comedy costumes stood at the front corners of the throne and fanned him throughout the ceremony. It was not the hasty careless fanning of mere modern mortals; they stood at the strict attention of the old days when a head was lopped off for a grimace, and one after the other raised his fan of feathers on a handle taller than himself and waved it once downward at a dignified speed, continuing to alternate with such exact time between the strokes that they must have mentally counted the seconds.

Two princes of the blood, dressed in robes of exactly that color, and whom I understood from a whisper from the owner of my raiment to be brothers of the recently exiled emperor, stood each on his mat on opposite sides of the wide-open front doors, ten yards or more from the throne. No other Annamese were allowed inside the throne-room so effectively graced by our broken double row of motley Europeans festooned about the first line of pillars on his Majesty's left. All the nobility of Annam was gathered in the sun-drenched, flagstone-paved courtyard outside the open doors which the emperor faced, but for the moment all one's attention was needed inside. Amid deep silence and formal attitudes the *résident supérieur* stepped nearer to the throne

and read in French a greeting in which he referred to his
Majesty's ascent of the same in 1916, recalling that he himself had been present on that auspicious occasion, that he
was overwhelmed with pleasure and honor at his recent return to a place so near his Majesty's sacred person, and in a
capacity now that implied a recognition of his constant dili-
gence in his Majesty's service, and so on and so on, to the
depths of French political rodomontade, with many references to the *Nation Protectrice* thrown in.

Then a young mandarin stepped up beside the "résuper"
and read in the querulously singsong Annamese language
what was evidently a translation of this masterpiece, written
in Roman letters. Thereupon the emperor dived down into
one of his voluminous sleeves, this very first motion he had
voluntarily made since our arrival seeming to bring him a
relief similar to that of a "living statue" at the drop of the
curtain, and dug out a document written in Chinese characters on a long strip of cardboard folded accordion fashion.
This he read in a better voice than his physique suggested,
though not without a nervous break now and then in his un-
melodious native tongue. From behind a dragon-climbed
pillar on the other side of the throne appeared an old mandarin with a straggling gray beard, looking in his New-Year
costume exactly like an ancient Chinese portrait cut out of its
frame, who read, in an almost perfect pronunciation that
seemed strangely incongruous coming forth from such a
figure, a French translation of the emperor's speech. This
fourth act of the exchange of platitudes over, the emperor
bowed low, the "résuper" bowed a trifle less low, and we
Europeans moved grudgingly back, not so far but that we
could still easily hear and see the chief actor in the ceremony,
who now for the first time sat down, with an air which
seemed to say that at least that was that. Every one else,

including even the *résident supérieur,* stood throughout the
entire throne-room part of the ceremony.

Meanwhile in the courtyard outside attention had turned
to activity. Scores of mandarins in the gay and fanciful
attire of Ming days began to fall into ranks. The Annamese
troops in blue, with brass-topped mushroom hats and imperial yellow leggings, but under command of a French
officer, and carrying their long rifles with needle-sharp fixed
bayonets French fashion, high on their shoulders, backed
to the edges of the court and out through the gateways. For
some time a great to-do reigned in the courtyard, but at
length restored order disclosed six rows of mandarins lined
up according to rank on as many strips of matting, each
holding before his eyes in clasped hands a somewhat less
splendid wand-with-mirror than that of the emperor. It was
typical of human society East or West that three rows of still
lower rank, no doubt the hard-working old souls on whom
the real labor of government fell, were lined up outside the
courtyard, where they could neither see nor be seen by the
emperor, but where they went through the same maneuvers
as those inside. Standing within arm's length of one another in exact rows some two paces apart, the assembled
nobles of Annam so vividly suggested a company of soldiers
or a gymnasium class about to begin its setting-up exercises
that one might easily have been struck by the absence of
dumb-bells. On the side-lines throngs of flunkies in conspicuous garments began to make those loud discordant noises
that represent music wherever the Chinese character is written, while others, in simpler costumes, added a weird vocal
dissonance in voices of which fully half suggested eunuchs.
The gymnasium-class aspect of the situation was not entirely accidental; the nobility of Annam was about to take

its yearly exercise. Loud noises not unlike the "music" that incessantly assailed the ears rang out in a series of semi-military commands, at each of which the rows of mandarins in their flowered robes threw themselves face down, slowly, as if, what with boots, the wands in their hands, and the insufficiency of annual practice, they found it no easy task, and touched their noses to the pavement. Just inside the main doors the two princes of the blood, also facing the emperor on his throne, were doing the same exercises, their movements evidently serving as a signal to those outside and keeping the prostrations in unison. There were several series of these, three at a time, amid much hullabaloo, the emperor meanwhile sitting motionless on his uncomfortable throne, except that he now and then mopped his face, yellow as the ensemble of throne-room decorations with the filtered tropical sunshine upon them, with the still folded pocket-handkerchief. Each time there was a dazzling flash of the many diamonds on his left hand, which he always folded again over the diamondless right.

In theory "ten thousand" mandarins of Annam—*ee wan* is a number so easily said in any tongue that reads Chinese—come to prostrate themselves in the great courtyard of the palace of Hué on the day of *Têt,* but something less than that number beat their foreheads on its flagstones that morning. *Lam lie,* the Annamese verb to prostrate one's self, means this stretching out at full length on one's face and is still descriptive in this great yearly ceremony, though at other times the Annamese nowadays usually contents himself with bending the bust as if he were hinged at the waist, and shaking his own hands. As they finished, the mandarins backed a couple of steps toward the side of the courtyard, then turned and marched to the side-lines, while others took in perfect military precision, and everyone seemed to take the matter very seriously, as if a slip would be as dreadful as during a guard-mount in our regular army.

Then came retired mandarins, in bright-red trousers under gowns reaching to the knees, and *no boots*. This, a whisper told me, is the sign of retirement; "I have taken off my boots," means to the Annamese mandarin what cutting off his *coleta* does to the Spanish matador, what the writing of his memoirs means to an American pugilist or politician. Each and every one of these old chaps was in stocking-feet quite plainly made in France, most, though by no means all, of the same color. They threw themselves down the same number of times as had those who had preceded them, some aged faces contorted as if they found the effort quite a trial. Two ragged rows of poor old fellows of low degree at the rear had not even been provided with mats, but had to bump their heads on the bare flagstones.

Between the two front doors almost directly in front of the emperor, where he could not have taken his eyes off them if he had tried, stood a hat-rack bearing aloft all the tropical helmets and uniform capes of those Europeans who did not carry their hats in their hands. A servant had taken that of the "résuper" himself, but many others had refused to run the risk of having some royal retainer make off with theirs. It seemed as if the hat-rack might have been put in some less conspicuous corner, but perhaps it was an intentional symbol, a constant visible reminder to his Majesty of who made him emperor, and who could unmake him again in twenty minutes if he bungled his rôle. I could also make out through a door at the back of the throne-room the imperial rickshaw. It seemed to be at least half of gold, with richly yellow cushions; and the imperial rickshaw-man— who with a few other low-caste hangers-on peered in now

Servants of the mandarins carry home after the ceremony the ancient Ming accoutrements of their masters

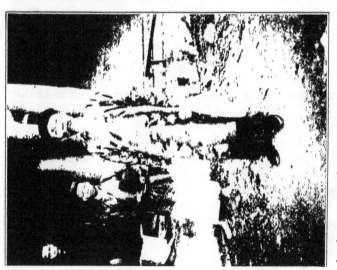

An Annamese mandarin all dressed up for his New Year's honors to his emperor, his servant behind

Some of the most effective of Annamese tombs are covered with pictures and designs made of broken porcelain dishes set in cement

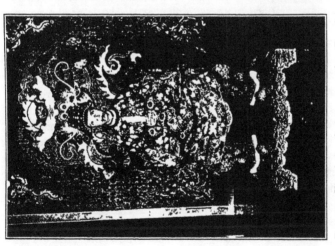

Emperor Khai-dinh of Annam on his French-supported throne

and then, after the custom at all Oriental ceremonies—was in an incredibly ornate livery, also mainly of imperial yellow. Though he uses an automobile outside the palace walls, the emperor needs a rickshaw within, for it is nearly a hundred yards from the throne-room to his semi-European living-quarters.

When the larger audience-chamber is available at the lunar New Year, trained elephants are brought from the imperial stables to do homage on bended knees before the Son of Heaven, but this sight was denied us. The kow-towing of the retired mandarins ended, his Majesty Khai-dinh stepped down from his throne, evidently no easy task in his heavy boots, for he moved on the polished floor like an octogenarian crossing smooth ice. He shook hands with the *résident supérieur,* then with the purple-robed old arch-bishop, and behind these three we all filed out into a semi-foreign dining-room at one side of the courtyard. There the emperor once more sat down at the back of the room, facing doors wide open on the yard, and again flanked by his two fanners, though these were not working now, possibly because it was after union hours. A young mandarin in-terpreter stood against the wall behind him; the superior resident of Annam took a seat on his left, and the rest of us subsided into the rows of chairs facing the emperor side-wise that filled the room. Khai-dinh knew some French, but like many others in the same boat he never ventured to speak it in public. Sometimes, before the interpreter had passed on the "résuper's" remarks, he gave a sign of having understood, but he never seemed to attempt to reply in French. He now looked more human, permitted some ex-pression to play over his features, among which that of relief was the most prominent, even smiled now and then. This showed that, unlike nearly all the mandarins that now mingled

with us, his teeth were white, but that he probably chewed
betel-nut. He smoked a cigarette as if he were accustomed
to devour them but was now on his good behavior.

The band played the "Marseillaise," after which the emperor evidently made a brief speech, though in a voice that
could hardly have been heard by the superior resident himself. The two more manly looking princes of the blood, both
wearing glasses, seemed to speak French fluently and to be
in many respects quite up-to-date, as they went about greeting
their many friends among the Europeans. Evidently there
was nothing wrong with his Majesty's voice when he wished
to be heard, for he went on talking to his respectful master
even after the fire-crackers had been set off, which feat was
as difficult as conversing in a subway express. The *pétards*
were tied in thick continuous bunches from top to bottom
of bamboo poles terminating in a few leaves that had been
set up at the four corners of the courtyard, and they kept
up a deafening bombardment unbrokenly for at least twenty
minutes, until they suggested the applause for a favorite
candidate at a political convention. The yard was filled with
white smoke and the flagstones carpeted with bursted
crackers, and still the bombardment went on. A little earlier
the booming of artillery had come from somewhere within
the citadel, probably an imperial cannon salute, but if this
still continued, as was likely, we could not hear it, so like
the firing of thousands of rifles was the bursting of fire-
crackers.

Meanwhile we had all been served iced champagne, in
which we drank the emperor's health standing; and there
were passed around plates of cakes and sweetmeats so elaborate that no one seemed to dare to touch them, though the
Son of Heaven himself munched a bit. A fat Frenchman
beside me wanted to know in a voice almost loud enough

to reach the emperor whether there was *pas moyen avoir un cigare,* and a moment later these and cigarettes were passed in jeweled boxes, which contained also the ingredients of the betel-nut habit for those who preferred that to smoking. Some of the servants who passed these things had the strained eyes and high cheek-bones common to eunuchs, and looked on as if the fun of life meant nothing to them, as if they were still wondering what had happened to them in boyhood that they could not be like other men, much as a blind man must wonder what sort of sensation is sight. Or they may merely have been tubercular.

There was evidently some way by which the initiated could tell when the bombardment was to cease, for the emperor arose and we all filed out after him just in time to hear the last fire-cracker explode as we reached the court-yard. We went on to the door of the throne-room, and there this queer medley of East and West ended with the Son of Heaven standing and shaking hands with each of us as we filed past him. I murmured New Year's greetings from the United States in his ear, but either he did not catch my French or he had never heard of so unimportant a place. His fingers were slighter than those of a school-girl, and his grasp weak and without cordiality, though this may have been due to lack of experience with our queer Western form of greeting. We filed out between ranks of gaily dressed flunkies, musicians, probable eunuchs, past the troops in the outer courtyard, to our automobiles and rickshaws and sped away through palace and citadel gates and across the big seven-arch steel bridge, soldiers at the gateways saluting as we passed, and the populace looking after us not so much with envious as with curious faces, as if the thought had never occurred to them that they might also be admitted to the great imperial ceremony. The last glimpse I had of his late Majesty Khai-dinh was of a slight form in ornate Oriental get-up, framed in the doorway of his throne-room and shaking hands with a fat and pompous French merchant who wore a golden Annamese decoration about a neck on which a once stiff collar had wilted beyond recognition.

I returned thus hastily to the grocery-hotel both because I could not decline the seat reserved for me in the chief's automobile and because I wished to restore the borrowed plumage before something fatal happened to it. Moreover, my shoes were rapidly changing from their false African to their natural Asiatic hue. But that duty and the eleven-o'clock *déjeuner* over, I hastened back across the river. The last few days had been very busy there, the market and the shops crowded, every one buying new mats, paper and real flowers, red paper lanterns, red strips of paper with Chinese characters written on them, and great quantities of other New Year's necessities. As in China the people of Annam must have money for the *Têt;* not only must they pay their debts at the lunar New Year, but they must have new clothing, redecorate their houses and the tombs of their ancestors, feed well those departed souls and themselves, and gird themselves for another Sundayless year of labor or indolence. Now the market was closed, though more shops kept open than in China, perhaps because many of the merchants were not real Annamese. On the other hand theaters were working overtime; temples were crowded with newly dressed throngs; in sampans, hovels, and houses the ancestral altars were laden with flowers, fruits, pork, fish, fowl, and boiled rice. The evening before they had scintil-lated with gilded and silver things that gleamed under candle, kerosene, and electric lights. Everywhere there was a great going and coming, every one making New-Year calls. A green bamboo pole, with a few feathery leaves still at the top, had been set up before each house and temple, a woven-bamboo ornament far up most of them as a kind of roosting-place for the spirits of the air. The theory is, if I understood an explanation couched in far from perfect French, that these invisible flying wraiths will accept this homage to them and do no harm to the inmates of any house before which such a bamboo stands.

The rickshaw-men had little chance to celebrate; their holiday resembled that of an Irish donkey on March 17. One of the chief New-Year sports even of those Annamese who usually walk was for once to ride in rickshaws, two and even three passengers in each vehicle. The women especially were in their newest and most resplendent garb—light and dark green, purple, rich brown, small children in every tone of red. Negro soldiers from other French possessions, their black faces emphasized under their white helmets, were hob-nobbing with the poorer people in the outskirts, evidently held in as much honor among them as their white masters. A number of ordinary-looking young conscripts from France also mingled freely with the populace, and here and there one met a negro and a white soldier arm in arm, as one may see them side by side in the same squad on the drill-grounds of Indo-China.

The Annamese seldom drink to excess, and they are not by nature quarrelsome or violent, but they dearly love gambling. So serious is this vice among them that the French now forbid games of chance except during the week or so of the lunar New Year season. Now one saw them gambling everywhere, men, women, and children. Women, even boys of six or seven, had set up gambling-boards in the streets, in the doorways of their houses, in the courtyards of those homes which had them, in the main rooms before the family altar. It was a simple game that engrossed most of them. A board was marked with chalk or paint into several squares, sometimes with numbers, some with crudely drawn animals in them. When all those who wish to take a chance have laid their money in the squares, the proprietor of the board throws out a handful of little disks from a bowl and counts them off four by four, the remaining number winning four times the amount of the bets on the lucky square. Besides this primitive form of fan-tan there were dice in a saucer with a cup turned down over them. When all the money is laid the cup and saucer are shaken and the result disclosed. In the public streets wagers ranged all the way from perforated brass "cash" to paper piastres; inside the larger houses especially much more serious stakes were the rule. Many French colonials criticize the government for gathering revenue through its opium monopoly and forbidding the lesser vice of gambling except during Têt.

Within the citadel much the same ceremony, on a smaller scale, as that at the palace, took place in each mandarin's home, with his relatives, friends, and the lower orders bringing the greetings. Among other New Year's decorations there were many flags all about this forest-shaded town, the tricolor less in evidence than a red and yellow flag that was evidently the imperial banner. Scores of the homes of the mandarins within the citadel displayed over their gateways the flags of all the Allies, that of France double size and in the middle. All the rest of the day I met mandarins coming out of their low houses in garden groves, or from those of others of the same rank, or along the roads and streets on both sides of the river, usually in rickshaws. Some even of high rank did not scorn to ride double, after the common Annamese custom. They no longer wore their ancient Ming

head-dresses or their knee-high boots, but still had on the gay
garments of festival, such as cerise robes embroidered with
flowers. I met several mandarin servants carrying home a
pair of boots strung over a shoulder, with a cloth-wrapped
bundle of holiday garments in one hand and the strange
head-dress left over from the days of the Ming in the other,
as if some of their masters also had been obliged to borrow
le smoking in its Annamese form, before they could bring
their annual greetings to their emperor.

One recognizes a mandarin of Annam by the somewhat
better material of his clothing and by a little wooden or
ivory baggage-check on his starboard bowsprit, bearing his
title or grade in Chinese characters. Some of them had
been so brave, or have obeyed the French so well, that they
wore on the other side French decorations enough to rival
a staff-officer. Not all the mandarins surrounding the emperor of Annam are noted for either their physical or—the
experienced eye could not but note—their moral beauty.
Many were pitted with smallpox, and more of them were
stoop-shouldered with loafing than were horny-handed with
toil. Like Chinese above the laboring-class, these tax-
gatherers from a hard-working people give no attention to
their muscles, scorn indeed to use them when there is any
way out of it, and are flabby and ungainly accordingly. Yet
some of the staid old retired mandarins looked like men who
had led a kindly and a scholarly life. Each generation the
grade of a mandarin drops a notch, so that the privileged
class does not remain perpetually the same, a scheme that
might perhaps advantageously be applied in other centers of
the human maelstrom. Titles of nobility are sometimes given
for distinguished services—such, no doubt, as betraying to
the French rulers independence movements among the natives—but these are no longer hereditary. I met one of

the princes of the blood on a suburban road that New Year's afternoon, still in his blood-red robes of ceremony, so out of keeping with his modern nose-pinching spectacles and the very ordinary rickshaw in which he rode. Here and there a coolie or a boy took off his palm-leaf hat to him, but that was the only visible evidence that his rank meant anything much to the populace, or to the prince himself.

The people of Annam still treat their puppet emperor as the true Son of Heaven, however, though they cannot but know that he is chosen by the French. It is as if they considered the French merely an instrument of fate, as some Christians manage to regard anything that happens as God's hand working in strange mysterious ways. Whatever he may have thought of this attitude of his loyal subjects, Khai-dinh did not by any means disdain the material conveniences of our upstart Western civilization. He never went outside his palace grounds except by automobile—a big imperial-yellow limousine with black top and red wheels, of French make naturally, and which had its blow-outs and other mishaps now and then quite like the Fords of the garden variety of mankind. Over on the French side of the river he had a suburban palace, a rest-house far from his crowded domestic circle. It is a very showy establishment in foreign, more exactly in continental European, style, with graveled driveways, *portes cochères,* plate-glass windows, the walls bright yellow with the intertwined letters AD on the gates. That afternoon it was gay with yellow flags, a color forbidden the ordinary people, though now and then a small child wears it with impunity—or it may be that this means the emperor once called upon its mother. Even in his palace within the citadel Khai-dinh had his apartments installed in European style, they say, though I cannot of course report this on first-hand evidence; his domestic realm was closed even to his French superior, for after all Annam is still Oriental. When the spirits moved him to spend an evening entertaining any cronies he may have had among the French colonials, he called his yellow limousine and repaired to his transfluvial palace. He drew and sculptured, not in the traditional Chinese-Annamese fashion, but after the manner of a not too talented pupil of the Beaux Arts. The French insist that he also was very happy, and they may be right. His salary for doing nothing was five thousand piastres a month; he had ten wives—his predecessor maintained a hundred, but economy is the watchword in official Annam since the war—and his dancers and all such necessities were paid for by the government. The "résuper" who really rules Annam and its emperor gets only fifteen hundred piastres a month and has only one wife, and as far as is officially known not even one dancing-girl.

On March 19 there was to be an even greater ceremony in Hué—the emperor's all-night vigil at the Temple of Heaven. Similar, though by no means comparable, to the imperial rite that took place yearly in Peking until the revolution of 1911 turned that Temple of Heaven into a tourists' picnic-ground and China into a masquerade-ball republic, this ceremony has long been given every three years; but the French had decided that this one was to be the last. Thus do the pageantries of olden days drop unnoticed one by one under the trampling feet of time.

CHAPTER IX

OF the eighteen to twenty million people of French Indo-China two thirds are Annamese. That does not mean that Annam has so many inhabitants. The Annamese are the predominant people of all the lowlands of France's Far-Eastern empire, not merely of Annam. Their own land, though nearly eight hundred miles long, is very narrow, containing barely sixty thousand square miles, on which between seven and eight million people manage to wrest subsistence almost entirely from a plain twelve to fifty miles wide between the mountains and the sea. Naturally they have gradually overrun the other divisions of Indo-China, submerging the other races there, just as the tricky, the less pleasing, the more sophisticated always drive out the naïve and the more lovable on this sad old globe of ours. Their Chinese religion of ancestor-worship, requiring every man by hook or crook to leave a son behind him, has of course much to do with this majority.

As far back as history mentions it, what we now call Indo-China was under the sway of the Cham, then of the Khmer, tribes of a certain Hindu culture who subjugated the land and drove the aborigines, if such their predecessors were, into the mountains. Later they in turn were conquered by what we now know as the Annamese. One guess is that this dour people originally came from Tibet or the lower mountains about it. They themselves say that they once inhabited southwestern China—Yunnan, Kwangsi, Kwang-tung, and Tonkin—at least five thousand years ago. Many of their customs and physical characteristics bear out this statement, but they are so mixed with the Cham and the other peoples they found in their new home that they have many traits not typical of the Mongol race, and one is every now and then surprised to find a nearly Aryan nose among them.

Whatever their exact origin, they came down from some-where to the north and filled, as tightly as a plump leg fills a stocking, this narrow strip of plain between the coast and the mountains, pushing back, killing off, and absorbing the tribes that preceded them. Highlanders to begin with, per-haps, they have now lived in tropical lowlands and rice marshes for so many centuries that they have gradually taken on tropical characteristics, hence it is not at all strange that they are the weakest and the ugliest of all those reputedly of the Mongolian race. Hardly of medium height, less vigorous than their neighbors, they are much like the Chi-nese, yet in many ways quite different from them also. They have been known to the Celestials for centuries by the name first given them when the two peoples came in contact with each other—the Giao-chi, or "Big Toes." The noticeable spread of the great toe away from the others, suggesting mountain-climbing ancestors, is still conspicuous among them even in this day of French shoes. Though the name no doubt had its origin in that scornfulness of the Chinese for any race but their own, in due season the Annamese began to call themselves Giao-chi also, just as they followed the Chi-nese example in calling their country Annam, Land of the Eminent South, or words to that effect. As I may have said before, the white man's name "Indo-China" is particu-larly fitting; France's Far-Eastern possession is certainly

the half-way station between the Chinese and the Hindus.
The Annamese are no more really Chinese than are many
of the Indian races that are called by that name, yet they
are quite unlike the Hindu-cultured Cambodians and have
nothing in common with the people of Laos, beyond the
Annamese chain, who are akin to the Siamese. In mere
physical matters they are not only smaller but darker than
the Chinese, tawny, though less so than the Cambodians,
with flat skulls, faces, and noses, protruding cheek-bones,
and large mouths that are made doubly conspicuous by their
permanently blackened teeth and thick lips swollen with
what we miscall betel-nut.

Thus we have come in leisurely sequence to the most
conspicuous, the most despicable perhaps, certainly the most
inexplicable point in the physical appearance of the Annamese. They have never practised mutilation of their women
in the Chinese manner by binding their feet; infanticide is
reputed to be very rare, if known at all; but about marriage
time, which in Annam is early in life, every Annamese,
of either sex, is expected to have his teeth lacquered black
by a process said to be very painful. Recalling what a
dentist can do to us in half an hour, it is not hard to believe
that they suffer during a task that takes day after day. The
lacquering loosens the teeth, but the *nhoc-nam,* or ground-
fish sauce with which every Annamese seasons his food,
tightens them again. The men are not so selfish as to force
the women to go through the beautifying process alone, as
in so many lands, but step up and take the same medicine
themselves, so that the mouths of both sexes resemble rat-
holes. Perhaps it is this that makes the Annamese seem
more stupid than the Chinese they in so many other ways
resemble—or perhaps it is merely their southern indolence

of manner, or the circumspection of a subject race as compared to freemen.

Every people has its own style of beauty, however, and to the Annamese a person is handsome only if his teeth are jet-black. "Any dog can have white teeth," say the Annamese, looking disparagingly at Europeans. To them white teeth are not only ugly but immoral! For the *congaie*, the Annamese girl, who has not blackened her teeth, is usually, if not always, some Frenchman's darling.

The blackened teeth alone would be bad enough, even if the people of Annam were not also addicted to a custom common to a large part of oceanic Asia. Almost all of them chew betel-nut, as we persist in calling it. It is really the nut of the arec-palm and the leaf of the betel-vine that often climbs this, mixed with lime to bring out the full strength of the ingredients. The wand-like arec-palms that rise straight and soldierly, as if they fancied they served some useful purpose and were proud of it, are the most conspicuous feature of any Annamese or Tonkinese village. Whenever a child is born one more of these slender trees is planted, with a betel-vine beside it, so that in time the infant also may have its "betel-nut." Large villages are almost hidden in arec-palm forests. This tree produces nuts of about the size of a walnut, in green clusters like a bunch of huge grapes, which grow, like cocoanuts, just below the leaves. These, sold in the markets, the shops, everywhere along the highways and the narrow trails, are cut up, wrapped in a betel-leaf—whence the misnomer "betel-nut," which does not exist—smeared with lime, and thrust into the repulsive mouth.

A French colonial who had tried betel-nut once told me that he had a sudden rush of blood to the head and felt warm

and excited all day long. Like opium, however, it was one
of those things I prefer to take on hearsay. It is strange
that in China, land of bad habits, this mild vice is unknown,
unless we count the lower half of now Japanese Formosa.
A few old French colonials get the habit, as they become
addicted to opium, *congaies,* and other customs of the East;
but most of the ruling race have more respect for at least
their outward appearance. The chemical action of the lime
on the other ingredients produces a blood-red cud, so that
betel-nut chewers look as if their disgusting mouths of apparently decayed teeth were full of blood, as if they were
in the throes of a hemorrhage—and didn't know it. Some
Annamese girls would be good looking but for this blood-
dripping mouth, repulsive even when closed, for the constant
use of betel-nut not only destroys the gums but leaves the
lips permanently swollen. On the other hand the lacquering
of the teeth and the chewing of betel-nut somehow manage to
save the Annamese from toothache, they say, though some
of us might prefer to suffer the pain ourselves rather than
pass it on to the beholder. The chemical action of lacquer
and betel-juice in combination seems to kill the microbes
that lead to the dentist's chair in other lands, and no wonder;
for surely no self-respecting microbe would take up its
habitat in an Annamese mouth.

In Hué and the two capitals alternately graced by the
French governor-general the younger people of the better
class show evidence of beginning to think of leaving off
the enameling of their teeth, and even of abandoning the
chewing of betel-nut. But both customs are almost universal among masses and classes alike wherever Annamese
is spoken, and many, like our rural tobacco-chewers, are
proud of the distance they can project the red saliva. This
seems to be a favorite indoor as well as outdoor sport, for

they spit the stuff everywhere, not only splotching with red every road and street in the land that is not already red by nature, but even the whitewashed walls of the homes of mandarins. In hiring an Annamese nurse-maid or cook one must insist that no betel-nut be used in the house, and even then one's best things are likely to become gradually speckled with red.

Though the race as a whole is not noted for its manly beauty, the women of Annam have a more pleasing appearance to Western eyes than do those of China—except when they smile. Their expression is more *piquante,* if you know what I mean. Those who become temporary wives of the French, and do not blacken the teeth, sometimes do not even chew betel-nut, are often pleasant to look upon during their younger years. To be sure these are hand-picked; but almost without exception, irrespective of age, the women of Annam are slender, sinuous, and graceful, with a sort of gliding walk, the countrywomen especially very erect, their arms swinging far behind them, as if they were constantly performing the feat of balancing their big palm-leaf hats. Many have beautiful hands, small, thin, and tapering, even though they do the hardest work of carrying and grubbing in the rice-fields. To Annamese taste the chief points of female beauty are black teeth, red heels—on bare feet, that is, not on shoes, as in the case of foot-bound China—and oval faces, in contrast to the round ones called for by Chinese standards of beauty. Great numbers of the women of the Eminent South have the longest hair that I—nay, even my wife—had ever seen, in certain cases reaching well below the knees.

There are those, however, who consider inwardness more important than outwardness, and for them let us begin by

saying that in disposition the Annamese are less gay, have
little of the sense of humor so highly developed among the
Chinese—unless it be that they put on a mask before the
white man. This they do, of course, like any subjugated
people, but one seldom catches them laughing even when
they have no suspicion of being observed—seldom, that is,
in comparison with that reservoir of laughter, the Chinese.
A Frenchman tells us that of all the people on earth the
Annamese have the greatest plasticity, are the most sly, cunning, utilitarian, and the most assimilative—though often
superficially so. They show outward respect to parents and
superiors, but seem to be insincere and incapable of deep
devotion—not unnaturally, one would say, seeing that the
race has been subjected for most of the past two thousand
years. Never showing his real thoughts on the surface,
conserving his own personality under all circumstances, the
son of Annam adapts himself, passively resists, triumphs
when he seems to be defeated. Those who know him well
credit him with a great love of his native land, especially
of the village where he was born. The French insist that
the Annamese are great thieves, which, with all their faults,
can hardly be said of the Chinese.

During all the centuries that China held Annam enslaved,
"like a kept mistress," it became Chinese. It took from
China its art, its morals, its writing, its costumes, its customs, its gods; it is so Chinese that there are still celebrated
in the temples of Annam festivals and formalities that have
not taken place in the Celestial Empire for hundreds of
years. Now it is France that rules, and the Annamese have
become French. If Russia had conquered them, asserts a
Frenchman, they would have icons in their homes and sleep
on unlighted porcelain stoves. Either they are naturally
copiers or they have found copying the easiest way in a hot

climate; long dominated, they seem to have lost through evaporation the "pep" of their probably highland ancestors. No doubt this explains why, although of old it was literary, artistic, responsive to the most subtle plays of the spirit, Annam never produced a single great personal work, a great poet, an original architect, a powerful moralist, a painter or a sculptor of genius. "The foreign model shines through everything admirable between the Mekong and the Gulf of Tonkin." The Annamese can work at the task in hand with infinite taste and patience; what he lacks in originality he makes up to a degree in ingeniousness; but the creative spark seems never to have flashed forth in him.

I suppose it is this copy-cat characteristic that makes him show no surprise at the inventions of the West. You cannot startle this ancient Oriental world with the mechanical marvels of the new. It accepts them, but it is not astonished. Give the yellow race the telegraph, and they send telegrams; the phonograph, and they listen; the railroad, and they buy their tickets and take their seats—granted that there are any left; the automobile, and a self-confident young man pours in gasoline and steps on the starter, knowing only that for some reason this makes the thing go. The force of this people lies in its shrewd plasticity; the Annamese do not resist, they adapt themselves; they espouse on the instant the practices and customs of the conqueror. Endowed with an immeasurable pride, they strive, not to do their best in their own line, but to imitate their masters, to outdo them in their own field. It is not because they admire them, one suspects; it is merely to prove that they are as smart as any one else. Thus Annamese students, with centuries of memorizing Chinese characters behind them, often outdo in French even the French youths in their classes.

Though they take so readily to Western inventions, no

Annamese will use a mechanical contrivance if he can do without it. With all the corkscrews and can-openers in the world within reach of his hand, your *bcp,* or Annamese cook, invariably draws corks and opens cans with his teeth. In putting fuel on his fire he prefers his hands to a shovel. You may show him better methods, but he continues to make sure of the condition of an egg by whirling it on its side; if it is fresh it will not whirl, according to the *bcp;* the older it is the more it will gyrate, he insists. Try it on your own "strictly fresh" eggs some winter, ye slaves of the land of cold-storage—and if he is right they may be whirling still when spring comes.

Though they sometimes eat sharks, the Annamese worship what they call a whale, really the dolphin or porpoise. According to legend, one of these acrobats of the sea once got under an emperor's boat and kept it from sinking until it could reach shore. Even students in French *lycées* still believe this yarn, and if one of these "whales" dies and is washed ashore, it is given honorable burial with much ceremony. The Annamese worship trees, especially if they are huge, or very old, or of strange shape; and to propitiate the demons or to win the favors of the good spirits that inhabit them they put under them little vases of the lime used with the betel-nut that even spirits are reputed to enjoy. Scores of these tiny jars may sometimes be seen at the foot of a single tree. No Annamese will cut down those trees, such as the banyan, that are especially sacred. The French sometimes have to chop down with their own fair hands trees that are in the way of civic improvements. At Tourane two Annamese converts to Christianity were given good wages and all the wood in a huge tree that was hindering progress, and earned fifty piastres for two days' work, fifty times their normal income. Being Christians, they did not of course care how many trees were cut down. There are other lands where so effective a superstition would be well worth entertaining

The religions of Annam are in the main those of China. Not only "whales" and trees, but big or queerly shaped rocks, the rat, the silkworm, the elephant, above all the tiger, which they never mention except by the honorable title "Ong Kop," have their worshipers. But the most general cult is that of their ancestors and of the village genii. The local god may be some mandarin who ruled the village centuries ago, some native son who became a great scholar, some former mistress of an emperor who aided her native town in some crisis; or it may merely be a beggar or an executed robber, some great calamity after his death having proved that his spirit must be propitiated, perhaps a new temple built to enthrone it. In return for all this adoration the village genius is expected to protect the village from drouth, epidemic, and similar catastrophe.

One can scarcely travel, however rapidly, through Annam without seeing one of these fêtes to the genius of some village or other. Parades riotous with color make their way along the narrow dikes, across the rice-fields, the fantastic costumes mirrored in the flooded sloughs. Not only do women take no part in the cult of village genii, any more than they can effectively worship an ancestor, but neither do any of the men except those village notables who are not in mourning and in whose family full peace and harmony prevails. I gather that if a wife has recently run off with a lover or wilfully blackened an eye of her notable spouse, or if a daughter has eloped during the year with a Frenchman but without benefit of clergy—though this is perhaps no such serious matter—the husband or father involved would not be available or eligible for the rites in honor of the village genius, but would pass the day in seclusion. An incentive surely to domestic harmony! The plebes of course have merely the honor of paying the bill, as in any other part of the globe.

There are many temples in Annam, but the largest of them are small compared with those of China, and in many details they are distinctly different. Elephants appear among the decorations; dragons are not so numerous. The roofs tilt with a longer, almost coquettish, curve; the tropical climate has given them a more luxurious brown; there is rather an air of equatorial languor about them. Most of them are better kept too, as if either the worshipers were more devout or there were better supervision over the caretakers. But this is perhaps merely another example of the superiority in cleanliness and order of Annam over China. Possibly it is due to the presence of the French, who have ruled over them during the life of almost all those now living, that the Annamese have a little more conception of the line between filth and its antithesis than is given to Celestial understanding. Or it may be that on the whole the people of Annam are less noisome in their personal habits than their northern neighbors because they are less poverty-stricken, and because total indifference in sanitary matters is more swiftly and visibly punished in so tropical a land. At any rate there is no such slovenliness, no such stench, in the cities of Annam as beyond the northern border; for one thing they are mostly on the coast, with water plentiful, and they are small, none of those enormous conglomerations of humanity to be found in hundreds of places throughout China.

Gaudily painted little temples, weather-blackened shrines, generally among trees, pass in constant procession as one hurries through the land of the Eminent South. Now and

again another procession enlivens the landscape—a long file
of people in their gayest robes, most of them carrying high
above their heads the parasols that are usually forbidden to
any but mandarins and foreigners, wending its way along
the dikes.   They are on their way to a temple, or taking part
in a wedding, perhaps a funeral, in which latter case they
carry with them gay paper imitations of everything the deceased will need in the after-world, from automobiles to
concubines.   Temple festivals are theatrical and musical
entertainments as well as religious ceremonies, even as in our
churches.   Probably the mass of the people distinguish no
difference.   The charming oasis of the *pagode,* as the French
call it, may suddenly have taken on life in the midst of
the rice-fields.   The dikes about it are covered with files
of people moving toward it; where there was once a road or
some other open space beside it there is nothing but streets
of makeshift shops that have sprung up overnight.   There
are improvised restaurants, women roasting cakes; sellers of
rice and *chunchum,* of sugar-cane and oranges, of arec-nuts
and betel-leaves, squat on their heels near their round flat
baskets—a whole village of fortune will have sprung forth
from the soil.   The swarming crowd rumbles and clamors
and shrieks with full mouths, for this is the time when they
are all gourmands and when the whole region becomes one
great family. Narrow wooden benches bear rows of custo-
mers seated monkey-fashion on their heels, stuffing themselves
with swiftly moving chop-sticks.   Every one is dressed in
his best, the villagers with floating black tunics, the band-
turban tight about the forehead, on which it leaves a whitish
streak untouched by the sunshine.

The temple itself, usually deserted, is full of natives,
chewing, spitting, shouting, their wooden sandals clacking.
An air of gentle yet barbaric splendor radiates through the

place; religious furniture, sumptuously carved and painted with lacquer or gold, gleams forth; parasols, silk banners embroidered with mottoes and attributes and moralities scintillate in the distilled sunshine. Everywhere, even in the most distant corners, candles and joss-sticks burn; blue clouds of incense cover with an impalpable veil the golden faces of the idols; the altars are loaded with offerings; pasteboard horses, richly caparisoned, spread their stiff legs. About the ritual vases, the big iron urns in which incense and paper prayers by the myriad are burned, sacred swans stand erect on bronze tortoises; every now and again the flame leaps high in an urn, devouring a package of bars of gold or silver, made of rice-paper painted white or yellow. Then suddenly, unexpectedly, two generals pop forth from the wings, their backs a quiver of waving flags, their lungs roaring forth challenges in a false key. With uplifted sabers they march upon each other and indulge in what is meant to be a terrifying pantomime, but nothing more serious comes of it than of most Chinese battles. Frightful noises resound from their armies following close behind them—two howling troops of ragged coolies shaking spears and standards. The stage becomes a whirling chaos of gleaming flags and shrieking soldiery, in which all visible likeness to a religious ceremony fades away into pure theatricalism.

I was constantly running across religious celebrations. Sometimes gay paper boats, their sails all set, were started off down a river to appease the spirits of the stream. Or it might be at one of those neglected little temples without door or roof which the slightest village maintains for its local gods. First the worshipers *lam lie,* kowtow to the stone or mud tiger at the entrance, a tiger with great bulging eyes, usually sculptured in deep relief on a stone screen. Then they go to lay their offerings on the altar—horses made of red paper, pasteboard gourds containing sticks of incense, rice-paper ingots of gold and silver. Fire-crackers explode, what the Chinese consider music howls and shrieks, crowds swarm, the temple flares with decorations in colored paper. In the front chamber there usually sat a shaven-headed bonze wearing a golden paper crown and dressed in red, singsonging Buddhist prayers from a ragged tissue-paper book. Beside and behind him men were beating drums, large and small, or pieces of bell-metal, of resonant hardwood, sometimes adding falsetto voices to the uproar. Countrymen in not too clean garments crowded close on either side, until men with sticks drove them back, again and again, sometimes by throwing lighted bunches of fire-crackers into the massed throng. Old women with sickening black mouths, contrasting unpleasantly with the gay decorations, seemed to be the chief worshipers. The mandarin in a gauzy black cloak who kept order knew enough French to tell me that they were praying for peace, but not enough to specify just what they meant by it.

Another time, elsewhere, strange sounds drew me to a house where men of professional countenance were playing on flutes, cymbals, tambourines, or their Oriental equivalents, while the people were lamenting in discordant voices. A family and its neighbors were praying about the bed of a sick woman whose body would not cease swelling for all the medicine-man's mud plasters. That concert of uproar had lasted since the night before; it was merely a question of who would tire out first, the music, the sickness, or the invalid. Before I left, fire-crackers were thrown about to scare off the evil spirits that were wilfully causing the illness, and if that did not drive them away the master of ceremonies was prepared to toss about handfuls of tissue-paper piastres, in the hope that the covetous devils would leave the body of the sick woman to fight for the money. If even this should not succeed, the funeral procession starts with a band, followed by banner-bearers, then by other ragamuffins carrying in a little paper temple the spirit-tablet of the deceased, portable tables laden with roast pig and other delicacies, and finally the gaudy bier, surrounded by howling mourners trying to call the soul back to earth, perhaps against its wishes.

As there is really no Annamese religion, so there is no Annamese literature, except the Chinese. Even their spoken tongue seems to be an ancient Chinese dialect. It is a monosyllabic language, depending on tones to give different meanings to the same words; and it is so difficult that those Annamese who know French prefer to converse in that tongue. A queer language indeed, explosive in pronunciation, so that the friendliest little chat sounds like a violent quarrel, and until one gets accustomed to it every conversation seems about to develop into a fist-fight—or at least its Far-Eastern counterpart, clawing and scratching. In writing, Chinese characters are used, therefore Annamese, Japanese, Koreans, Formosans, Chinese of the north or south, can all converse readily enough on paper; though as they do not pronounce the characters at all alike the spoken word is of no use among them. Half a century ago the French Jesuits gave the Annamese a romanized script, and now thousands read their newspapers in it. In fact the government has made this alphabetical writing obligatory in the schools, and it is far more widely spread than a similar effort in China. But it is no such simple matter as the uninitiated imagine to represent tones by an extension of accent-marks. With the reform goes the ability to talk to their neighbors on paper too, and the old classics are being lost to the younger generation, even as in Korea and Formosa under the Japanese.

Polygamy is still legal in Annam, though for economic reasons it is no longer usual. It remains a not uncommon practice for the wife who has tried in vain for eight or ten years to bear her husband a son to put on an old woman's bonnet and go out and buy him a second wife. Not a bad plan, surely an improvement on the extramarital secrecy of the West; it no doubt makes for a more congenial companionship and incidentally solves the servant problem, if ever there was one in Annam. Yet the Annamese wife has a better social position than in most of the Orient.

Speaking of wives, in Annam kissing—except in the not few cases in which Frenchmen have taught a different style—consists in approaching the nose to the face of the loved one and sniffing, much as if one were smelling a flower. The harder one sniffs the more it proves one's love—which is sometimes a real test!

Naturally a ditch has dug itself between the younger and the older generation in Annam. Other customs, other manners, other points of view have grown up since the rule of despotic emperors changed to the rule of protective Frenchmen. When the old ancestral altar is replaced by a chest of drawers topped by a mirror it is not merely a question of furniture; something has changed in the heart, in the essence of things. The fathers wish to remain true to the spirit of old Annam; the sons wish to be "même chose Français." Observing the two generations side by side, one has an impression of two different classes, almost two different races. The dissimilarity shows itself in the slightest matters of every-day life. Take, for instance, the well-to-do Annamese families the traveler finds dining in the more or less French hotels along the main routes of travel. The young people, often dressed entirely in European garb, their black hair cut in our fashion and glossy with brilliantine, eat their *tête de veau* and *poulet rôti* with ease, talking and laughing freely, while their constrained, embarrassed, yet always dignified parents, in their long gowns and the Annamese head-dress, handle knife and fork in one hand at one time, as if they were chop-sticks, and hardly succeed in swallowing a mouthful. Especially in the ports and the larger cities young Annam is growing up vastly different from his fathers. Far from reading the old classics, he knows only the *quoc-ngu,* the Annamese language transcribed in our alphabet, which he even beats out on a typewriter. At Saïgon or Hanoï he is resplendent with modernism, agitating, scheming, getting rich; but at Hué he seems to have taken refuge in the legendary past, in tradition, in the memory of his ancestors. How long even this spacious town on the banks of the River of Perfumes will remain what it still is, the natural place of refuge of the exalted spirits of the great princes of other times, seeking throughout the "protected" kingdom for a place to which our Western civilization cannot track them, is not hard to guess: just about the time necessary to finish the railway that is to unite the Annamese capital with Hanoï on the north and with Saïgon to the south; the time needed to replace the little hotel-grocery, celebrated among all the colonials of Indo-China, with the tourists' palace already planned; the time it will take to build a few factories in which fishermen will be the workmen and princes and mandarins the bosses.

Ah, well, the world changes. Not every visitor to Annam can see the prostrations of the "ten thousand" mandarins at Hué, and soon that ceremony too may be gone forever. The legendary Annam, the traditional Asia, is passing

away. Roads, the automobile, the telegraph have upset all
the old customs. Old-timers cannot tell a story of the
olden days—of late in the nineteenth century—without sigh-
ing, "Ah, in my time . . . but we shall never see that
again." We shall not, of course; yet there is no just cause
to weep at our misfortune in arriving too late in a world
grown too old. There are compensations. Western customs,
introduced into Indo-China, have not destroyed the picturesque; they have merely transformed it. In the place
of the adventurers turned administrators who, living like
little kings far from control, inspired respect in the natives
by tricks akin to sleight-of-hand, surrounded themselves with
congaie like Oriental sultans in their harems, and dispensed
justice in the shade of a banyan-tree, like some tropical
Saint Louis, there is the Parisian boulevardier, far from
his element, watched over by a wife who will see to it that
congaie become nothing more romantic than seamstresses
and cooks' assistants. After all, the sedan-chairs that once
crawled along the Mandarin Road by which Chinese officials went and came among their posts in Annam were no
more worth coming to see than are autobuses, jammed so
full of natives that their feet stick out from both sides of
it, *congaie* wearing French shoes, an old Annamese dowager
with a modern umbrella under her arm, "boys" with a golden
tooth or two among their black-lacquered ones, bicycles
among the baskets on the roof of the terror-spreading
vehicle, an autobus so crowded that it looks as if the passengers were transporting it, like ants dragging a dead fly.
Come to think of it, there is nothing more amusing about
the myriad old temples of a mummified Far East than about
a Buddhist priest in his saffron robe carrying a fountain-
pen and riding a bicycle in his bare feet. The old *nha-qué*
bound to market with a string of "cash" over one shoulder

may be gone, but in his place there are Annamese youths, still wearing black band-turbans above their misfit French clothing, counting out paper piastres behind the bars of the Banque de l'Indo-China.

CHAPTER X

HURRYING ON TO THE NORTHERN CAPITAL

I WAS up at four the morning after the imperial ceremony, in sufficiently good mood to refrain from kicking the "boy" who had called me according to orders, and
off in a heavy rain by a rickshaw assured the evening before by a combination of heavy subsidy and threatened
penalty. The train from Hué to Dongha, completing the
central stretch of the railways of Indo-China that begins
at Tourane, ran close outside the moat of Hué citadel, the
walled imperial city stretching from river to river. Beyond, a rich plain was almost completely covered with rice,
a wet green plain backed by the mountain ranges, bulking
against the western sky, that were never far distant on the
left. The scantiness of the country, the paucity of its arable
land, seemed to be emphasized here; for Annam gets very
narrow indeed north of Hué, so narrow that it all but
breaks in two. Yet it was surprising how many people
were crowded into this slender strip of earth, how many
things of interest to the hurried traveler too, for that matter.

At length, hardly an hour beyond Hué, we rode out from
under the clouds as from under a roof. For the climate runs
in streaks up and down this narrow country. The weather
again became, and, what was more to the point, remained,
splendid, so that almost the only time I did not have brilliant sunshine during my two months in Indo-China was
during that enforced delay at Hué. Another hour and we

ran out of track, and were set off at 7:30 at a mere station, where I stepped into an autobus in which I rode until 8:30 that night.

There were plenty of Annamese in the back four fifths of the vehicle, though it was not packed as the autobuses of Annam often are. For at this New Year's season most people were either already at their ancestral homes or had no intention of coming. Just how the driver and his unfailing assistant were induced to work at such a time was a mystery, but that perhaps is one of the advantages of French rule. These autobuses run as regularly as the trains with which they connect, whether there are passengers or not, for at least there are the mails. In fact on the whole they run a little faster than the trains, which is perhaps one reason their fares are higher. My Scotch blood evidently having surged to the surface during my delay, I had taken before leaving Hué a second-class ticket, partly too, I fancy, in order to prove that the company would have to sell me one, in spite of my complexion. There had been no argument, though white men cannot ride among the natives in fourth class on the trains. But the Annamese agent at Dongha, as if he could not bear to see the race that ruled over his land mingling with his fellow-countrymen, insisted that I ride first class, that is, in the front seat, behind the driver this time. Or there may have been another reason; for when my recovered baggage was placed in the closed box at the rear of the car—also a first-class privilege, since freight and express, the parcel-post and the baggage of native passengers, was all piled up on the railed roof of the vehicle or tied along the running-boards—he mentioned casually that of course it weighed considerably more than the fifteen kilograms even a first-class passenger was allowed as free luggage; and as the rate for anything above that amount is nearly as high as for human flesh, I felt it only fair to slip a couple of paper piastres into his limp palm, at which he not only did not protest but even thanked me in imperfect French.

This time I had a fellow-passenger of my own color. A Frenchman of sturdy frame and studious face, a khaki patch held in place over one eye by a cord that had left a thin white line free from sunburn diagonally across his intelligent features, had also stepped off the train. As the custom in England and its newer American counterpart of strict incommunicativeness between strangers unexpectedly meeting on the road does not apply among the hospitable French colonials of Indo-China, I soon discovered that my companion, though ostensibly in the customs service, was a novelist whose latest romance against an Annamese background I had finished reading the evening before. I might have been embarrassed at being discovered by so important a personage, an official to boot, occupying "European accommodations" at the price of a native ticket, had I not quickly learned that the novelist had not even paid second-class fare for his first-class seat, but was traveling on a government *réquisition,* which cost him nothing more than the asking.

He had been in the customs service of Indo-China since early manhood, but chancing to be on furlough in his native land when the World War broke out, he had joined his regiment at once, fighting unscathed all through the war, until, three days before the Armistice, he had lost an eye. But the government had been kind. It had kept him on the pay-roll as a customs officer, but let him run about the country at government expense, to such things as the ceremony we had just seen at the court of Hué, in order that he might gather material for more writing. For your

Frenchman realizes that even an honest novel, true as to local color, is useful propaganda; and Indo-China has a longing to be known, in France as well as in the world at large. Hawthorne and Whitman, I recalled, had not been paid their government salaries in order that they might go on producing what was perhaps even better literature than that of my new traveling companion. Nor could I remember having heard of any of our crippled war veterans receiving government aid in the production of art or letters.

We made the constant good speed of a limited express, along a road raised a foot or two above the rice-fields, here dry but green, still flooded back toward the foot-hills. I could in fact have ridden a little less swiftly with more pleasure. For there being rarely any turn in the road, and no other vehicles, gasoline-driven or otherwise—luckily, since the roads of Indo-China are for one car at a time— we went over the many short bridges just wide enough for so ponderous a conveyance as ours with the roller-coaster feeling of a day at Coney Island. It was a gravel road in which grew grass that seemed to have sprung up during the last few days of rain; and there was never a fence or other protection from it even at the villages through which we roared so madly. Striking peaks stood out among those rows of ranges perpetually following us on the west; at the mouths of the several short rivers that looked like seas in the raging wind we were ferried across in the usual decrepit old *bacs*.

At Donghoï or Quang-binh we were the first guests in a brand-new hotel, subsidized by the government in order that the few French travelers who go up and down the *Route Mandarine* may have all the advantages of home during the *déjeuner* and siesta that break the journey there.

During that Parisian ceremony we picked up a French colonial burned a reddish bronze by half a lifetime at a country post beneath the equatorial sun. He went on with us for a few hours to his bungalow at the place where another *bac* came across the sea to us at the call of a water-buffalo horn in the hands of a ferryman. Before it had fought its way to the southern shore there was ample time to enjoy the coolness of an interior in marked contrast to the facial and temperamental heat of its chief occupant, who, apologizing for the absence of his *congaïe* to do the honors, had his "boys" serve us drinks cooled with the ice that was thrown off to him each forenoon from the south-bound bus. Without this daily necessity he could of course no more have endured life in his isolated station than without his respectful servants and his female companion. Most of the conversation ran on the selfishness of a few of his younger colleagues in expecting their own countrywomen to accompany them to such posts of "exile in the wilderness."

Every house or hovel of the natives had standing before it the tufted bamboo of the New-Year season, that signal to the spirits of the air that the people who live beneath it are pious and not to be molested—something akin to the hobo signs of our own land. In many of the villages the populace was childishly enjoying itself in swings made, supports and all, not too securely of bamboos crudely lashed together. Toward the middle of the afternoon we found ourselves making toward a great wall of mountains at right angles to the main ranges. It looked as if this ponderous autobus could not possibly pass such a barrier, at least without the united assistance of the passengers, and I recalled with some misgiving the ancient story of second-class travelers being obliged to get off and push, while those

in first class had merely to walk. For the day was still
uninviting to physical exertion, and my special front-seat
privileges might not be honored in such an emergency without the two-piastre agent at Dongha to protect me. But
the road found a way up and around and over the steep
spur, twisting itself into hair-pin curves to climb a slope
up which an old-style Chinese road went straight and un-
swerving, with the hardiness of the pioneer, to the remnants
of a gate at the lowest point, not far from where our less
virile modern route surmounted it.

To all intents and purposes we had come to the end of
Annam. What the Chinese named the Eminent South
Country was usually reckoned as beginning on the north
at the Gate of Annam, as this pass has been called for
centuries. This was the old Annam-Tonkin boundary;
there is still the vestige of an ancient wall built along the
summit by the Annamese to protect themselves from invasion, and many great battles have been waged there. To-
day the official boundary is much farther north, and does
not signify anyway, for there is a fiction that Tonkin, the
northern knob of the Indo-China dumb-bell, is now a part
of Annam, ruled over by Koang-de, the Son of Heaven at
Hué.

The climb had opened out a great amphitheater of a valley,
checkerboarded with rice-fields, a stretch of the sea with a
curving beach that flashed in the afternoon sunshine, several other spurs that almost hindered our progress, and more
rows of ranges, with densely green forests in the hollows
high up on some of the ridges. On the southern side of
the Gate there had been no forest, only a light brush; but
it looked as if the northern slopes, blue-black now in the
slanting sunshine, were all thickly wooded. Long pasture-

lands, rolling and bushy, dotted with red herds, almost completely crowded out cultivation for some distance.   There
were few inhabitants, but many tiger temples, all set in
clusters of bamboos or trees, as if the wilderness that had
driven out the rice-fields brought the dreaded beast that much
nearer.   The mountains had pushed us so close to the sea
that for some time beaches and even islands seemed but a
stone's throw away.

A slightly different human type appeared beyond the Gate
of Annam, stockier, the women perhaps a bit better looking, or more nearly good looking—so long as they kept their
repulsive mouths shut.   In fact purists among the French
anthropologists of Indo-China insist that the real Annamese
are not in the handle of the dumb-bell at all, but in Tonkin, because south of the Gate so many tribes have been
Annamited, so to speak, mingled in blood and culture with
the conquerors from the north.   Unlike their relatives south
of the Gate, the Tonkinese were dressed in a cinnamon or
tobacco-juice color that suddenly became as universal as
black had been farther south, as denim blue is among the
masses of China.   The countrywomen, then their men, and
finally all the hand-laboring class, took to wearing long cotton cloaks of this reddish brown hue.   I found later that
this is colored with *cunao,* the vegetable dye in which the
masses north of the old boundary dip their clothing, so
that all Tonkin wears the same conspicuous livery.   More
exactly it is inconspicuous, in much of Tonkin; one might
fancy it had been adopted as a protective coloring, not only
so that betel saliva would not show on it, but because so
much of the soil of the Tonkinese plains is reddish that
everything, earth, water, people, their clothing and their
cattle, anything that comes in contact with the earth, took

on this *cunao* color. Centuries of toiling in flooded rice-fields reflecting a tropical sun had indeed given even their faces a similar tint.

There were fewer male Psyche knots here than farther south, hair-cuts for men being now popular. The women had suddenly taken to skirts, in place of the voluminous thin-cotton trousers of Annam proper, and dressed their hair differently, wrapping the braid once about the head and letting the rest hang down like the tail of a Hindu turban. But the most conspicuous change was that the palm-leaf hat of toadstool shape, which I had grown to associate forever with the country people of Annam, had given way, among the women only, to a most astonishing head-shade. Of grindstone shape and size, being easily two and a half if not three feet in diameter and perfectly flat on top, with a brim six or more inches wide forming a perpendicular circle about them, these astounding hats made also of leaves, perhaps of the banana, looked like a tub set upside down on the head. More exactly they sat on a little round support tied to the top of the head, and were so unwieldy on this slight fulcrum that whenever the wind was blowing or the wearer under motion the struggle to retain her headgear seemed to be much more difficult than the carrying of her shoulder-pole burden. The men continued to wear the smaller cone-shaped mushroom hats that had roofed the rural population all the way from Cochinchina, as if they realized how foolish they would have looked in these immense grindstones, or knew the futility of trying to compete with their women in ornamental matters.

The graves were now well weeded knobs on top of large raised circles of earth; the towns, almost as compact as those of China, were surrounded by high walls of growing bamboos. The more straggling towns south

With each new year the Annamese clear of vegetation the graves of their ancestors, back to remote generations

I asked a living caretaker to fill the place of one of these of stone which guard the entrance to a royal tomb of Annam

In the heart of Hanoï, northern capital of French Indo-China, stands a delightfully picturesque lake of goodly dimensions

Annamese girls hold Sunday morning flower-market at this corner of the city-girdled lake of Hanoï

of the Gate of Annam had been encircled, if at all, by hedges of cactus or wild pineapple, concealing nothing; here every village was completely hidden, with an opening here and there through its bamboo wall like that to the lair of a jungle beast, so that with Tonkinese villagers going home consists in crawling away into the jungle like the tiger they so dread and honor. This lofty bamboo hedge is a vestige of pirate days, and of battles between towns and clans. Near the coast cocoanut-trees did their part toward the concealing, and of course the soldierly arec-palm with its clinging betel-vine was everywhere. Once or twice we passed fields of mulberry-trees, for Tonkin also produces silk. Women in the grindstone hat stood on little platforms and screened rice by pouring it out in the wind, rice to be hulled later by these same women stepping with their bare feet incessantly on the end of a heavy beam that drops its hammer-head into a stone or wooden mortar.

It was well after dark when we came to a last *bac,* across an arm of the sea that seemed in the black night as wide as the British Channel, and were gradually poled and pulled and sculled by sleepy coolies toward the lights of Ben-thuy, where the railway picks up again. Another three years and trains will be running between Dongha and Ben-thuy; we had seen the half finished embankment now and then along the way. Within twice that time the traveler should be able to go entirely by rail the whole length of Indo-China, clear on to the Yang-tze perhaps, possibly even to Angkor, connecting with the lines of Siam, which already run to Singapore.

There were no accommodations for foreigners at Ben-thuy, merely the river-mouth port of the city of Vinh, where we were soon housed in the almost French hotel of a

Spanish—er—lady of fortune. Vinh is a large town, for Indo-China. Three hundred and ten houses, a whole section not far from the hotel, had been burned that day as an unintentional addition to the New Year's celebration, and the night air was still strongly scented with the conflagration; but this catastrophe had left only an unimportant vacancy in the civic area. The French showed little sign of interest in these popular misfortunes, so long as their own spacious part of the town, with its uncrowded dwellings on broad half forested lawns, remained undisturbed. Is it because they no longer hold in honor their own labyrinthine old cities that the French have given such an atmosphere of bourgeois order to the towns of their Far-Eastern empire by making them checker-boards of straight, right-angled streets, just as the Japanese have done in Formosa and Korea?

Another "boy" risked his life by calling me at four again, though the train on which I wandered northward all that day long did not leave until two hours later, from a station a few blocks away. That journey from Vinh to Hanoï began as rather a stupid ride, but it turned out better than the morning promised. The little train, with its single three-class coach at the end of a string of modified cattle-cars for the populace, sat lower to the ground and was in some ways less comfortable than the autobus. A stone embankment from two to six feet above the rice-fields formed the basis for railroad and highway, which flowed together every little while into the same narrow bridges, with a coolie at either end to sound a warning. The plain, of more or less width according to how curious the mountains were to come down and look at the sea, was one vast paddy-field. Birds were numerous for a tropical land. Herons lay in wait for careless frogs at the edges of the rice-fields; the *crabier,* a brown bird showing a patch of white, like a flag of truce, when flying, plied its customary quest for edible crabs; a little reddish bird that seemed to have copied the garb of its human neighbors flitted here and there across the leisurely moving foreground. Water-buffaloes, almost one in three of them of the albino type, were plowing belly-deep in the slime of the paddy-fields or loafing along the dikes; whole Oriental families of them lay immersed in mud-holes, completely covered except for the ends of their snouts and their sagacious little eyes, recalling those tales of Annamese pirates hiding themselves indefinitely under water by breathing through two reeds thrust in their nostrils. Now and then one of these ponderous pachyderms presented his massive head threateningly toward our train, as if about to attack this new type of animal, but always decided at the last moment not to risk it and loped off into the flooded paddy-field on either side with a splash of wet mud.

In places the land was so flooded from the recent rains that only graves, dikes, and the tops of the half-grown rice appeared above the broad expanse of water—except of course the villages and temples in their clusters of trees, standing wherever possible on a knoll too rocky to be cultivated to advantage. Villages close to the road were frequent, graves still more so, the dead and the living inhabitants both too numerous. The plain, flat as a billiard-table, the water and the exact rows of flooded rice shimmering like silk, was dotted with red cattle, some also plowing, and with redder people of all ages and both sexes, in various forms of undress, all toiling for their rice in the inundated fields. More exactly it was all one vast field, divided into all manner of queer shapes by narrow green ridges six inches above the general level. Brown men in faded tobacco-brown clothing—still more often

women, who seem to do most of the work—groped about
up to their thighs and biceps in the slime. Some were immersed to the waist; some paddled about in sampans; others
stood in pairs on the dikes and tossed water from one
field to another in a basket of woven bamboo splints hung
in the middle of a long rope, or toiled alone shoveling
water from one level to another with a huge wooden spoon
mounted on a framework.

The reddish-brown garments that had begun at the Gate
of Annam were universal in the rural parts of this region.
Some of the men in the fields were naked except for a
shirt tied up about the armpits, but the women were more
or less covered, though they are more careless than those
of China about exposing the person. Trousers for women
had for the time being entirely disappeared, though they
were to appear again about Hanoi; a sign, I suppose, of
the fast life of cities. Along the road close beside us women
under shoulder-pole loads of anything, everything, trotting
in constant files, like trains of leaf-bearing ants in the
jungle, often left their long, sun-faded, red-brown cloaks
swinging open, and not concealing all that the once white
diamond-shaped breast-cover beneath leaves visible. Some
frankly wore only that and the knee-high skirt, as if
this season of hard labor was no time to be prudish in
small matters. Almost all wore those great basket-like hats,
some faded and frayed, some fresh from the markets to
and from which endless streams of them forever jogged.
A picturesque figure is the Tonkinese woman of the people,
with her flat umbrella-hat, her loose, cinnamon-colored, knee-
length jacket, her short skirt or very loose thin black
trousers, her clacking wooden sandals in town or her noiseless straw ones in the country, her black-lacquered teeth
bloody with the betel-juice driveling from the corners of

her hideous mouth. Invariably she has a well built back, a pretty brown in tint, and suggesting to our society leaders how they too might have perfect forms—merely by carrying a hundred pounds or so across their shoulders to market several times a week.

There were stretches where the land was almost bare, the fields yellow-green, with brownish graves, the foot-hills terraced, some of them cut up by bush fences but apparently uncultivated now. The forerunners of the mountain range were without vegetation, except for clumps of trees, among which the palm was the most common. In other places, where the demands of husbandry had not killed them, were whole forests of trees white with blossoms, bamboos that were like smoke spirals of blond gold, great kapok-trees, without a leaf on their whitened branches, but bearing immense bunches of flowers that turned orange by translucence against the blue of the sky. Finally the mountains came down so close to the sea that there were heaped-up hills cultivated in patches, though here, unlike China, the ratio between soil and inhabitants has never been such that anything more than the level land must necessarily be cultivated.

Here and there on the muddy mat of the fields stood slender triangular rafts anchored or mired in the slime, raising in the air, with strange immobile gestures, disjointed arms, like gigantic field-spiders. Most of them bore on this base a rudimentary house, a roof of woven palm-leaves closed at the back with an old paddy-winnowing basket, a bundle of straw inside taking the place of a sleeping-mat. They were the shelters of the fishermen who come here whenever there is water enough to make it worth while to plunge into it the big square dip-net at the end of the balanced pole suspended at the front of the raft.

Some were without the nets now, the bare bamboos on which these are fastened seeming to claw the air in their eagerness to be of use again. In places there were scores of these fishing devices, each with its little hut, its net balanced with stones and raised and lowered by a rope inside the hut, so that the fisherman does not need to expose his already bronzed hide to either rain or shine.

Some time in mid-morning, masses of jagged rock, similar to the "Marble Mountains" of Tourane, began to rise from the plain, growing ever more numerous. They were identical, I was to find later, with those fantastic rock isles that dot by thousands the northwestern corner of the Gulf of Tonkin. This region has indeed been called the terrestrial Bay of Along, which is no misnomer, for these rocks also once stood out of the sea, before the earth came to fill in between them the flat plain that flows as level as the ocean all about them. Some of these gigantic formations, which were to follow me far down the West River into the Chinese province of Kwangsi, had patches of hardy vegetation on them; some were as bare as the forbidding mounds of stacked bayonets they suggested. They were of most curious shapes, forms as tormented as if the mountains had been tortured in their youth, some like rocks torn jagged by uncounted centuries of dashing waves. Now they grew up among the rice-fields, and continued for hours, fantastic, of every possible formation, attitude, posture, striking peaks and ridges with perpendicular, horizontal, diagonal strata, covered with thorny scrub vegetation wherever it could get a foothold. Some of those queer rock hills, half covered with plant life, looked like velour fedora hats carelessly tossed out on the plain; others resembled the slack heaps of a region of pulsating industry.

All the rest of the day we rode among those mountainous

heaps of rock, those phantoms of stone. Sometimes that afternoon the whole western horizon was cut off by a capriciously peaked range so hazy as to seem a gauze curtain, at other times so close that it appeared to hang threateningly over us. But always there was this vanguard of isolated rock heaps standing sentinel along the plain I made the journey between Vinh and Hanoi three times before I finally left Indo-China, and I never tired of those eccentric nonchalant piles of stone, on land and sea, of which the "Marble Mountains" of Tourane are the southernmost outcroppings and the bandit-riddled cliffs along the Si-kiang near Nanning the most northern.

The arable land was still more intensively cultivated and inhabited north of Thanh-hoa, a hot "citadel" of well built structures along orderly streets, which there is time to go and see if you will miss the midday meal at the station presided over by an Annamese woman with unlacquered teeth whose French is suspiciously fluent.   Thanh-hoa station well outside the town is the luncheon-place of all foreign travelers between Vinh and Hanoï, whether by train or by automobile, and track and road run so close together much of the distance that acquaintances made there can be renewed from time to time during the journey.   Those in the motor-cars now and then sped past us within handshaking reach, tossing over their shoulders gibes at our slowness, though we were not so slow at that.   The towns grew larger, with some more or less European houses, an old church sometimes bulking above the trees.   The mountains gradually retired to infinity; French appeared in the platform crowds, the Chinese merchants in our car increased as Jews do in trains nearing our own metropolis. Crowds were returning from holiday jaunts on this last day of the official *Têt* season.   French boys, and girls too for that matter, with nascent mustaches and bare knees, who had never been in France, were on their way back to school; French and half-caste hunters filled our car with dogs and guns, with dead rabbits, wild chickens and ducks, bagfuls and bunches of still less commonplace game. Though we took on more cars as they were needed, our coach was so overrun with standees that the mind was unwillingly carried back to the subways of another continent, while the fourth-class cars were almost as packed and jammed and chaotic as the soldier-abused trains of China.

Passengers were piled three deep from engine to back platform by the time we reached Hanoï at six, and I found the city so busy that I had my first and only ride in a *pousse-choléra*, as the French quite fittingly call the iron-tired buggy-wheeled rickshaws usually patronized only by the natives. Certainly I should have had something akin to cholera if the journey to the post-office for my first mail in a long time and back to the Hôtel de la Gare had lasted much longer.

CHAPTER XI

HANOÏ, northern capital of French Indo-China, is somewhat larger and less obviously tropical than its southern rival, Saigon. It is quite a city, with expensive modern
buildings, electric street-cars—found nowhere else in the
colony—railways in four directions, many automobiles, both
of the taxicab and private limousine variety, several excellent
hotels; in short, it is a little Paris of the tropics, with some
advantages that even Paris does not have. Those hotels
were a constant surprise, though I had seen almost their
equal in other parts of the colony. Not only were they
all you could expect of the French themselves, but their
rates were surprisingly reasonable for these exorbitant times.
Though I am getting ahead of my story again, we had later
on two large rooms with bath, electric fan thrown in,
excellent French food and plenty of ice, for three adults
and two small children at 250 piastres a month. True, there
were cobwebs visible in the corners of the high ceiling,
bright little lizards paraded the walls, and the plumbing
might have been more strictly up-to-date, but he is an inexperienced traveler who expects perfection anywhere.

In the very heart of Hanoï, with the principal foreign
streets on some sides of it and the native city on the other,
is a large lake, delightfully blue and restful, bordered by
a stone-faced embankment spaced with huge old trees. Out
in it rise two little islands, one reached by a causeway,

the other needing a boat, bearing respectively a famous old temple and a kind of pagoda. The beautiful, lazily tropical view across this broad deep lake in the heart of a city is one of the sights of the Far East, and gives Hanoi quite a distinctive atmosphere. In a well shaded corner on its shores there is, especially on Sunday mornings, a flower-market very similar to the one near the Madeleine in Paris, except that this one lasts the whole year round, and in place of the *bouquetières* of Paris boulevards the sellers are black-toothed *congaïe* in long cinnamon-brown coats, their swollen lips reddened with betel-nut, yet quite as commercially skillful and in their Oriental way just as coquettish as their Parisian counterparts.

Rue Paul Bert, named for a former French commander, is to Hanoï what the Rue Catinat is to Saigon. Along it are some very up-to-date government and private buildings, well stocked stores, and cafés overrunning the sidewalks. The tram-cars across this lead along the lake and through the native town to even larger government structures in a great park of the outskirts, now admittedly the head-quarters of the governor-general, though even he hardly dares openly admit this down in Saigon. There are other parks, one with a big stone water-tower that looks like a medieval dungeon, many streets of good foreign houses, most of them gay in Buddhist-yellow stucco, a big museum left over from a former exposition, and all the other adjuncts of French civilization. As in Saigon, there is an imposing municipal opera-house, where a company subsidized by the government, at the cost of the natives, comes to sing each "winter" for the French residents, not to be outdone by that other Paris on the opposite side of the earth in any of the cultural things of life just because their lot happens to be cast so far afield. Most of the

year the municipal theater stands idle, however, with a wel-
coming air toward anything that promises to be a relief
from the monotony of the silvered-screen nonsense offered
in another part of town. On my second visit to Hanoï
its pretentious façade was adorned with the paper of an
"Oriental Magician," whose performance was as worthy
of the solemn throng in full dress that filled the house
as would have been those of his rivals elsewhere. The very
atrociousness with which he massacred the bit of French
needed to accompany his tricks had about it a tang of the
occult East unable to express itself in our crude Western
medium—which was strange in an Italian who called New-
ton, Massachusetts, home, and whose ultra-Oriental wife
and chief stage assistant admitted in unofficial moments that
she was born in Kansas.

The rush and swirl of street life in Hanoï was even more
nearly incessant than that of hotter Saigon. Hawkers,
improvised restaurants, hundreds of rickshaws, most of
them thumping their wooden wheels on the ill-fitting axle,
queer carriages, wheelbarrows again for the first time since
leaving China, man-drawn freight-carts, automobiles bellow-
ing their demanding way through flocks and shoals of
pedestrians, all bore testimony to the importance of the
northern capital. Superficially everything was French, down
to the tiny bottles containing those *pierres à briquet* required for the gasoline-driven cigarette-lighters of France,
which one saw in the display-windows of native as well as
French shops. The big department-store across the street
from our hotel opened at dawn and closed from eleven
until two, like almost everything else, so that its reassembling
force was constantly breaking short both our night's sleep
and our afternoon siesta. But the red tape of buying there
was as entangling as in France, with the added difficulty

that prices quoted in francs and paid in piastres had to
be figured according to the daily rate of exchange—often
to our decided advantage. There seemed to be a general
taste for French bread, and bottles by the coolie-load were
so cheap and plentiful, in contrast to China, that every possible thing was made out of whole or broken ones—walls,
garden borders, sidewalk edges, playhouses. But there did
not seem to be much Frenchifying of native life except in
these external details, and even with those the millions of
the masses have little to do.

Late January in Hanoi was cloudless, almost as hot as
in Saigon, more than ten degrees farther south, so that
even in white again I was none too comfortably cool. By
night it was often too hot to sleep well even stark naked
under a languid electric fan, and one's dozing was made all
the more fitful by the rattling hubs of the *pousses-choléra*,
those iron-tired, almost springless rickshaws of the masses,
and of the larger coolie-pulled baggage and vegetable carts,
that made a hubbub beneath our windows all night long
like the passing of a regiment of lumber-wagons. Sometimes there might be a lull from about two until four in
the morning, corresponding somewhat to the daytime siesta,
but even then the streets were by no means so nearly
deserted as they were around noonday. Plenty of good
rickshaws, with wire wheels on large pneumatic tires and
ample springs, as noiseless and comfortable conveyances as
those of Peking and far better than the ones to be found
in Canton and southern China in general, plied the streets
of Hanoï. But they were used almost exclusively by foreigners, one European each, while the bone-breakers in
which even mandarins were glad to save an Indo-China
nickel served the natives.

The rickshaw-men of Indo-China are so hungry for

work that they always know, whether they understand him or not, where a possible client wishes to go. A score of times I had the same experience; all foreigners in Indo-China have had it: a mob of rickshaw pullers, seeing me come out of a hotel, a shop, a government office, the home of the lone Protestant missionary couple in Hanoi or of the customs officer turned novelist, rose up like a battling mob along the sidewalk, each vociferously offering his little seat on wheels, those behind thumping the others with their shafts, so common a trick that none of them show anger at it, as if it were all a part of the day's work, of the eternal struggle for rice for their thin bodies and the many dependent upon them. "Rue de la Soie!" I cry to the uproar. All begin to shriek, to howl in chorus: "Moi connaître! Moi connaître!" I step into one of the vehicles at random. The others give a little smirk as of amusement to cover their chagrin, to save face by pretending that they were not keen for the job after all, while the lucky fellow speeds away straight before him, as if he knew the way perfectly. But he goes too straight ahead; the way to an Asiatic goal cannot be so direct as that, even in this less labyrinthine part of the Orient. I begin to grow suspicious; at the end of several full-speed minutes I stop him with "Mais, ce n'est pas—this is not the way to the Rue de la Soie, is it?" He has no idea what I am saying, longer experience will show me; all he understands is that I have said something. So he turns around and flees as rapidly in the direction from which we have come. I call out again, and though he still does not understand, he pretends to, and feeling that he must do something to satisfy me he forks off at random, to the right, to the left, no matter which, and continues to trot, now and then turning his head to look at me more or less surreptitiously, like a clever old horse, as if to gather from my expression some notion of where I wish to go.

All very well for the old resident, who knows his way about town and is well aware that the two-legged horse between his shafts does not know a word of the French he so glibly pretends to understand. But it is hard on the new-comer, who has neither of these advantages, who does not know one street from another until he can read the signs on their corners, who speaks no Annamese, particularly so on the naïve American accustomed to put his faith in the truthfulness of the human kind. After he is lost completely he appeals perhaps to a native policeman, only to find that the officer knows even less French, and so, he discovers one by one, do the natives round about, even those in full European tropical dress. So that unless he happens to run across a French official or resident, which is unlikely in many parts of town or anywhere at certain hours, he is in for it. Perhaps, if he is lucky, he can make his more or less human horse understand that he wishes to be taken back to the place from which he started, or to a police station, where at least he can telephone for assistance, if central happens to have a smattering of French. Besides, it is no pleasure to drive these poor fellows far, with their thin chests heaving and their bare brown backs gleaming with sweat. Yet it is perspiring work to walk; the trams go only along a fixed route, and automobiles are expensive.

The very next day I would find the same coolie, or one looking exactly like him, shrieking with the same effrontery, "Moi connaître!" if I asked him to take me to the corner of Broadway and Forty-second Street; and at the end of the run, wherever that might be, he would stand holding out both hands cup-fashion in that engaging Annamese manner, as if he expected a fortune for the job. It is only a poor ruse to earn a few cents, for these *pousse-pousses* are the most miserable and the least astute of the Annamese who serve the French and such few white foreigners as come to Indo-China. The "boys" who work for us are much brighter and know far smarter tricks. Certainly they are ingenious, if somewhat less so than their Chinese counterparts, capable of serving a ten-course dinner without cook-stove, dishes, or cutlery; but they are so artful, so cunning and sly for all their outward servility, that even he who tries to be continually on his guard is sure to be periodically duped.

Though the streets in their own section of Hanoï bear the names of French heroes and politicians, the rulers from the West have not forgotten that it is after all a Tonkinese city. In the native town on the farther side of the lake—which is nothing like a native town in the Chinese sense of the word—the streets are also named in French, but not for the French. Instead, they have preserved as much of the old atmosphere as is compatible with sanitary requirements, including the ancient street names. The blue and white metal placards on each corner bear literal translations of the old Chinese-Tonkinese names for the trades once, and in many cases still, practised in them—for after the fashion of the East, those craftsmen or merchants carrying on the same work gathered in a single street or piece of street, instead of scattering to various parts of town.

Thus the traveler can wander for interesting hours through the indigenous quarter intersected by the trolley, into the sweetish-scented Rue des Sucres, through the Rue des Cercueils, lined with heavy wooden coffins in the Chinese style—

for the wealthy, massive sarcophagi richly carved, lacquered, gilded, or painted, each bearing the Chinese character for longevity; for the poor, thin bare boxes. The Rue des Médicaments is full of the ancient type of medicine-shops, its air pungent with the odors of dried barks, herbs, deer-horns, roots, plants, magic powders, tiger bones, talismans, all the somber and mysterious pharmacopœia of China, everything with which to combat the evil spirits, influences, fatal breaths of the Black Kingdom. In Furniture Street the tools of long ago are still in use; crude planes fly; saws sing; a chisel cuts its way through brass; a center-bit, still run by a string wound about it, creaks; files set the teeth on edge; chips and shavings dance madly about among unfinished pieces of furniture on the bare floors of open booths from which escapes a dry odor of varnish. Here and beyond are the shops of the inlaid mother-of-pearl things, from tables to jewel-boxes, for which the Annamese are famous—things to which steam-heat is so fatal, as the gatherer of souvenirs discovers soon after arriving home, though they stand the steaming heat of the tropics well enough. The people of Annam and Tonkin are good carvers and designers in the old models, but they are plainly not originators; there is more than a suggestion of the Chinese in all their work. Silk merchants carry on in the Rue de la Soie as they did centuries ago; Copper Street, a block long, is strident with workers in copper and brass; the Street of the Forgers—in the honorable sense of the word—teems with workers in heavy metals; there is the Street of Rice, of Veils, of Iron, of Flax, of the Cantonese, a street with shop after shop full of the gay paper things used in funerals, a street of workers in lacquer— for the Annamese lacquer other things besides their teeth—

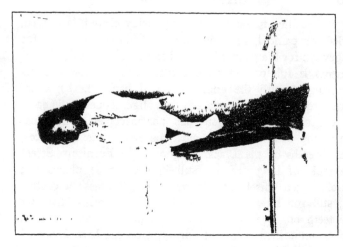

Thi-ba, who did her best as guardian of our children, was equally set against bobbed hair and skirts

The ladies of Annam lose any claim they have to beauty when they open their mouths on black-enameled teeth

For days one may steam in and out among the fantastic rock islands of
the Bay of Along

Tropical vegetation sometimes commandeers sustenance on the rock peaks

and so on, as long as the hardiest wanderer would care to stroll in such a climate.

The trolley goes on, through the Rue du Grand Buddha, past the temple of a great statue that is small compared to similar figures in China, Mongolia, and Tibet, on along a shore of the big lake, as distinguished from the *petit lac* in the heart of the city, to the Village du Papier, where native paper is made of bamboo shavings or of bark. The brown outside of the bamboo gives second-grade paper, the white inside first-quality, and most of it is turned into false money to be burned at funerals and graves. The raw product is cooked to a pulp and then pounded in a granite mortar with a stone pestle. Women, standing before the vats in which the pulp floats, swirl the water and lift out on bamboo slats the film that form on top, then lay each sheet on a soggy pile that would seem to defy taking apart after stacks of them have been pressed to squeeze out the water.

On one side Hanoï is bounded by a wide boulevard on a high dike along the Red River, which comes down out of China and spreads its fertility in a long straight streak diagonally clear across Tonkin, a dike not high enough, how-ever, for sometimes it lets the river into the city. Here one may muse upon the contrast between East and West while gazing at the telescopic perspective of the longest bridge in the Orient—as the French, if not the Tonkinese themselves, will proudly tell you—a bridge which in one sense is very ugly and in another almost beautiful. Eight hundred and ten meters from end to end, it carries across the Red River all the railway trains leaving the city except the daily one to and from Vinh to the southward; and just then it was being widened to carry automobiles also, so that no longer would motorists be forced to go down a steep and often slimy bank to a miserable *bac*.

One train across the bridge follows the Red River north-westward to Laokay and goes on two days farther into China by a line marvelously engineered through magnificent mountains, to Yunnanfu, whence the French have now and then had hopes of pushing their trains clear to the upper Yang-tze. Across it, too, goes the branch-line to Langson and the "South Gate" of China, by which I left Tonkin on my way back down the West River of Kwangsi to Canton, up which the defeated Tai fled centuries ago before the conquering Chinese. We were soon in uncultivated jungle, as north of Saigon, though the undergrowth was much thinner here, with brown fields and slopes of wild hay now and then, and stations that consisted of a sign-board and a woodpile. But every little while there were a few huts and some cultivation. Then came mountains covered with trees and underbrush, more and more abrupt rocky mountains, and the sun, so long imperious, suddenly disappeared for good and all the seventeen days back to Canton. Though the altitude was not great, within an hour it grew so cold, in contrast to the month behind me, that I changed to my heaviest clothing, thereby reducing my baggage by half. At the end of the train a special car carried a lone general, with whom, though I did not then suspect it, I was to lunch at the *Résidence* at Langson. As I alone graced the first-class division of the three-part car, one might have thought that a simple way of cutting down expenses and paying French debts would have been to let the general share the compartment with me, particularly if we were to sit down to the same *déjeuner*. But the French cannot treat their great men in that simple fashion.

The world had become little more than low mountains punctuated with forts on rocky eminences when I reached the place from where the little Peugeot of the *résident* was to carry me over the border into suddenly and totally un-Tonkinese scenes. The Foreign Legion serves in these picturesque strongholds along the Chinese frontier, a picturesque crew themselves, whom the French find it safer to confine to such isolated posts than to turn loose on Hanoï and other cities. Though no German travelers were allowed to land in the colony, there was a whole company of Germans among these guardians of the frontier, as well as many Russians and sprinklings of at least a dozen other nationalities, adventurers, down-and-outers, fugitives from justice—for there is no extradition from the Foreign Legion—above all men who do not care a tinker's damn so long as life remains interesting and as free as possible from dangerless monotony

The usual route for those from the outside world who visit Hanoi is by rail or automobile from Haïphong, or rather, vice versa, also across the great bridge. There were always the same scenes on these journeys through Tonkin, but one never seemed to tire of them—broad endless stretches of rice-fields, women in long copper-colored coats and grindstone-shaped hats skimming along good roads under shoulder-pole loads, boys and sometimes girls loafing on the backs of water-buffaloes grazing among flocks of white ducks, others of these ponderous animals plowing belly-deep in slime, still others in their glory, with only eyes and nostrils protruding, beautiful gates into low temples, banyan-trees of four or five trunks, with little vases of lime and often a few tombs under them, villages of huts among the feathery bamboo groves, a tomb with a flat-topped tree over it, a boat with a sail moving through a rice-

field, though no waterway is visible, two women watering
a field by means of a basket between them in the middle
of a long rope, graves of different shapes dotting the dead-
level country near-by, cactus hedges, almost naked countrymen washing their legs beside the track, a girl toiling with
a hoe almost as big as she, a man who owns no buffalo
plowing in deep water with his cow, a little hut thatched
with straw surrounded by a grove of very green trees, still
larger groves in the distance with white buildings peeping
out of them, a beautiful tree spread like an open umbrella,
its branches almost touching the ground, roofs coyly curling
up their corners, still another apparatus, like a huge corn-
popper hung on three poles, for lifting water from one field
to another, sometimes a big wooden spoon manipulated by
one man, still more likely by one woman, two pagoda-shaped
pillars at the entrance to a tomb, implying that the deceased
was a scholar if not a gentleman, a coolie laboriously making his way through the rice-fields by a dike-top path not
wide enough for the richshaw he is dragging behind him,
other such vehicles with two, even three people in them,
scampering across the flat country behind small runners,
dim mountains forever in the distance—and there ahead
lies Haïphong, an important city and port now, the first
houses of which sprang up about the barracks of the French
cantonment in the days when France and China disagreed
as to the "protection" of Tonkin.

I had heard so much of the Bay of Along among the
French colonials, confirmed by what I had seen of the
terrestrial part of it from Tourane to Nanning, that I realized
the foolishness of leaving Indo-China without spending a
few days cruising about it.   That would have been impossible, there being no regular service and I still unable, for

all my more than a quarter century of toil, to buy a yacht
or even charter a steamer, if the French authorities had
not been so proud of their famous bay that they would
not hear of my turning my back on the Far East until
I had given them my unbiased opinion of it. So they
lent us the *Tuyen Quang,* a comfortable floating chalet in
the customs service, with a picturesque Corsican captain
whose French outdid our own in foreign accent. I say
"us," for this time I took along not only the family I
had brought from Canton but Thi-ba, lacquer-toothed Tonkinese nurse-maid of our children.

We steamed away one sunny morning before the heat and
humidity became unbearable, down the river by which steamers from China and the rest of the outside world come to
Haïphong, and within two or three hours found ourselves in
the midst of the justly famed, or rather, the most unjustly
little known, fairy-land of Along. It was like roaming
among mountain-tops at sea. The rock formations were
unlimited, fantastic, incredible—round rocks springing sheer
out of the bluest sea on earth, rocks like mushrooms, the
waves having worn them away about the base until they
seemed to stand on stems, rocks that looked as if they
were floating, or were upheld by pedestals incredibly small
for such massive things, rock islands of the most fantastic
shapes to which islands can aspire, some with holes washed
clear through them, some looking supernatural where gashes
of white rock met the black shadows thrown by them,
cliffs, precipices, palisades, with vertical, horizontal, diagonal, zigzag strata—the sheerness was so remarkable that
we could scrape the sides of them with our large steamer
and be in so little danger of striking the bottom that the
sailors were not even told to heave the sounding-lead.

How many thousands of these rocky islands there are

floating on the blue waters of the Bay of Along only the
architect of the universe knows; the human mind could not
count them. Yet never were there two of the same shape.
With every hundred yards forward we found ourselves
looking through another narrow vista upon row after row
of pointed rocks, always varying in size and form, in distance and color, new ones with every new opening, though
one would have thought Nature had already rung all the
changes possible, used all the models and molds in her fac-
tory. Each was of some unique configuration we had never
seen before, as if they were all parties to a masked ball
every member of which had succeeded in getting himself
up in some novel way to surprise and delight the beholder.
Morning, noonday, or evening, when the sun rose or when
it set, great vistas of them stretched as far as the most
piercing eye could see in any direction we chose to look.
Calcareous rocks washed down during the centuries to the
hard basis of which they were made, broken by weather,
water, and time, with windows, arches, doorways, now a
tree standing forth in silhouette in one of these, here an
island depicting a whole cock, from comb to tail, another
looking like a group of black monkeys made of stone, some
veritable mountains of stone slabs laid together like huge
bricks, some with tiny crescent beaches, whole horizons of
fantastic peaks, monuments of every possible form—and
beyond, more vistas of heaped-up rock through every narrow
opening. Magnificent as they were, they seemed at times
rather pathetic too, standing, floating, here for so many centuries in their unrivaled beauty, yet unknown to almost all
the world that prizes so highly many a vastly inferior scene,
unknown even to most of that European nation to whom
they "belong." An endless wilderness of rocks so poignantly
beautiful in their stillness, their solemn isolation, their

majesty. . . The far famed Inland Sea of Japan hardly seems worthy of a place on the same hemisphere.

Many of those steeple-pointed islands are as bare as the sea itself, but vegetation covers them wherever it can grow, so that some are green as a spring meadow. On the larger and less impressive ones there was sometimes a complete cover of bush, with plenty of small game, the captain said, where they are not too sheer. But ordinary trees cannot get foothold on most of those gigantic needles; only some contorted cypresses, intertwisted lianas, represent the forest, wild pineapple here and there humping its wicked backs. On one of them is a little cemetery of Frenchmen who died of fever or dysentery far from their native land.

There are grottoes and tunnels in many of these floating mountain-tops. We took a life-boat one afternoon nearly two miles through one of them. It was dark as a Paris sewer, the bottom, clearly seen beneath a flickering torch, covered with millions of oysters half an inch thick that recalled the sand-dollars on the coast of Maine. The grottoes, too, were reached by small boat, then by climbing steep stairways of stones roughly piled up or carved in the rock. The greatest of these led first into a sort of reception-hall, beyond which opened a narrow tortuous corridor, its walls perpetually sweating. Though two solemn Annamese sailors with sizzling torches of waste or rags in an iron cage at the end of a pole, on which they occasionally poured thick oil, preceded us, we advanced by feeling with our fingers, the smoke pricking our eyes and suffocating us, our elbows tight against our sides. Then suddenly at a turn came the sight that gives this cave its name of Grotte de la Surprise. A vast amphitheater of tumbled rocks, into which streaks of daylight fell as sheer as at the bottom of a crater, yawned at our feet.

The light of the torches wavered capriciously on rock walls striped with green, with purple, with violet, a setting and lighting as fantastic as that of any Broadway musical review. Stalactites flowed down from the great vaulted roof like a cataract of stone, nay, of pure marble, stalagmites large as century-old tree-trunks climbing to meet them, some already forming great pillars that gave the place the aspect of a mighty cathedral. Misty shafts of light played on pulpits carved by nature, on pillars almost as symmetrical as man could have fashioned, on great shimmering heaps of stone with the same semi-glossy sheen one sees on pure-camphor piles in Formosa. Certain columns seemed to be formed of millions of shells piled up as if by some pre-human, pigmy bricklayers; others were like the trunks of massive trees, their stone roots twisting themselves into the stone soil like those searching for nourishment among the ruins of Angkor. Here hung a colossal stone beard, there a marble veil with a gleaming white fringe; in places the cold water dripping forever down through the centuries had made stone things that looked like mammoth frogs, a monkey, a turtle with a scaly back; in certain vistas the grotto suggested the interior of a vast tobacco-barn in the drying-season. Maidenhair ferns had crept in as far as they dared; now and then, doubled, quadrupled, by the echo, sounded the piercing cry of a bird of which we saw nothing, except the gigantic shadow of its wings.

This endless forest of floating stone islands is a fisherman's paradise. Each evening and sometimes oftener my wife and I dived into the incredibly blue sea—though the Corsican captain, to say nothing of the Annamese crew, evidently thought us mad—and saw between us and the bottom, hundreds of feet down yet seeming so near that we felt in danger of striking our heads, fish of every kind and color,

Of many caves and grottoes in the rocky islands of the Bay of Along
this is among the largest and most impressive

Sunset on the Bay of Along

An excursion to the open-air coal mines along the Bay of Along is time far from wasted

Campha is one of the picturesque places of exile for French and Annamese alike, in the interests of the coal syndicate

pinkish fish of the tint of the albino water-buffalo, red, purple, green, white fish. Natives in henna brown peered forth from some of the smaller grottoes; more of them were at home in their fishing-boats, square golden-brown sails of which often broke the deep blue surface. Whole clans of fisher-folk spawn, live, and die among these calcareous rocks, satisfied to leave this, their native land, only now and then to sell their fish and buy the few things they need that cannot be found here among these clustered sea-bound spires. Our steamer now and then called in, by three short blasts of the whistle, all the sampans and sailing-craft within hearing, and examined their papers. Finding these in order, and neither opium nor girls in their holds, we bought fish and sea-monsters of them for the next Parisian dinner and parted, outwardly at least, friends. It seems that with its thousands of hiding-places for malefactors, the Bay of Along has been notorious for two crimes: the smuggling in of Chinese opium, and the smuggling out of Annamese girls. Old women still lure girls away and deliver them somewhere in the bay to Chinese junks, which sell them in the open market farther east. Enticed, drugged, kidnapped, hidden among the islands and in the grottoes, these girls have supplied a trade between wicked Annamese and Chinese men of the pirate family that has flourished for centuries, and even the French have not yet been able to do away with it entirely. When pursuit grows too warm the miscreants slit open the bellies of the girls so that they will sink quickly, and by the time the pursuers overhaul them all traces of blood may have disappeared in the blue waters.

Three heavenly days we cruised about the Bay of Along in our private yacht, and we might have gone on for thirty and found something new every hour among the floating rocks of every shape stretching clear to the Kwangtung coast of China. The French authorities, and certainly the Corsican captain, did not seem to care how long we stayed. But all things must have an end. We turned back much against our will, and by noonday there was steaming hot Haiphong in the offing again.

CHAPTER XII

MUCH as we all hate to be fed plain knowledge, preferring our learning disguised with the sauce of entertainment, like castor-oil in orange-juice, I fear we must taste a few of the bitter spots in the history of Indo-China before we can properly savor the present position of France in her greatest Far Eastern possession.

All the land from Tonkin to Cochinchina was conquered and colonized by the Chinese more than two centuries before the beginning of the so-called Christian era. From that time China ruled the region off and on; it was in fact five times a Chinese colony. Once, shortly before Christ, a woman of Annam governed for three years, but after another brief hiatus or two China held unbroken sway from the third to the tenth century, until the revolution of 968 A.D. During that millennium Annam took on a complete Chinese culture, and has kept most of it down to this day. Then there were various native dynasties until 1407, when, under the Ming, China again ruled until 1428. Even after that, though there was no interference from Peking, and the Manchus held Tonkin only in name, the people of the Eminent South, like Siam, Burma, and other former dependencies, paid a modest tribute to the northern emperor, as the easiest way out of risking more fighting. Koang-de, the Annamese Son of Heaven, was still considered a vassal of the emperor of China—the occupants

of the throne at Hué are in fact still proud to claim
descent from the Chinese imperial family of before the
days of the pigtailed Manchus. Toward the end of Chinese
domination the Annamese could function even in China
proper as mandarins, generals, and still higher officials, so
that the line between the two peoples was almost obliterated.

In the mess that followed the Manchu conquest of China,
a Tonkinese fisherman founded a new dynasty, which ruled
at Hanoï until the end of the eighteenth century. Then,
the country having naturally broken in two in the middle,
a rebellion overthrew the ruling Nguyen family of the
south and the Tai might have taken the country in hand,
had there not arisen that epic hero among the Annamese,
Nguyen-anh, who in 1802 took the name of Gia-long. This
founder of the present dynasty united under one rule what
are to-day three of the five divisions of Indo-China—
Annam, Tonkin, and Cochinchina—establishing his capital
at Hué, being the first to group under the jade scepter
everything from the frontiers of China to the banks of the
Mekong.

But his victory was not so complete or so simply won
as this may sound, and strictly speaking he did not rule
as master, for he had to pay for calling in outside help.
As usual it was a squabble between native factions that
gave the less naïve Europeans their chance. Though they
had already begun to visit these shores in the way of commerce during the sixteenth century, the French first had
official contact with Annam in 1787, when the future Gia-
long was fighting to recover the position of his family.
Finding himself, in his war with the Tai and three brother
usurpers, in imminent danger of being driven out of his
native land, he ill-advisedly followed the suggestion of the
French bishop of Adran and sent an embassy to France

asking for protection. He got it, with a vengeance. Also the wise bishop, who thought this a fine chance to counterbalance the growing political power of England in India, got a splendid tomb and a lot of Indo-Chinese streets named after him. Fearing perhaps that the embassy would not put things strongly enough, the bishop went to France in person and got promise of help from Louis XVI, or whoever ruled in his name. Before the assistance was delivered, however, Gia-long-to-be had to make a treaty with Louis promising to cede to France the islands of Touron and Poulo Condore off the coast of Cochinchina and give the French a concession at Tourane. Then the French sent troops from Pondicherry and helped Nguyen-anh to overthrow his enemies and to acquire by 1801 sway over all the present Indo-China except Cambodia and the Laos, in short to become Gia-long the Great.

Though Gia-long died in 1820 without perhaps suspecting the truth, this opening wedge eventually led to the establishment of French authority over all Indo-China. But the successors of Gia-long showed themselves "very ungrateful" to the French. His immediate successor, his natural son Minh-mang, broke off with Europe in order to get the support of China, and after considerable rough work, including the massacring of many native Christians, died by falling off a horse, a failing he seemed to have in common with some modern princes, leaving behind him seventy-one children, of whom forty-nine were sons—not a bad record for a man who died young. The choice among these must have been difficult, and it does not seem to have been particularly successful, for the son who followed him under the name of Thieu-tri left no great fame behind him. But then came Tu-duc, who massacred many more native Christians and their European missionaries. Though they probably wanted to be martyrs anyway, the killing of the ecclesiastics was made the pretext for the declaring of war. A Franco-Spanish squadron took Touron and finally Saïgon; Tourane was seized by the French; Tu-duc, besieged in his own capital at Hué, gave up all Saigon Province; and by 1867 all lower Cochinchina had passed into the possession of France and became the French colony it has remained ever since.

Cambodia was already considered a protectorate of France; for Norodom, father of the present octogenarian king, Sisowath, had for better or for worse placed his country under the protection of the French in 1863. The French gradually crowded upon the Chinese in upper Tonkin, to make up for the British advance in Burma, and there was long and sometimes severe fighting, with "some splendid feats at arms," according to French historians. There was an opposition or anti-imperialistic party in France, but as usual this minor opinion was crowded into the background. This time the French intrenched themselves in the citadel of Hué and put on the throne a new emperor, the old one fleeing among the Moï after massacring several thousand more native Christians. The war for the possession of Tonkin lasted a long time. In 1873 Dupuis and a hundred French soldiers captured Hanoï, though it was the Portuguese and Dutch who had long had "factories" in the rich delta of the Red River; and China, which had given her Tonkinese vassals no more assistance than she did the Burmese against the British, was at length forced to acknowledge all Tonkin to be under the "protection" of France. Thus by 1885 the whole of present-day Indo-China, from end to end and from Siam to the China Sea, a country about the size of Texas, therefore larger than France, was consolidated under French rule;

except that the Angkor region was added later. Plainly speaking, though the French talk of "treaties" as if an equal sovereign people had requested them to take over the task of governing, not only Cochinchina but all Indo-China was stolen bit by bit as a result of the simplicity of Gia-long and the killing of those French missionaries in 1858. Bright little pupils will recall that the French had similar schemes afoot in Mexico at the very time they were fighting for Saïgon, and in Asia one realizes that the Monroe Doctrine has certainly changed the face of America from what it might have been.

The French conquest of Indo-China, some of it by trickery and some of it, notably the Tonkin, by real warfare, is merely a part of Western covetousness in the Orient, not the individual sin of an individual nation. We can condemn that Western aggression without losing the right to give full praise to the French soldiers who did the dirty work, just as we can condemn modern industrial exploitation without charging present conditions in Indo-China particularly to France. Once we grant the righteousness of "imperialism," of the conquering "for their own good" of colored races by the white, once we accept that trite tricky phrase of imperialists, "the white man's burden," any possible charge against the French is quashed. It is the old question: Is it good or is it bad for white nations to take over weaker peoples who cannot govern themselves well in our sense of the word—and who are so well worth exploiting? Is it better to be chaotic, "backward," but independent, or modern and exploited? Is it better for a country even as civilized as France to take hold of these poorly governed races, these inefficient countries, and make them settle down to business and behave themselves, even if the "protector" does pay himself well for the trouble? Great minds set in cement will tell you, but I cannot; I find my judgment depending on the color of the day, the way I have slept, my breakfast, the mail I have received; it is a perpetual struggle between my reflected and my indignant self. And of course each individual will condemn or praise this modern way of acquiring colonies that are not called colonies, of subjecting people who are not admittedly subjected, according to his background, his environment, his wealth, and the job he holds, perhaps also to the breakfast he has eaten.

At any rate exploitation is visibly the *raison d'être* of the French in Indo-China, though the Indo-Chinese are no more exploited than are the great mass of our own people at home by those few who have the strangle-hold in industrial matters, and by no means so much as are the people of "independent" China by their own legal and bandit rulers. One of the trump-cards in this modern game of colonial exploitation is a tariff. There are swarms of customs officials whose duty it is to see that nothing gets into or out of Indo-China—or even through it, for that matter—without paying heavy charges, swarms of Frenchmen with native assistants who examine every spool of thread that comes in from anywhere except France, so that it takes all day to get a few dollars' worth of "foreign" goods through the customs. Things from France pay no duties, submit to no formalities, any more than the French need passports or lose time in landing. But all others, whether persons or things, are put to trouble and expense. A box of cigars selling for three dollars in China costs seven dollars in Indo-China, though its Philippine place of origin is as near one country as the other. Every kind of French drink is available, but no others; even British whisky can be had only if it is smuggled in. Every box unloaded from the average ship comes from France; everything not of local origin in the average shop is French, even those things which France produces much more poorly and much more expensively than other lands. A Ford coming direct to Indo-China pays 45 per cent duty—125 per cent if it comes indirectly—and sells for about eighteen hundred piastres, or more than nine hundred dollars gold. The little cars for which the French are noted cost from thirteen to fifteen thousand francs, so that it depends on the exchange of the day which car you can afford. There are not only import but export duties on everything, even paddy, or unhulled rice, nay, a duty even on the gunny-sacks it goes out in. More than that; everything merely passing through Indo-China, as the shortest or most convenient route between two parts of China, is opened, carefully examined, and assessed, though in this case the charges are called "transit dues." Indeed, the more toothsome things from foreign lands are not infrequently consumed by the examiners and the empty cans sent on to the consignees.

Does all this money, paid in the end by the inhabitants thereof, go to the "protected" country? You have three guesses, if so many are needed. *La Métropole,* that is, France, gets real returns from its Far-Eastern possession; it is no altruistic "white man's burden" the French are carrying there. Every year Indo-China sends France a check for about twenty million piastres That nice little filial Christmas present of ten million dollars comes mainly from the *douane* and *régie,* that is, the customs and the tobacco, opium, and other government monopolies. Besides this the "protected" people pay the cost of military occupation, not to mention many millions more in official salaries and the like.

But what France officially gets out of Indo-China is a mere drop in the bucket compared to what Frenchmen get by individual exploitation of a land where they have special privilege. French commerce has a virtual monopoly in almost anything except rice and betel-nut. There is plenty of iron, innumerable other natural resources, but the French encourage no modern industries in the colony, because they prefer to import from France the products of their own factories, so that after all it is the French capitalists and workmen at home who are "protected." Take sugar, for instance; they export the crude at low and import the refined at high prices rather than help the natives to have their own refineries. Perhaps the best example of modern industrial exploitation of a "protected" people is the coal-mines in the northeastern corner of the Tonkin, which we visited on the second of those never-to-be-forgotten days in the Bay of Along.

The mines of Campha or Hongay, on the northern shore of that great wilderness of floating rocks, are open cuts, like those of the Japanese at Fushun near Mukden, or the iron-mines of Daiquirí in the mountains of eastern Cuba. There is no flaunting of the dreaded earth-dragon by digging down into the earth. Black terraces, mammoth stairways, are piled up the reddish hillsides, great amphitheaters cut in the hills, their walls so smooth and so sheer that one might think the coal was cut in huge slices, as from a gigantic cake. This precious region was discovered by a French forest-ranger wandering the woods along this coast no longer ago than 1905 and 1907. To-day the cuts are so large that the natives pickaxing on the slopes look like ants on gigantic black stadiums scaling the heavens. The roads through them lead from one grade to another, on and on, cutting through the villages, following the edge of the bay that is sprinkled much farther than the eye can see with those fantastic protruding rocky mountain peaks.

When we visited Campha, the black quarries swarmed with workmen, clothed in once reddish-brown cloth, now so dirty that they blended into the background against which they toiled. According to the mine officials and foremen these Annamese coolies are very lazy miners; certainly they seemed unwilling, after the manner of slaves, as if they were asking themselves who is benefiting by all this hard labor to get out of the hillsides the black stuff that is of no use to them. In fact the atmosphere of Annam in general is unwillingness, when working for Europeans, in antithesis to that of China. These beings dressed in sooty rags, these men wielding pickaxes with thin arms, have little to gain by their grueling labor under an imperious sun. There were women on the slopes also, their mouths bleeding with the sustaining and comforting betel-juice, and behind the coal-wagons *nhos* ten years old, their worn faces under the coal-dust seeming forty, bent double their gaunt little bodies, half covered with black rags and tatters, their bare feet covered with a hard sole of the dust in which they forever trot for ten or fifteen cents a day.

We were carried in chairs and on horses up the slopes from where the cars of coal are loaded into barges with little houses at the stern, a kind of Paris green scattered over the top of the coal to keep the workmen from stealing a little of it to sell. We went so high that we could look down not only upon all the town below, but across a great stretch of the blue rock-strewn sea. There was not a temple or pagoda in the native town, not a flower, not a single bamboo hedge before the native houses, no more slim straight arec-trees topped by a parasol of leaves, no smoking incense, but belching chimneys, and pickaxes. Instead of the pastoral quiet of other Tonkinese villages there was a great roaring as of a waterfall, as of some great battle— the noise of the sifters. In contrast to this super-civiliza- tion there are wild animals in the surrounding bush; tigers come now and then to eat a coolie, when old age makes them more cunning than swift and strong, for they do not need much strength to carry off a mere human being.

But soon the 10.30 whistle blew, halting the work until two in the afternoon, and we came down for the *apéritif* in one of the houses where the French live in the comfort they will not be denied even in the wilderness—and where even the women could not understand why my wife and mother, why our not yet four-year-old son for that matter, would not join them in a cocktail.

The hardest job at the mines is to get workmen, to bribe coolies to work here in the bush, and to keep them from running away again. Everything has been tried, and nothing works. As soon as the Tonkinese has a few piastres in his substitute for a purse he leaves the mines and returns to his rice-fields—and who can blame him? At the time of *Têt*, which also is nearing the time of harvest, all wish to escape to their ancestral villages again, and then especially they run away by the thousands. Every ruse and stratagem is tried, for the massed overseers and guards do not suffice. For instance, wages are paid only for the last fortnight of the preceding month, so that the workmen must either remain or lose many days of toil by running away. In order that they shall not starve, however, and out of pure philanthropy as it were, the company gives those who have worked well a piastre every ten days, which they call "making an ad- vance." Another scheme to hold them is to build a big cov- ered market, a movie booth. Not long ago one bright ad- ministrator discovered a still better plan. Missionaries installed at the mines would keep there at least the Catholics, he thought. So an Annamese father of the Spanish missions was imported and a little church constructed for him, and the new parish already has some seven hundred coolies whom the confessional and a fear of future damnation keep from running away.

Sometimes, on the other hand, when floods carry away the dikes of the Red River, devastating the rice-fields so that famine settles down upon the delta, the *nha-qués* flock to the coal-fields by whole villages, to find the rice they cannot get at home, and then there are as many as twenty thousand coolies dotting the great black stadiums, and a good year for the mine syndicate. As each new mine opens, at every new terrace begun, a Chinese man comes to set up his four planks and lay out his bowls of rice and provisions, often before a single shovel-stroke has been struck, as if he smelled profits from afar as the vulture smells carrion. He will be rich, this fat, physically flabby fellow with his freshly shaven head and his smooth, imperturbably smiling face, from the profits garnered from their wages, while the new coolies are still only poor ragged and dirty miners, longing to run away.

The coolies of Campha and Hongay are of no importance to the court at Hué, and not only is there no mandarin to rule over them, but not even a French functionary, except a gendarme who pompously decorates himself with the title of commissary. The real master is the mine; the mere people are nothing; as in all this modern world of industry property is everything, human life a mere pawn. The syndicate owns everything for many miles round about: the fields, the woods, the houses, the roads, the railways that carry the coal down to their jetties, the barges, the whole port, even the church with the sharp steeple, everything from the bowels of the earth to the slightest sprig of grass that may force its way through the coal-dust. If a village stands in the way of a new mine, so much the worse for it; down it comes; and when the syndicate constructs a new one farther on each native is made to pay part of the cost of his new house, so that he will be bound to the soil like a serf. The company is self-sufficient too; it produces everything it needs, from its tools to the rice for its coolies; and it is rich enough to be beyond the dreams of avarice, were there any such locality. The sixty-four thousand shares of stock offered at sixteen million francs a few years ago are to-day worth more than half a billion. The net profits the year before my visit were more than the total capitalization, not counting a twenty-million-piastre reserve.

One might conclude that at least this kingdom of coal brings its tribute to Indo-China, to debt-ridden France. Not at all; it does not even furnish the colony the coal it needs. Almost all of it goes to Japan, which pays well. Saigon and Hanoi demand coal in vain; such factories as there are have to send their orders to Cardiff, and the railroads fire with wood, devastating the forests. After the fashion of modern industrialism, that present-day descendant of feudal tyranny, unknown stockholders suck the marrow from the country, dividing the profits among themselves, and leave nothing either for the colony or for France. As in France, the rich run away with the money that should be paid in taxes and leave "nothing but the hatred of thousands of coolies."

As in these coal-fields, so it is with most rich enterprises in Indo-China; many a scandalous fortune has been created there since 1914, yet the public treasury takes no account of them. Not only is there no tax on war profits but not even an income tax. For the laws of France do not apply, and the law of the colony is to exploit it and the people thereof, not the Frenchmen who make their fortunes there. Nowhere in the world perhaps are war-profiteers more favored than in this rich French protectorate, for they can keep everything for themselves, down to the last piastre. "They are as miserly with their gold as they were with their blood when the war was on," a French traveler bitterly puts it, adding that all those enthusiastic young men who conquered Tonkin gained for their country were the swollen profits accruing to the holders of stock in such things as the mines of Hongay. It is a misfortune that the people liberated by France from the tyranny of their mandarins, he goes on, fall now into the power of these new tyrants; bad, because little grains of misery make a mighty ocean of revolt, and just over the frontier of China there are something like half a billion yellow men who are gradually waking up. "For the true mandarins of to-day are no longer those lordlings in yellow robes and silk tunics, so proud of their long overdue finger-nails, whom we saw bumping their heads on the palace pavements at Hué, but negotiators and financiers, adventurers who now carry no rifles on their shoulders but operate far from the jungle, by thrusts of the stock exchange."

As we have already descended to statistics, let me go on to say that Indo-China is now credited with about 20,000,000 inhabitants, of whom two thirds are Annamese, 1,300,000 Cambodians, more than 1,000,000 Laosians, and half a million aborigines of various races. To be still more statistical, the latest census, now some years old, gave the total population as 18,983,203, of whom 16,256 were French and 1191 "foreigners." Most of the French and nearly all the "foreigners"—that is, non-French Caucasians—are in Cochinchina and Tonkin, more specifically in Saïgon and Hanoï.

To-day there are some 30,000 Chinese and other alien Asiatics not included in the round figures above; and for the 18,000 Europeans, more than 90 per cent of them French, there are fully 40,000 Eurasians!

Many French colonials think it would be better to abolish the pretense of "protectorates" and really rule the whole country in name as well as in fact, make it all a colony, like Cochinchina, in order to do away with the sleek practices of the native mandarins and other functionaries, particularly in Annam. Either, they say, let us have a direct and undisguised French administration or return to a real protectorate, with kings and emperors who would not feel themselves annihilated, who would have the impression of being guided, counseled, even directed, but never dominated. On the other hand the French way of ruling through native chiefs pushed along by Europeans is a good system, and it is hard to see how native go-betweens of some sort could be done away with entirely.

For the French officials, particularly those higher up, being French as well as officials, rarely know any other language than their own; and therein lies perhaps their gravest fault. For they and those they rule over are at the mercy of any scamp who poses as an interpreter. Some French functionaries get official credit for knowing one of the native languages, but they seldom speak enough of it to get along in court, for example, without calling in the *interprète*. Just as there is a pidgin-English along the China coast, there is in Indo-China a pidgin-French, using only the infinitive of verbs and always the *toi* form, so that "Toi connaître?" takes the place of "Savez-vous?" and so on, irrespective of tense or gender. It is an amusing tongue, which "boys" probably find as queer and as hard to learn as we do their quarrelsome Annamese. As in the case of foreigners who

become so fluent in the bastard English of Chinese treaty-
ports, it would require little more effort to acquire a speaking knowledge of the native tongue.

Individually the French officials of Indo-China are agreeable gentlemen, at least on a par with their counterparts in
other white man's colonies. But the government atmosphere
is much like that of old Spain: no one seems to come out for
his health or primarily for the benefit of the natives. While
there is not the "squeeze" of China or the graft of Tammany,
still there are ways of turning a politician's honest penny.
It is less dishonesty, however, that constitutes the official flaw
than lack of ardent personal interest in the task in hand.
"The soul of the missionary and the educator is what the
'protectors' of such a people should bring to their task," a
French *publiciste* asserts. "But few officials will accept the
sacrifice of wasting any more time and energy than necessary in a place reputed inadequate to their merits. The only
thought of the average French colonial official seems to be
to 'make a hit' with his superiors, for his own benefit and
advancement, and get back to the fleshpots of Paris as soon
as possible. He has no ardor, no initiative; the ethnic and
social milieu being closed to him, his business becomes mere
routine; he does everything with only one thought in mind—
his career."

The French have of course done much good for Indo-
China. They have improved the cities, planted parks, opened
ports, built roads such as the Far East had never seen before;
and some one would certainly exploit the people if the French
did not; their position is decidedly preferable to the anarchy
over the Chinese border. But the guardians pay themselves
well for their services. The government departments are
greatly over-staffed; even the hurried traveler gets the impression that the colony is a refuge for deserving wards

of the government who cannot be accommodated at home. The Council meets once a year in Hanoi and once in Saïgon, which among other things gives a change of scene, a "winter" and a "summer" capital, with lots of travel pay for mileage between them. The higher officials in particular are shifted often from one division of the country to another, whereas there should be two quite distinct sets of rulers, dividing the colony on ethnographic lines; for Cambodia is as different from Tonkin as Morocco is from Réunion.

The majority of the French officials in Indo-China are from the Midi, like most of her colonials. The speech of many of them sounds almost Italian, to say nothing of that of the Corsican river-captains and the like, who speak with a genuine foreign accent. This is natural, the Midi being nearer the sea and having few industries to absorb its ambitious sons. Yet they do not love the tropics. Most of them are frankly bored with life in this distant possession and, outside their routine tasks, are interested mainly in café pleasures and the joys of feminine society. There are some exceptions, of course, some who do their gymnastics every morning and some who become mighty hunters before the Moï. Now and then a scholarly fellow takes advantage of his ethnographic opportunities. But on the whole there is little unnecessary mingling with the natives, little outdoor life, except under café awnings, few excursions, fewer *piqueniques* than one would expect in a land of good roads to delightful places and automobiles in which to reach them. Lest I be accused of pessimism, let us listen to a critic of their own nationality:

The Frenchman imports into the Orient the immortal principles of absinthe and café gatherings, as the German does his beer and the Englishman his sports. Individualists, rarely knowing any modern language except our own, we have therefore a national self-

sufficiency and a suggestion of provincialism, which betray themselves the moment we escape from the superficial cosmopolitanism
of Paris—of a part of Paris and a certain stratum of Paris at that.
Café habits and the customs of the politician, narrow-mindedness
and prejudice, disparagement, the faults of individualism, give our
colonial officials an incapacity for agreement and of organized
collaboration, a tendency to ignore realities, and to pay themselves
with words. All the colonial official's thoughts seem to be turned
toward his past, toward the *Métropole;* the society he has left behind still obsesses him. He learns nothing, and he can teach
nothing. The discouraging reality that surrounds him quenches
his eagerness to know. How often that has been impressed upon
me when I wished to document myself on Indo-Chinese conditions!
To most Frenchmen the delightful landscapes of Annam, the artistic
tombs of Hué, the noble adaptation of a temple to its site, all that
remains dead-letter. Most of them are as disdainful of the ancient
people they have come to rule over as was the famous governor,
Maurice Long, who did not know a word of the language, of the
history of the country he ruled, and forged for himself the most
erroneous, even the most pernicious impressions of its future destiny.

An old British captain, sailing the Far East for the past
forty years, and familiar with most British colonies, insisted
that, unlike his own people, the French do not coddle the
natives of their possessions. England, he asserted, caters
to the natives, gives them education and too much self-rule,
and is all the more despised for it. Asiatics do not understand kindness and sympathy; therefore the French are respected. You must not mix sentiment with the ruling of
inferior races, or for that matter of any other subject races,
he went on; "for instance, you do not seem to be having an
entirely happy time in the Philippines." The French themselves assert that there is more liberty under their form of colonial rule than under that of the British. I rather doubt it.
Though the outward French attitude of equality irrespective
of race or color may sometimes give that impression, in the

end liberty in French and British colonies probably sums up to about the same total.

It is true that the color-line is less tangible in Indo-China than in American or British colonies. French boys are deferential and even obedient to half-breeds, even to well dressed natives, such as an American or English boy brought up in a colony would scorn to glance at. Native and Eurasian boys of Indo-China act toward white boys as if they quite expected to be accepted as their equals, though that attitude does not exactly hold among adults. This freedom of intercourse has its good points—and certainly its bad. Yet the Frenchman is at heart no democrat; the line of cleavage is social rather than racial. There is every stratum of French society in Hanoï, from the haughty governor-general to the conscripts from manure-heap villages in rural France, and the common soldier is closer to the native rank and file than he is to the high officials of his own race, the governor-general socially more allied to high-class natives than to his own clerks and troopers. Yet on the whole it is better to be white. At the *guignol* near the tiger-cage in the big park about the palaces of the governor-general the Annamese policeman raps on the head native children who do not behave, but is very deferential to the white children who sit elbow to elbow with them. On the other hand the sweat-dripping French soldiers who come out of their cloth-inclosed cages between the acts of these popular outdoor Punch-and-Judy shows and smoke a cigarette before going back to their stifling duties as showmen again are regarded by the upper-class Annamese more as servants than as lords. There are not only French children with their amas in the front seats, and half-breed ones already posing as French, as they will through life, but purely native children as well; and not far away the adults sit or saunter and listen to the good band concert, or cluster before the monkey-house and other cages, without any outward evidence of that racial dissonance emphasized in our own or British colonies. The best hotels in the colony make no distinction between French and Annamese, or any combination of the two races ; the Annamese wife of a Frenchman "will be admitted to any circle in France to which the social position of her husband corresponds." Yet Indo-China is almost the only place left where one still sees white men, and women, slap and otherwise manhandle their servants, and some Frenchmen speak to native railway men and the like in a way that in any other country would bring them the quite proper request to betake themselves forthwith to where it is reputed to be warmer than in the earthly tropics.

A French novelist whose background is Indo-China rates its "scourges" (*fléaux*) as—in the order of their appearance to the newly arrived colonial perhaps—sun, "boy," *congaie*, alcohol, gambling, opium, and madness. Most of these are self-explanatory. The "boy" alone is sometimes enough to drive the exile to drink, if not to madness, and it is not infrequently he who more or less surreptitiously brings in the *congaie*, perhaps his own sister, sometimes even his own wife. The *congaie*—normally a perfectly respectable Annamese word for girl—is in colonial vernacular what in France is known as *petite femme*, and by many other names, some of them far less complimentary, in every land. As our own pretty but stupid girls go into the movies or the "Follies," those of Annam become the temporary wives of the French. There is a lot of romance about the *congaie*, from those of the "Madame Butterfly" temperament, until one finds that she is sometimes hired by the week, like a *bonne à tout faire*, and is often passed on to a successor with the furniture.

Nor is she the Oriental doll she is painted by romantic Latin
novelists, though during her first few terms of service she
may have youthful charm and perhaps be pretty.   Many
Annamese mothers do not blacken the teeth of their daughters because they wish them to live with Frenchmen, especially if they are the daughters of other Frenchmen, which
is said to make an ardent combination much sought after
among colonial Lotharios.   But the *congaie* must love her
François indeed if she eschews betel-nut for his sake; she is
more likely to teach him the habit.   There is little visible
public opinion against these temporary matings, though it
is said that the best class of Annamese look down upon the
practice at least as much as do the most nearly prudish of
the French.   As in France, marriage is very difficult and
its unofficial rival very easy; one may even take the *congaie*
back to France as a servant.

One sees half-breed children now and then even in thatched
hamlets far from the centers, while there are plenty of both
children and adults of mixed blood in any city.   Wherever
there is a Catholic community cynical French males suspect
any one in the slightest degree off color as having French
blood contributed by the "missionaries."   The opposite combination, with the male Annamese the "protector," may
sometimes be seen—a Frenchwoman in Annamese trousers
in some wayside village or peering forth from some native
den in the cities.   There were several instances in Hanoï of
Frenchwomen legally married to Annamese, most of them imported after the war.   The wife of a furrier who won a
gold medal and his French bride at the Marseilles exposition
of a decade ago never went out, but stood looking through
her *grille* like a captive animal.   The Parisian wife of a
barber in Haïphong lived in the not too large room of the
barber-shop, with a bed off in one corner behind a bamboo

screen that did not even conceal from observant clients that she was soon to contribute to the Eurasian population. The government is now refusing licenses for such marriages, but that naturally does not do away with similar unions as long as Frenchwomen are ignorant of the color-line or indifferent to it.

The French think that they cannot live in the tropics without a pith helmet, a cholera belt, wine, and a woman. One might add ice in the place of song. They have a curious belief amounting almost to a superstition that to take off *la casque* in the sun, even the reflected sun, be it only for the instant needed to mop the brow and sweat-band, will almost surely be fatal, so that every little while the thoughtless "foreigner" is startled by raucous shouts of warning, and assailed with screams of dismay if he so much as thrusts his head out a window without his helmet on. Yet they constantly see the natives bareheaded, and either I must conclude that this, like the cholera belts with which even the women seem to torture themselves, is an unnecessary burden or that my own head is more *dure* than those of the notoriously hard-headed French.

Of the eighteen to twenty million inhabitants of French Indo-China only the males over twenty years of age among the perhaps seventeen thousand French residents can vote —for the deputy from Cochinchina to the French Chamber of Deputies and for a delegate without a vote from the "protectorates." Naturally those elected are Frenchmen. The number of French in Indo-China might have greatly increased of late, contends one party among this slight electorate, were it not for more or less official opposition. "For many of the rulers, the free Frenchman, the Frenchman who is not a member of the administration, is regarded as a

troublesome intruder, an unknown incumbrance, a suspected
person, a constant addition to the problem. This anti-
French politics arose from the spirit of autocracy of those
Cæsars with clay feet, Long and Baudoin, with their avowed
hatred of every French civilian in the posture of a man."
This party insists that there should be a "white proletariat,"
that many a young Frenchman, released from the army there,
for instance, could live well in some part of the colony with
his "companion," and even contribute a large progeny, to the
advantage not only of himself but of France and Indo-
China. If only the government would find some means of
helping him to raise and educate his children, they insist, he
would be far happier than at home and gradually help to
bridge over that gulf between the French and the natives.
The point of view of this group is that of Brazil: that there
is nothing wrong in mixing racial strains, legitimately or
otherwise, that on the contrary this mixture of races should
help to cement together more closely the different elements
and perhaps breed a stock that would better endure the
climate than does the pure white. In other words, they
would emulate in human form the success of breeding hardy,
tick-impervious, but runty tropical cattle with India bulls.

Offhand the impartial observer would say that there should
be a "white proletariat," that not merely French capitalists
and officials should have the advantages France's "protection" of this part of the world offers. But the governing
class insists that there shall be none, or no more of one
than is unavoidable, and for that reason does not now allow
conscripts to be discharged in the colony when their time is
up, even though, unlike those of higher social standing, they
may be willing to marry their *congaie*, produce legitimate
offspring, and agree to remain in the colony for life. Nor
do those in power encourage the coming of colonists from

France. Yet, contend the self-appointed spokesmen of the
"white proletariat" who are so bitter against what they call
the "anti-French" policy of the officials, it was precisely
because of the sacrifice of these *"petits blancs"* that France
lost many of her other colonies.

Some of the complaints of the Annamese against the
French are so well put in one of the novels of my companion
from Hué to Hanoi that I cannot do better than to quote
him:

You have seized Annamese in the streets of the large cities, with
all possible vexations, for the sum of two piastres owing to the
government, yet you subsidize each year a theater troupe at the cost
of 80,000 francs [written when exchange was much higher than now]
merely to amuse a handful of French during the three winter
months. You have inaugurated the régime of the *corvée* for the
building of roads, or of buying out of it at a high price, promising
the population that for this it would be exempt from payment in
kind, yet by roundabout means you continue to requisition the inhabitants of the villages for nothing more than that you may be
able comfortably to roll along in your automobiles.

In other words road-building in Indo-China is quite as it
was under us in Haiti, by *corvée,* or payment of road taxes
in labor. For three piastres a man could buy off from the
ten days a year required of him, but the *coolies volontaires,*
who had even to bring their own food, were often taken far
from home and sometimes kept for months. When food
gave out they renounced their nominal wages, glad to get
home at so slight a sacrifice. As in Haiti, the explanation
of the officials is that subordinates in the field did things
contrary to the orders of those higher up, but this must be
entered in the column of dubious excuses.

But to go on with the plaints of the Annamese against
their "protectors," as interpreted by one whose history and

temperament have made him as nearly sympathetic as the average Frenchman ever becomes:

The money you so cruelly cause to be sucked from the population you spend almost entirely on your own luxuries and pleasures, your own well-being; you spend next to nothing for the good of the natives, to help them to profit by the procedures which modern science puts within the reach of industrious, laborious people. The poor people everywhere say that the government deceives them by using tortuous schemes to increase imposts that are already heavy. They say that your protection is not what it seems to be on the surface, that while a European can go anywhere, except sometimes among the wildest tribes of the far mountains, there is still almost as much robbing, kidnapping, virtual banditry as ever among the natives when no Frenchman is looking on. You let the people be ruled by native mandarins, pure bandits whose immorality is no longer doubted by anyone—former "boys," liberated criminals, head gardeners who have known how to please by combining pretty parterres and by offering flowers to the women of your officials, intriguers and unscrupulous adventurers, beardless youths who have won the favor of your ladies, sons of mandarins with the most corrupted habits—whereas under the old régime this important mission as father and mother of the people was confided only to men of forty or more whose worth was proved. The greater part of the mandarins to whom you have accorded your confidence are rascals who exploit the people in the most shameless manner. We call them patented pirates, differing from real priates only by the brevet given them by the administration, with the aid of which they can legally pillage more easily and with less loss of honor than real pirates and smugglers.

You do next to nothing for the higher education of the Annamese, for fear, you say, of making outcasts [*déclassés*] of them, as if advanced instruction could make a degenerate of a man. It is said everywhere that you wish to keep the native at an intellectual level low enough to be able more easily to make him your slave. Thus you are false to the mission you gave yourselves to civilize the people. You cannot understand what attachments you would create between yourselves and the Annamese if you set yourselves resolutely to teaching them everything you know, without *arrière-pensée*. You have an example in the Chinese, who, though they treated us more severely, had nothing to regret for having inculcated in us all their civilization, all their knowledge, to such an extent that Annam became a China in miniature.

You have too much pride; you disdain the natives too much; you believe yourself to be of a divine essence compared to us whom you keep at a distance, as if it were a question of a vile, abject race, worthy at most of being your servant. You are jealous of our slightest qualities; you cry out against our slightest faults, which for the most part you have noticed among the scum of our race that surrounds you, and which you attribute to all of us in general, without knowing that the true honest Annamese takes care not to approach you, not being able to support your arrogance, your conceit, your insults.

Yet though the Annamese, particularly of the Tonkin, fought long and valiantly to keep from being "protected" by the French, and there have been some revolts since what is considered the final conquest of all the Indo-Chinese empire, notably that abortive scheme to poison all Caucasians one evening in 1916, on the whole they now seem contented, or at least reconciled, and fairly friendly. Do they perhaps see the advantages of French rule, and recognize that some one would exploit them if these aliens from the West did not; or is it merely the fatalism and the infinite patience of the East that gives them the outward appearance of comparative contentment?

CHAPTER XIII

OVER THE MOUNTAINS TO LAOS

EARLY April found me back in Hanoi, this time as a family of five rather than a foot-loose individual. It was not the place I had left two months before. Constantly heavy skies gave it a gloomy oppressive atmosphere not at all like those brilliant days of late January. Almost perpetual rain, even though it was not always heavy, made the life of the city less chic, less lively. With even the big wide streets covered with a light *couche* of mud and water, the large French community seemed to dress in its older clothes rather than in its Parisian best. In a hundred ways the change in weather made other things different. But the natives, especially the toiling masses, were evidently used to a season that had befallen them yearly for who knows how many centuries; for, covered with big pancake hats and palm-leaf rain-coats, they splashed about in their bare feet almost as happily as in the brilliant month of January.

Luckily Sunday managed to be fine long enough to confirm my reports on the zoo and *guignol* and the band-concert in the governor-general's park, and convince all three generations of my family that a month in the little Paris of the East would be the great contrast to life in China which my first glimpse of it had promised. It was still brilliant too, and already hot, when I took the train next morning for Vinh, through a land everywhere lush green now, to be met at the station that evening and carried home by the

244

résident in person. For though I had not known it until a
day or two before, the journey through Laos, Indo-China's
largest, most distant, and least known division, could only
be made more or less officially, with the willingness and
connivance, sometimes the actual help, of the French authorities. That part of it which I proposed to visit could
hardly be reached even on foot without government permission and aid, and only those whom the governor-general
considers *personæ gratæ* may expect either. The time will
soon come when that great region northeast of Siam will be
made the commonplace stamping-ground of tourists, but
so far the roads were only started and the hotels not yet
begun even on paper. Still, the French were not averse
to begin to let the outside world from which tourists eventually come know what will some day be in store for them.

The *résident* did me the honor of driving his big Peugeot
next day himself, though to save face he took along his
native chauffeur, as well as a "boy" to act as general servant.
We turned back north for thirty-five kilometers along the
railway by which I had come, then swung sharply west from
the macadam road upon a gravel one that was by no means
poor. At the first village officially recognized by the French
the army turned out—a score of Annamese soldiers in white
knickerbocker uniforms and red wrap-leggings, with the
familiar brass-tipped mushroom hats, all of them barefoot
except the sergeant, whose heavy high shoes on the ends
of his thin legs gave him a resemblance to a diver about
to descend to the bottom of the sea. With stiff leather
cartridge-boxes in the pits of their stomachs, their French
rifles with the long sharp bayonets, usually carried sidewise
high on their shoulders but now held stiffly perpendicular
before them, and as spick and span as only native troops
under European command can be, they stood at rifle-salute

behind their young French officer with raised sword, the very personification of the East under Western training, while the *résident* leisurely got out and inspected them as deliberately as if it were a pleasure to stand motionless in full dress beneath a tropical sun. Once these formalities were over, however, and arms had been grounded, the two Frenchmen shook hands and fraternized like exiled brothers.

While they are hardly a military people, any more than the Chinese, the Annamese had compulsory military service for all men between the ages of eighteen and sixty long before the French came. In fact they were so often called to arms that the field-work was largely left to their wives, which is perhaps why the women seem even to-day more at home in the fields than the men. Nor has the country lost its militaristic aspect under the French. Besides the white conscripts from overseas to be seen at important points, native soldiers are constantly in evidence. Astonishingly well groomed and set up compared to the armed ragamuffins of China, they commonly salute all Europeans with a gravity that further distinguishes them from the saucy, leering uniformed coolies of the soldier-ridden land to the north.

Naturally, most of these *linh* are Annamese, though each of the four protectorates has its own soldiers, nominally under command of its king or emperor—"semi-volunteers" they are usually called, and quite properly. For even to-day it is no business of the king or emperor, much less of the French, whether or not they are volunteers in the true sense of the word. Mandarins or other officials tell each commune how many recruits it is required to furnish, and they are duly furnished, without embarrassing questions. The notables of each village choose those who shall leave it for eighteen months of service, at the ratio of one recruit to every six adult males, and naturally they do not include their own sons

among them. Their training over, the youths may return
to their homes, but are subject to call until the age of sixty.
Many prefer to remain under arms longer than is required,
and with this system France—or the native sovereign—has
a reserve of very respectable size, some of whom have served
five, ten, and even fifteen years. The French assert that con-
scription is hardly necessary, that most of the soldiers of
Annam are real volunteers, that all the men of Annam
wanted to go to France at the time of the war to fight for
the "mother-land." If so, this indicates a patriotism, or
at least a wanderlust, not in keeping with the manner of
most of them, though it is true that a visible pride shines
forth in the brown faces of those few native soldiers, usually
noncommissioned officers, who display two or three French
medals across their breasts.

An hour or more later we crossed a river by a *bac* and
raced comfortably on along grass-grown roads for the rest
of the morning. The rice-fields had given way to brush and
forests, the plain to ridges and ravines, to a semi-wilderness
in which the scarcity of people was in great contrast to the
endless files of cinnamon-clad coolies of both sexes jogging
under their shoulder-pole burdens, the files of wheelbarrows
carrying produce to market, pack-animals among which our
snorting conveyance created a panic reminiscent of the early
days of the automobile, and to the crowded hat-roofed
markets themselves, close beside and even in the road, on
what might be called the Annamese side of the river. For
though we were still geographically in Annam, almost no
country in the world is so narrow as this one in the vicinity
of Vinh, and almost nowhere do conditions change more
quickly, once the crowded, rich, flat coast-land between the
Gulf of Tonkin and the Annamese chain has been left be-

hind. Already we began to meet tribespeople very different from the Annamese. Barely two hours from the railroad there appeared women dressed from just above the nipples barely to the knees, in primitive skirts wrapped about the lower waist, carrying heavy loads of wood, with a forehead-strap similar to that of our Indians. They were Muong, that is, "wild people," though their wildness showed mainly in their timidity as they slipped off into the jungle below the raised road. We had not merely changed regions at the *bac;* we had entered a new world, stepped back several centuries.

We raced incessantly westward, for all the grass in the road, along which a path meandered as constantly as if forever dodging the evil spirits that can only move in a straight line, like a rifle-bullet, never encountering another vehicle— except once, when we missed by inches meeting head on at a brush-hidden turn the only automobile of the day. Toward noon we stopped at a Muong village, where we picked up a French colonist with holdings scattered among the foot-hills of the Annamese chain. The two Frenchmen of course were already acquainted, and there was the usual *apéritif* before we sat down to a surprisingly good *déjeuner* in a more or less public rest-house. More exactly it was no longer surprising to find good meals provided even in the wildnerness, for your Frenchman will not endure gastronomic hardships; and since good meals are always more important to him than arriving, nearly three hours had slipped away before there was any indication that we were to move on again.

Meanwhile, on the heels of our arrival, the Muong chief of the village, closely followed by three or four retainers in bare feet, loose white panties, and more or less picturesque regalia, had come to welcome my high-rank companion. The chief wore a blue suit, instead of the usual black or cinnamon brown of the Annamese, and in honor of the occasion and of his own standing he had a blue cloth wound turban-fashion about his head. Also a volumnious cloak of mosquito-netting or cheese-cloth with huge sleeves, in which he clasped his hands together in a manner that increased his resemblance to a Chinese Buddhist priest, covered him to the bare ankles He and his satellites brought us, as the city fathers of Muong villages do all important visitors, according to the *résident,* a basket of eggs and several bottles of what looked like water. Knowing that such a beverage would be an insult to a Frenchman, I made inquiry and found that the bottles were filled with a native liquor of such deadly voltage that even my wine-loving companions did not venture to sample it. While the chief acted out his respects, the most lowly of the attendants laid out the ten eggs on a brass platter and set it with two of the bottles of rice-alcohol on the earth floor before the seated *résident.* Only then did the chief speak, accompanying his greetings with many low bows, showing none of the friendly half-gaiety of the Chinese, but rather an air of being inwardly frightened. The *résident* replied, somewhat carelessly, with a bit of the native tongue that was at least fairly fluent. Then the chief and his attendants withdrew, and the eggs and the bottle stood where they had been placed until we departed, when they were either retrieved by the chief or fell to the lot of the rest-house servants.

The colonist went on with us to the night's halt by a road now crawling along the edge of a precipice, now across serried ranks of what my companions called *montagnes russes,* sharp ridges over which we incessantly bounced, alternating with constant drops to low filled-in runways in place of bridges, a wilderness all about us. But after all,

tropical jungle has less of interest, at least after the first
visit, to any one except the trained naturalist, than the seem-
ingly greater variety of flora in the temperate zone. There
was still something left of the afternoon, for all our gener-
ous midday halt, when we reached the military post of
Cuarao, across the river from the highway and a mud and
reed garage offering tropical accommodations to a car or
two. One of its several white buildings of an official character, which looked so imposing against the background of
Muong houses and jungle, had rooms for the three of us,
opening off the soldier-trodden compound and roughly comfortable except for the heat.

There are three crops of Indian corn a year in this region;
and among the small craft of various sizes on the river below
were many narrow little boats full of ripe husked ears that
gave the scene flashes of color. The Muong prefer rice,
according to the *résident,* but the land left them is so hilly
that the toil of raising it is more than they will endure.
Wild-looking Muong mail-carriers, each with a small bag,
hung about the rowboat ferry between the garage and our
quarters as if they were in no hurry whatever to cross and
be off on their fifteen kilometers of the Postes et Télégraphes
relay. It was a reminder that the mail service of Indo-China
under the French is by no means the equal, in proportion
to the difficulties involved, of that of China under inter-
national tutelage. But on the other hand one can telegraph
anywhere within the colony, from almost any hut, at a cent
a word, in English, French, or the native tongues, and be
sure of prompt and accurate delivery. The traveler long
inured to the unreliable, expensive, often hopeless telegraph
system of China, unfortunately not under foreign manage-
ment, could forgive the French almost anything for this
boon. During all my journey through Laos I never took the

trouble to write letters to my family in Hanoï, with the
probability of reaching there again before they did, but spent
a few cents each evening for a telegram, and kept as closely
in touch with them as if I had gone home each evening; for
never once was I more than two hours in receiving a reply.

I have spoken before of the complete security of Europeans almost anywhere within France's Indo-Chinese empire,
whatever the complaints of the natives. No doubt it was
to make us feel doubly safe that soldiers beat a hubbub on
bamboo sections all night long about the post as a proof that
they were awake and on guard. But there are dangers, according to some of the tales with which my companions
whiled away the evening. The *résident* of one of these wilder
provinces, for instance, had broken five ribs when his automobile ran into a deer unfamiliar with modern traffic rules.
A French soldier stationed on the Tonkin border was at-
tacked by a tiger, an animal reputed always to take its victim
by the back of the neck; and as this man chanced to be
carrying a blanket-roll across his shoulders, he killed the
beast with his knife—or his bayonet, for he himself was
never clear on that detail—without getting a scratch. Tiger
stories are legion in Indo-China, and many of them are as
free from doubt as this one, which is fully authenticated
—or documented, as my fellow-travelers put it.

The *résident* drove me a few miles farther in the morning,
halting at the edge of another river, where we had made
telegraphic rendezvous with the authorities of the next province. Here and there a path went off up into the woods to
clusters of Muong houses; now and again we met a file of
these jungle people sidling along the edge of the road. The
men did not look greatly different from the Annamese. Their
eyes were a little less oblique, their faces at close range

shaped more like our own; there was a bit more wildness, naïveté, timidity, or something countrified about them; but the surest way of telling apart the males of the two races was the manner in which they carry their burdens—the Annamese on the shoulder-pole, the Muong in baskets on their wives' backs. The men themselves sometimes carry in baskets also, and even larger loads, but only when the available supply of females makes it necessary. The women who trail behind them could not possibly be mistaken for those of Annam. They were much less independent, each hiding behind her husband at sight of us, following close on his heels as they hurried silently on. They wore little above the waist except the loads they carried on their backs, secured by a band across their foreheads. A cloth about their heads and another barely covering their plump breasts were evidently concessions to the prudish world of the highway, for at home in the bush a blue-embroidered skirt from the waist to the lower thighs seems to be all that Muong public opinion requires. A long bodkin protruded from a queerly arranged knot of hair worn somewhat to the side of the head. The long round basket on the bare back drew taut the supporting cord across the forehead, a small board with two holes in it keeping the two strands apart. Each woman wore at her left side a section of bamboo as a pocket, and carried by another cord over one shoulder a canteen in the form of another piece of bamboo, several feet long, and filled with river-water with which to quench the thirst of her lord and master. Some of the brick-colored male savages bore a lance over one shoulder, and most of them had a long tobacco pipe of tiny bowl thrust like the bodkins of the women through their knot of hair, or worn in the belt like a cutlass. There was some evidence of tattooing, but the naïveté of their faces and manner and the attitude of the half-naked women were the most typical features. Between the men and the women there seemed to be a deep social gulf, something like that between servants and masters among the wealthy of other lands.

Here and there within sight along the road were a few Muong houses, all standing man-high on piles, a kind of gang-plank with cleats forming an outside stairway to a rounded veranda under a low overhanging thatch roof at one end. Men squatting over their long pipes and children at play evidently monopolized this portico, which the women only approached with the obsequious manner of those who feel themselves intruders. A smaller veranda at the other, always the southern and sun-baked end, served them as kitchen and place of recreation. Most Muong hamlets are far from the grass-grown highway, and one can scarcely blame them for preferring solitude and simplicity, though their roosters and cur-dogs probably make the nights as hideous there as the soldiers with their bamboo drums had ours at the post of Cuarao. The *résident* whiled away the time with stories of this "wild" timid race, one of which concerned a great chief of the Muong who had always gone about as naked as his forefathers of pre-French days, until, having been decorated with the medal of the Legion of Honor, he went to Vinh and bought himself a magnificent jacket to pin his decoration on. Since then he had never been seen without the jacket, and his brother was always following him with envious eyes, though whether he envied him the medal or the jacket was not clear.

We had waited nearly an hour when there appeared on the other side of the not very large stream a sumptuous Fiat strangely out of keeping with the wilderness about us and a startling contrast in transportation to the leaky old *bac*

by which I crossed to it amid the blessings of the *résident*
of Vinh. It was to have been there at daylight, but it soon
became evident that even a high-priced Italian car cannot
move faster than the chauffeur that drives it. We were off
as soon as my modest baggage had been stowed away, along
a still grassy road cut between the steep mountain-side and
the stream, the scars of the evidently recent road-building
already almost completely obliterated by the impulsive tropical vegetation. Here and there a path meandered along
the road, and on it passed picturesque Muong women in
scanty garments, all of them carrying baskets and some of
them suckling babies as they walked, climbing the rocks as
high as possible whenever they caught sight or sound of us.
Birds of rich colors flitting in and out of the jungle gave
us as hasty glimpses of themselves as did the Muong women
who sought refuge in the thick underbrush on the stream
side of the road. There were flapper birds, too gaily dressed
to be useful or even virtuous members of ornithological
society. One of them had a brilliant blue back, tail, and
wings, red feet, and a velvety-brown throat above a snow-
white breast that gave it the appearance of wearing either a
low-necked evening-gown or the white shirt of a dinner-
jacket. Its fantastic Semitic beak and cardinal-red head was
topped by a purple hat adorned with a single aigret. There
were matronly birds in black, with wings of the rich brown
of Tonkinese clothing, actress birds in exaggerated, even in-
decent costumes, birds that changed appearance entirely, as
if they had suddenly put on a disguise, when they opened
their wings and showed the under side of them; there were
birds that were mere streaks of white, flashes of fire in the
sunshine, birds with tails longer than themselves, birds that
made a noise like the pounding of a section of bamboo with
which Chinese watchmen make nights miserable, or Buddhist

bonzes call upon the charitably minded. Yet they sang less than did the crickets or katydids, less than the queer members of the lizard family sunning themselves on the rocks, confirming a memory that the whistle or call of jungle birds is often monotonous but rarely musical. Once I caught sight in the stream below of a ridiculous member of the duck family, swimming and strutting about among his modest female mates in a costume so gaudy and incredible that he must have designed it himself. We were so closely flanked by the prolific vegetation that this part of the trip was like taking a journey through the heart of the jungle in an easy-chair, or on the magic carpet of Arabic legend. Memories of the tiger stories I had heard the evening before, and elsewhere, crowded upon me. There were panthers in these forests too, and herds of gaur, a wild cattle like the aurochs, two meters high, of little trouble to the people but very dangerous to the hunter. Yet the only visible peril was the constant tendency of the road to make hair-pin turns on the sheer edge of great gorges.

The chauffeur, dressed in full European style even to his tropical helmet, seemed to be a mixture of French and of several Indo-Chinese bloods. Instead of driving like the madman that most chauffeurs of Indo-China resemble, making every turn an attempt at suicide, every downward slope an effort to hang up a new speed-record, he was so overcautious that I no longer wondered at his failure to be on time at the rendezvous. While I am not one of those who like to fly along the brinks of precipices, I rather prefer that to crawling like an ox-cart when a stretch of straight wide road lies in clear view ahead. Twenty kilometers from the *bac* he halted where we should have been three hours before, at a village which seemed to be named Muongsen, and announced that he could not reach our destination that day.

It happened that my trip through Laos was absolutely set in cement, since I had to be somewhere else at a definite date, and this fellow and his chief, the *commissaire* of Xieng Khuang, had been advised of that fact by urgent telegrams from the governor-generalate itself. But the Caucasian part of him seemed to have exhausted itself in his appearance without touching his character. Or perhaps he had once run into a water-buffalo or spilled himself down a mountain-side.

I was protesting against halting for the day while it was still fully an hour short of noon, when a white man unexpectedly turned up. He was a tall, good-looking, splendidly built fellow, with the appearance of a big blond Frenchman who had lived all his life in the open; and he wore the blue uniform of a French colonial officer. Yet he was no Frenchman for all that, but a native of Bavaria, who had lived as a boy in New York—at Sixty-fourth Street and Second Avenue, he still remembered. Now he could speak only French—besides Annamese and several tribal tongues of Indo-China—and was as Gallic in temperament as he was blond. Having entered the Foreign Legion when he was fourteen, he had been with the French ever since, and was now a second lieutenant in command of a village station higher up on the plateau ahead. With him was a French-Annamese woman of possessive manner, though no startling beauty, who called him husband.

Hospitable as he was handsome, he insisted that at least I could not go on until we had performed the Frenchman's midday rites. We had to prolong the *apéritifs* an hour or more before we could sit down to a several-course lunch in a hut grocery of very respectful serving manners and a not total ignorance of French cooking. For according to the lieutenant and his no less hospitable companion, it would have been a great breach of bush etiquette not to wait for

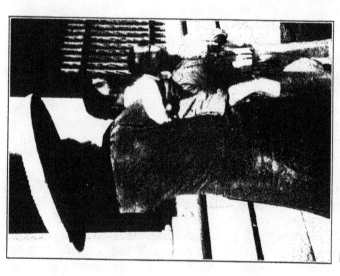

The women of Tonkin combine hat, sunshade, and umbrella in one unwieldy contraption

The Muong women wear little above the waist, except the loads they carry

The guard turned out to greet my companion, the *résident* of Vinh, at the first village on the way to Laos

The Muong chief of our noonday village came in state, bringing eggs and native fire-water

the other "European" in the village. He was the chauffeur
of the general-in-chief of all Indo-China, and had been left
behind with his car *en panne* while the general had climbed
on into the mountains in a Citroen "caterpillar" that had
been serving him as baggage-trailer.

This other "European" turned up at last and proved to be
a Guadeloupe mulatto, who lost little time in claiming that
his grandmother had once been a great personage in Bor-
deaux—which, after the way of French ladies, was not at
all impossible—and who either had never heard of American
conventions where negroes are concerned or judged from
my hand-shake that I had outgrown any such prejudice.
Simple and naive, yet with all those amusing little idiosyn-
crasies of courtesy and their opposite common to the French,
he was a bit bashful at first, until convinced by my manner
that I accepted him as a social equal. His misgivings had
plainly nothing to do with color but with the natural gulf
between a mere corporal turned general's chauffeur and a
traveler sponsored by the governor-general himself. Thereafter he was at his ease, and his big eyes rolled like those
of a minstrel-show end-man whenever he heard anything
even mildly surprising, and he became convulsed with gaiety
at the slightest suggestion of anything humorous. The lieutenant thought I might get more willing service out of my
chauffeur if we invited him also to sit down with us; and
what with the Muong and the Laosian servants who waited
upon us, the mixture of races about the rough but well
garnished table at which we finally gathered could hardly
have been increased without going in search of other
individuals.

The conversation hovered chiefly about the women of Laos.
The lieutenant asserted, and was borne out by his wilderness
companion of the sex under discussion, that to touch the

hair or breasts of a Laosian woman is a more serious crime than actual violation. In fact Laosian law prescribes a much more serious penalty for the former than for the latter indiscretion, and the lieutenant in his judicial capacity had often been called upon to try cases under this strange code. Naturally, he explained, again abetted by his lady-love, what the Western world considers the lesser of the two crimes might be committed entirely against the will of the victim, while the other. . . In brief, here was an example of Oriental wisdom to which the other side of the earth has not yet attained.

In a case of what, in the language we were then using, is called *tromper le mari*, the Laosians again outdid us in their sense of justice. By their law the lover is punished for the first offense, the woman for the second, and the husband for the third! For, as the lieutenant said, and his domestic partner again agreed, the woman who is party to such an act a second time must have some of the guilt; and the husband who is so inattentive as to be *trompé* three times is either a fool or is knowingly permitting it, and deserves punishment in either case.

The gentleman of color from Guadeloupe confirmed all these statements and added the information that when the husband, or the "man," is a soldier, like himself and the lieutenant, or is for any other reason away from home for six months or so at a time, it is impossible for him to avoid betraying his wife, or she him. This recalled to the lieutenant that the code of Laos allows the woman a divorce without contest if the husband stays away from her longer than the length of time he said he would when he left. What an importation this would be in our civilized West! One might fancy that it would make the men of Laos more punctual, more aware of the value of time, than the subway

victims of our great metropolis. Yet it is not so, far from
so. The lieutenant contended that this is a very just law,
for the suffering of the woman from long absence, whetted
by the uncertainty of the return, is obviously more than she
can stand, more than she should be expected to stand. His
own darling feebly denied this, but the men agreed with many
sage shakings of the head. It is as bad as expecting a man
to live six months without a woman, they went on, with
extravagant gestures, as if trying to clinch the argument
with the most ridiculous analogy they could hit upon. Gradually the tone of the conversation drifted to the other side
of the shield, the subject of parents. Both men asserted
that they had loved their mothers but not their fathers. "A
man's mother can only be one person; there can be no doubt
about her," the mulatto argued, with all the gravity of a
chief justice, "but his father may be any one of thirty-six."
Whereupon there were general roars of laughter and agreement, while the typically French dinner came to its end with
demi-tasses as naturally as a sentence does with a period.

CHAPTER XIV

EN PANNE!

WITH the influence of the lieutenant I managed at last to get under way again, not without hope that we might reach somewhere before nightfall, since the sun was still almost directly overhead. At Muongsen there begins one of the greatest automobile climbs I have ever seen, up and up and forever up through the jungled ranges of the great Annamese chain, an ascension unforgettable both for its magnificence and its danger. We climbed abruptly to an elevation of fifteen hundred meters, a full mile above sea-level, without moving forward a mile on the map. The road, forever clawing itself a place in the flank of the mountain, constantly making great detours, looking always for an opening, a gap to slip through, writhed like a tortured snake, struggled fiercely upward, grew dizzy with effort, took breath again, and climbed valiantly onward. On the left, or, worse still, on the right, the abyss always yawned. Our wheels touched the edge of space and flung stones off down sheer wooded slopes into *le vide*—emptiness; in many places there were curves so sharp that we had just room between the jagged mountain wall and the bottomless pit to make the turn by backing and filling where the slightest miscalculation might have meant destruction. Even then we barely got by without striking a lamp on the recently blasted mountain-side or dropping a hind wheel over the edge. I began to understand why a man, particularly an aging half-caste, whose lot in life required him to drive even now and then up or down this fly-footed route, might easily become too nervous ever to speed again and might grow to have the downcast view of life in general of this crawling imitation of a chauffeur.

Between the trees of every size there were glimpses here and there for an instant of the great Annamese chain we were struggling to surmount. The narrow little boats fighting their way up the rapids of the river we had crossed again at the beginning of the climb had long since disappeared; the river itself was gone. Giant ferns, valleys full of banana-plants, perfect tenement clothes-line mazes of jungle vines, range after blue range of the densest forest-jungle sank beneath us, and still the climbing continued, steadily, inexorably, forever. It was like duplicating by automobile my wild journey through the jungles of the upper Malay Peninsula, now two decades ago. Sometimes, when the road was completely exhausted, it went a little way on the level, but only long enough to catch its breath, as quickly as do the barrel-chested Indians of the Andes, before digging its toes into the mountain-side again. The air became fresher; the humid scent of the tropics disappeared; with every wheel-turn it was more pleasure to breathe. Behind and below us lay an ocean of branches, a vegetation so compact that it filled the vast ravine of the visible world to its very edges, like an overflowing bowl of greens, an immense panorama of verdure dotted with densely black patches of shade that looked like the mouths of caves.

There were many long thatch-roofed bridges, some of them curved, some with sharp angles, bridges of timbers and rough-hewn planks evidently cut on the spot, some covered with woven bamboo splints, bridges supported only by the upright trunks of trees along the sides of them, so that even

the least nervous of travelers could not but have wondered
whether they would always hold the weight our heavy car
suddenly put upon them. Many similar bridges had been
abandoned and left to disintegrate into the jungle again, because the road had been cut farther back into the hillsides.
When this new road gets officially opened and there are cars
in both directions—many cars, the French hope and believe
—there should be magnificent possibilities of accident, for
rarely indeed can one see five yards ahead, and often fog
half or fully fills and conceals mighty ravines into which a
false twist of the chauffeur's wrist would have sent us crash-
ing among the jungle tree-tops hundreds of feet below. I
looked anxiously askance at the graying fellow at my side
on whom my life depended, and was startled suddenly to discover that after all he was a mere savage in loin-cloth and
bare feet, however much his half-French features and his
wholly French garb might strive to conceal it.

It was an expensive luxury for the one or two automobiles
a week that traveled over it, this road up the face of the
mountains, costing seven hundred piastres a kilometer, about
seven hundred dollars a mile, even in this continent of low
wages. The workmen were paid only thirty-five piastre-
cents a day, and must furnish their own food; hence one
could scarcely blame them if they did not hurt themselves
with work. Piles of stone, broken or to be broken, lay in
long carefully slope-sided heaps at frequent intervals along
the way, recalling France and its *cantonniers;* but the road
was built rather in "American style," according to a French
engineer I met later, especially on the curves, because the
famous old highways of France were not designed for speed-
ing automobiles. We passed scores of Annamese men, nearly
all of them gaunt and sickly looking, thin, lemon-yellow,
feverish pictures of misery, squatting in miserable grass huts

that had been thrown up for the road-building, or dawdling along the way. Always with the air of being half scared to death at sight of a white man, they were pitifully obsequious, all snatching off their hats and most of them even the rag they wore about the head under it, at the same time backing against the mountain wall or to the extreme edge of the precipice and bowing low with the palms of the hands together. I have seldom seen human beings as sad looking as these Annamese road-builders. There was no gaiety, no life at all compared with the harder working and more miserably living Chinese, though one was still constantly puzzled to know whether this related race was merely suppressed, depressed by French treatment, or naturally gifted with solemnity. At any rate we rode frequently through bowing ranks of bareheaded coolies in rusty clothes and with fever-stricken faces, who could not have greeted me more obsequiously had I been the governor-general himself. In fact more deference was shown me on this trip into Laos than is received by most European sovereigns of to-day.

It astonishes us from the temperate zone of the West that the Annamese or Tonkinese prefer the malarial and overcrowded rice-lands of their coastal plains to the rich upper regions of their country. But the most wretched of them have a horror of the hills, even though their ancestors seem to have been highland men; so that it is always a difficult job, often requiring actual governmental force, to get even a few hundred coolies from the plains, where they are often half starved, to come up and help build these roads; and the few French exploiters of highland plantations look almost in vain for workmen. Criminals sentenced to hard labor are sometimes used in such enterprises, and often the *corvée*, calling for forced contributions of labor on the roads, has had to be invoked. In the cities it is no uncommon sight to meet a column of these miserable fellows, wretched already, though perhaps only the recruits of a labor agency, marching to a train under command of a half-breed, like a file of condemned exiles. When moving from one camp to another almost all these downcast fellows carried a cloth-tied bundle in their hands or at the end of a bamboo over one shoulder, so that they resembled a tropical imitation of a procession of American hobos "hitting the ties."

There seemed to be no women in these road-building camps, which perhaps accounted for half the appearance of misery, the great susceptibility of these plain-dwelling descendants of hardy highlanders to disease in the hills furnishing the rest of it. But it seems to be psychological more than physical, according to the French; ancient superstitions make the mere thought of living in the mountains sickening to them.

Higher up there were two or three villages that seemed to have inhabitants of both sexes and all ages, some of whom we now and then met making their way along the winding, perpetually climbing road. The sound of our horn drove them mad. The more fearful tried their best to climb the sheer earth or rock wall of the blasted mountain-side; the others, as if imploring us to be merciful and realize that they would run away if they could, snatched themselves bareheaded and, placing their hats against their stomachs, tried to break their spines in kowtowing to me as they might to a long dead emperor suddenly returned to earth. A few, less obsequious, or less quick-witted, watched us pass with open mouths and stupefied expressions, bawling children scurrying in and out between their legs. Near the top of the climb there suddenly appeared horses and other pack-animals, and the panic we created among these unusual carriers in Indo-China could not easily be described. We passed not a

The racial mixtures of French Indo-China include full and mixed blood of the four races of mankind

The Miao of Laos are sturdy mountain dwellers using primitive methods of transportation

Miao women of Laos wear festive garments that are more elaborate than colorful

Along the trail in the kingdom of Luang Prabang

few traveling pigs along the way too, for wherever there is Chinese culture there must also be pork. Though they are credited with infinite patience, the Chinese will not drive pigs to market. But the Annamese, more afraid of work perhaps, rather than more patient, usually try to, with a cord tied to each porker's leg. This may possibly be easier than the Chinese way of bodily carrying them, two on a one-man shoulder-pole or one between two men, so that carrier and carried, bound to market in this undignified manner, seem fellows in misery. In Hanoi and the larger towns of Annam this more certain form of transportation may also now and then be seen. But the Annamese pig is ordinarily driven, which is hard on motorists. For most of the pigs we met were too strong for the holder, and yet not quite strong enough to get away entirely and dash themselves over the mountain-side. Therefore, as they seemed bent on suicide in any form—and who could blame them?—the car always had to wait while the would-be pig-driver and several of his fellows united in one mighty tug of war that dragged the squealing animal out from under our wheels. For the most foolhardy of Annamese chauffeurs, however disdainful of the pig-driving populace, would scarcely have risked running over one of these porcine obstructions on this pathway along the bottomless pit.

It was in many ways a delightful trip, doubly so because one knew even without being told that very few travelers had ever made it. But good things often come to a violent end, though to tell the truth I had felt it in my bones that trouble lay in wait for us. I claim no prizes as an automobile driver, but I certainly could have given that mixture of races in French garb several pointers on how not to drive up a high mountain. Again it was overcaution rather than recklessness

that worked his undoing. Never would he let the car get a
reasonable start, with the result that it had to pump its heart
out to make a snail's pace. I carried no driver's license for
Indo-China, and should not have considered it courteous
to my host ahead to practise with his new Italian-minded
car on such a road if I had; hence I was totally at the mercy
of this mingled son of caution. A dozen times we snorted
to a halt before the maltreated engine quit entirely, fairly
near the top. The chauffeur's mental reaction to this emergency seemed to be to sit where he sat until the Goddess of
Mercy or some one else came to help him out, with the probability about a week off of another car passing. When at last
I prevailed upon him to get out and look at his engine, at
least out of curiosity, all he knew was to lift the hood, when
he fell into contemplation before the motor, mute with stupor,
as if he had discovered this strange machine for the first
time, until I expected him to bow down and kowtow in the
dust before it. He seemed to know as much about the work-
ings of automobile engines as of the gods in his temples,
and to have the same dread of looking into the secrets of
their power. But then, when I came to think of it, even I,
effete product of a garage and repair-shop on every corner,
knew no more about it than he did, so that after all he had
been right, and there was really nothing to be done except
what he had started to do—calmly to sit and wait for help.

That was no easy task for a man whose hair is habitually
ragged of edge because he cannot endure to hold the peni-
tents' seat in a barber-shop, and when we had been broken
down long enough to prove that neither of us could do anything useful about it, I walked on. Gusts of rain had fallen
during our climb, pedestrians each lopping off a banana-leaf
as an umbrella and dropping it where the shower ceased.
But the second-hand one I picked up at the next emergency

proved that as an umbrella a banana-leaf is waterproof, at least to the tropically inexperienced, only when one sits down under it. Luckily the showers were short and not very intense, and within an hour or so I was striding over the summit and down upon a few simple buildings. It was a military post named Nong-het, which turned out to be the station of the Bavarian-born lieutenant and his mixed lady-love, who had indeed invited me to stay with them on my return, should it happen that the rains made impossible the itinerary I had planned. Much good that did me now, with the hospitable pair still down at Muongsen.

The Annamese sergeant in charge massacred a few words of French, beating them out between his black teeth in a clogged stream from his betel-nut bloody lips, and there was no great difficulty in getting enough of his confidence to seat myself in the faded cloth easy-chair under the thatch roof of the lieutenant's earth-floored porch. In fact it was not long before I could have coaxed his cook to cook me something, if we had been able to find anything to cook. Obviously I could not broach any stores there might have been inside the lieutenant's thatched house, though it was locked with a piece of jungle twine, even had I been sure that the sergeant would permit it. In the long thatched barracks across the smooth earth parade-ground there were different kitchens and "beds" for the Annamese and the Laosian soldiers who made up the garrison, the former sleeping on wooden platforms, Chinese style, and the Laosians on soft springs of woven bamboo; and there were similar differences in cuisine and other customs. But that made it all the more difficult to convince the sergeant that surely there must be something native that could be made edible for "ung Flançais," as he persisted in calling me. Plainly the lieutenant or his protective companion had taught the sergeant the solemnity with which the rites of the table should be treated, and the sacrilege of mixing culinary breeds.

Finally, thanks to my well known persistence and persuasiveness, there appeared some rice and the toughest chicken for its tender age that I have ever met in all my travels, nay, on Broadway itself. This trial over, and a path worn in the parade-ground while we discussed beneath a sardonically grinning moon the propriety of my continued presence in the post, the sergeant at last consented to have collected for me in an outhouse a bundle of straw and a ragged blanket which I was just as well pleased not to have seen by day—or even by torch-light; and just as I was dozing off there came the choral shrieks, growing slowly louder, of a great gang of coolies whom the chauffeur had requisitioned to push the car over the summit to Nong-het. The suspicions of the sergeant and his post having been allayed by the chauffeur's acknowledging me, I found somewhat better quarters, now that my cot had come, out in the half-finished stone garages into which the Fiat had been coolie-handled. The chauffeur being hopeful, for some reason, of making the wop contrivance go on again in the morning by gasoline rather than by coolie-power, we turned in, he, somewhat less downhearted, curled up on the back seat of the car. Perhaps he thought whatever injuries the car had suffered would heal during the night.

He actually did get the thing under way again, long after sunrise, on three or five or seven of its four, six, or eight cylinders, as the case may be, and we covered twenty-seven kilometers along a now merely hilly road. Early during that feat we met and paused to chat with a French lieutenant driving back to Muongsen the Citroen *chenille* that had carried the general-in-chief to Xieng Khuang, the same in fact that had crossed the Sahara the year before; and but for that fatal optimism of motorists so long as their wheels are turning we might easily have had him repair whatever damage had been done us. Apparently neither of us thought even to mention our difficulties of a few miles back, yet almost as soon as the "caterpillar" was out of sight my substitute for a chauffeur halted before another cluster of huts, called Sala Nam-lien, and refused even to try to go farther, saying that something disastrous would happen to us if we attempted to proceed. As nearly as I could make out from his ignorance of his father-tongue, the car was certain to explode and strew itself and us all over the Annamese chain if he annoyed it any longer. Possibly Italian cars do succumb to such fits of Latin temperament; at any rate I was in no position effectively to argue the matter, and assassination is regarded as more or less reprehensible even thus far from the haunts of civilization.

Though I only suspected it then, I was destined to know Nam-lien better than I know my own birthplace, nay, than Paris or Rio de Janeiro. It consisted of a dozen thatched huts with earth floor and wattled walls on either side of the wide space that served as road, one of them the *sala* or resthouse for French travelers. Two bare woven-bamboo cots and a rough wooden table comprised the furnishings of this, unless one also counted the soft layer of dust on the earth floor as a rug. A few things such as eggs were purchasable about the village—though I should have been in hard luck indeed if I had not taken official advice and brought a few canned supplies with me—and a native was available to boil water and do the simplest form of cooking.

There I spent the rest of the day, sitting in the automobile, the only really comfortable place in the vicinity, reading, with a walk for exercise' sake thrown in. During that time I had much intercourse, in so far as that is possible without a common speech, with one of the principal tribes of the region. I had known the Miao, or, as the French call them, the Méo, in southwestern China, though there my acquaintance had been mainly with the "Flowery Miao" in their extravagantly colorful dress. These were "Black Miao," a much more independent tribe, and with almost no color in their black or dark-blue garments, sometimes set off by a dull red or purplish wine-colored scarf about the waist. Both men and women, often riding on horses, were a wilder tawnier type than their flowery relatives, their sturdy independence as plainly to be seen as their bare feet; for none of them, of either sex, had ever tortured their feet with shoes. Their sunburned hair and eyes were more nearly brown than black, and both sexes wore the hair long. Most of the men had carelessly wound turbans of dark cloth, a few of them wore Chinese skullcaps and dressed their hair Chinese fashion, old Chinese fashion, more exactly, for the majority still had queues, often hanging unbraided loosely about their shoulders. Another custom among these sturdy mountaineers is the wearing about their necks of heavy silver rings of all shapes. These are evidently concerned with their tribal superstitions as well as being their idea of combining adornment with safe banking. All silver money that falls into their hands is turned into rings; men, women, even the children, all wear them, large and small, from mere twisted silver wire to veritable horse-collars, some with open ends, some fastened with silver padlocks. Sometimes there are as many as half a dozen on a single neck, even of men on their way to work in the jungle. The richest of them clanked like perambulating pawnshops whenever they moved.

A critical observer might have wondered why they do not spend for shirting some of the silver dollars they turn into neck-rings. For the men wear a shirt or jacket that covers everything except what a shirt is most expected to cover, leaving bare a foot or more of the waist, with the navel as its central point of departure. But to every race its own ideas. The girls are not prudish, yet not at all forward. For their jackets, open almost to the navel and giving frequent half-glimpses of the breasts, were plainly designed for comfort rather than coquetry, as were their plaid skirts reaching hardly to their bare knees. The women walk with a powerful yet not ungraceful swing of the hips and a saucy flirting of their short pleated skirts, of which they are perhaps quite unconscious. Some of the men wear the tattooed blue panties ending in ruffles just below the knees that are common in Laos and the Shan States, but this is evidently due to extratribal influence, just as are the flowered silk gowns a few of the well-to-do among them wear after the fashion of the Chinese. The men, and sometimes the women, carry crude daggers in home-made sheaths; some had a long slender rifle, a few of them crossbows of a simple form, and most of them smoked or carried in their sashes pipes of sometimes elaborately tortured shapes. They use pack-oxen as well as little horses, but most of them, of both sexes, carry in a basket on their backs, though Chinese influence perhaps has led some to fasten two baskets at the ends of a short, stiff whole bamboo over a shoulder, thereby losing all the advantage of the long and supple shoulder-pole of China and Annam.

Some consider the Miao merely Chinese who in centuries gone by drifted down from the north, with a history similar to the Hakkas, but it is probably a better guess that they are of a more nearly aboriginal tribe than the Celestials. Sturdy enough in their natural habitat, they must live at least three thousand feet above sea-level to be either happy or healthy, just as the Annamese must stick to their miasmic rice-plains; and they never descend below that altitude if there is any way out of it. Of all the races of Indo-China the Miao are probably the most self-sufficient. In common with some other mountain tribes of Laos they burn off steep hillsides, normally every nine years, for their cultivation. When they need new fields to plant, they fell the biggest trees and set afire great patches of the jungle-forest, destroying wood and lumber enough to supply a large city for years to come. This burning is partly to drive off the blackleg fever and partly to give room for grass for their cattle; and as cinders make good fertilizer for a few years, their crops are abundant until it comes time to burn off another mountain-side. As this burning by patches has probably been going on for centuries, much of the Laos is not so forested as one expected it to be, but often covered with those half-grown forests which the French call *brousse*. Yet with all the uneven growth there are many magnificent panoramas of densely forested ranges.

I spent that night in the *sala*, and when, late next morning, it was still evident that the substitute for a chauffeur did not propose to do anything about it except to settle down there in the vain hope that some day some one might come along who might do something to help us out, I set out to walk. It was still about fifty miles to Xieng Khuang, but certainly there was more prospect of reaching there on foot than of having help turn up within the same length of time. Moreover my supplies were distinctly limited, even if the loss of time could be made up by abandoning the best part of the trip and returning as I had come. Besides, I am far better at walking than at waiting, and nothing

The chief sport of the mountain dwelling Miao of Laos is the making of assorted neck rings of silver dollars that might better be spent for shirting

A Kha woman of the semi-wild tribe that is said to be the aboriginal race of mountainous Laos

The Miao women of Laos take no back seat for their men

after all is more delightful than walking, especially on so splendid a route for it—high enough not to be too warm, the great jungle-forest opening new vistas, springing new surprises at every turn, at every rise of ground, so few of the tiresome human race as hardly to bother at all, and at every corner the chance of an adventure. So I swung off almost light-heartedly, even if to the mingled worry and disgruntlement of the worthless chauffeur, who evidently lost face with the village by this flaunting of his services and protection.

I had walked about ten alluring miles, or perhaps merely kilometers, when to my vast astonishment a big automobile came suddenly down out of the west upon me. In the capacious back seat, the top stowed away behind them, rode the general-in-chief of the French forces in Indo-China and a colonel aide. Having waited in vain for the conveyance that was to have brought me to Xieng Khuang in time for them to return by it, they had been forced to drain the province of its last thing on wheels, the Berliet—one car of each make seemed to be the rule here; once the road was officially opened they should know which performed best—of the *vice-commissaire*. Never have I been more pleasantly treated by a chance passer-by on the road. If the general's importance weighed heavily upon him he was an expert at concealing his burdens. To be sure, the fact that he also had been the guest of the ruler of Xieng Khuang whose hospitality I had been—enjoying? no, let us say suffering—since stepping into the Fiat of distressing memory, and that, having expected me two nights before, they had about come to the conclusion that I had been eaten by a tiger, may have had something to do with his geniality. For it seemed that the donkey masquerading as a chauffeur who had been sent for me had not disclosed to the harassed head of the province an inkling as to our plight, though one can telegraph in Indo-China from almost any tree-top.

The general was strongly of the impression that I should come along with them rather than continue my walk until the returning car overtook me, and the semi-guest of a government does not flout the opinions of its chief military officer. In fact the general had an insistent way about him, though it had on the surface none of that big-stick gruffness of too many of our own army officers. The change from walking to riding left me somewhat chilly; the general insisted that I put on his coat, which had been lying in the seat beside him. I protested that the insignia of such high rank did not become me, that he himself might need the garment. His reply was typical of an old campaigner in many lands, of one who had served France in almost all of her colonies:

"*Je n'ai jamais froid, jamais soif, jamais faim, jamais chaud.* When any of these things threaten me, *je fume une pipe,* and they disappear in a puff of smoke"—and suiting the action to the word he lighted up again.

We were soon back at the *sala,* where there remained enough of my meager supplies so that I could do my share toward providing a luncheon. While we ate, the fellow who had been sent to fetch me told the general some badly pronounced tale of why it was dangerous to try to go on, lifting the hood to prove it. Again it seemed to be something to the effect that he could make the car go all right, but that if he did so the engine might blow up at any moment. He seemed to convince the general, who was probably no automobile expert, and naturally the colonel always agreed with a superior of such high rank; hence there was nothing left but for me to agree also. I might have stayed on at Sala Nam-lien and, if the Berliet and its Annamese driver had the luck that had been denied the Fiat under the inexpert ministrations of the son of caution, have been picked up by it sometime next day on the way back from turning the general over to other transportation in Muongsen. But the general insisted that I give them the pleasure of my company as long as possible, and on second thoughts it was better not to trust myself to spend another night within reach of that mixed-breed chauffeur.

Besides, it was a pleasure to travel over that great mountain-side road once more, even though I might be less successful in climbing back to the plateau, and although the platform-bed in the rest-house of Muongsen was several times harder than the cot I had left over the mountains. The lieutenant of the Citroen "caterpillar" had the Guadeloupe-driven car ready for action again, and in spite of all the decorating Muongsen had done for him the general insisted on continuing eastward toward nightfall, leaving me alone in the riverside *sala* like the janitor of a ball-room amid the embellishments of an abandoned banquet.

I set out once more next morning before daylight upon that great climb from Muongsen to the plateau of Laos. This time fogs all but hid the world about us and made the road-gangs along the way seem more miserable than ever. But this Annamese chauffeur knew his trade and his car much better than did his predecessor in my affections, and while a man not so disgusted with a continual run of bad luck as to be willing to take some risk for a change might have complained at the speed he made on the brinks of bottomless precipices, we were soon at Nong-het over the summit again, then back at Sala Nam-lien, still adorned

with the stalled Fiat, in time for a skimpy lunch. From
there on, the Annamese let no grass grow under his wheels.
In fact I wonder if any ever grew again in some of the
spots they touched in our semi-aërial dash across the eastern half of Tran-ninh. It was startling to be able to race
what seemed hundreds of miles along an excellent, even
though grassy, automobile road through so primeval a region.
There was some more climbing, though it was by no
means so strenuous as the ascent up the face of the Annamese
chain, and at length, beyond a waterfall that came down
the mountain side within hand-shake of the road in a beautiful cascade of many strands of silver among jungle and
forest choked rocks and, dashing under the highway, dropped
far down below to form a reunited stream, we came out
of the great forest that had surrounded me ever since the
first afternoon out of Vinh. Here, a hundred kilometers
from the border of Annam, amid a plateau growth of
scattered oak-like scrubs, there was much open country, of
reddish rich-looking soil, though few inhabitants. In fact
all Laos, largest of the five divisions of Indo-China, being
about the size of Italy and not unlike it in shape, has, if
the recent census was accurate, only 818,755 people, of
whom 280 are French and eight—count them, eight!—are
"foreigners." About us lay vast rolling meadows of great
beauty, as virgin as a world in which animal life had not
yet been created. The general-in-chief, who had seen most
of them, thought this great plateau of Xieng Khuang the
finest region in the French colonies. There were some
cactus-trees of striking forms; then the mountains closed
in again on a narrow valley that seemed once to have been
broken up into rice-fields, though this may have been an
illusion. Small villages appeared once more, this time of
the real Laosians, villages of thatched houses raised on poles

well above snakes and possible floods, with a bit of cultivation about them. Each house had rounded gable walls at either end, one a kind of family veranda all but covered with a curving roof of thatch, where visitors are received and the family does its gossiping, the other a granary and store-room, where the cooking also seemed to be done. The walls of the houses, everything possible, in fact, were made of strips of narrow palm-leaves folded over a stick, forming panels overlapped like shingles. Many small but stout horses dotted the landscape here and there. I had not seen a grave for days; the Laosians dispose of their dead like real Buddhists; the Miao pile heaps of stone over their corpses.

This time fortune showed me unusual favor and we made the whole trip from Muongsen, including the stop at Sala Nam-lien, in a single day, as we might have done three days before but for the over-cautious chauffeur. In fact we turned up at Xieng Khuang toward the end of the daily siesta, and I spent the rest of the afternoon in French formalities with the colonial officials of that distant but little known Garden of Eden.

CHAPTER XV

HAVING ended on Saturday instead of Wednesday afternoon the first stage of a journey that at best had seemed in the beginning hardly possible in the time available, I made a tight fit even tighter by spending Easter Sunday in Xieng Khuang. For the *commissaire,* so long absent from the world at large that time had come to be a mere academic expression to him, had done so much to make my stay agreeable that to have hurried away again next morning would have been to increase a common French impression that to Americans personal convenience is more important than courtesy. Visitors do not come often to Xieng Khuang; besides, there are things of interest there, and whatever is worth doing, be it only a journey, is worth doing well.

There was the *commissaire's* zoo, for instance, a score of pets ranging from some distant member of the leopard family to monkeys that looked like puffballs, fittingly domiciled in his garden, with or without chains to assure their allegiance to a master from whose hand the fiercest of them ate with murmurs of pleasure. There are said to be more species of animals in the forests and on the plains of Tran-ninh than in almost any other space of similar size on earth—tigers, panthers, bears, gaur, gibbons, monkeys, deer, pythons, boa-constrictors, and a host of lesser serpents; a cobra was chased out of the yard of one of the French residents that very day; and the museum maintained this quarter-century past by a tropic-emaciated Frenchman was easily proof that the province is an unspoiled paradise of the ornithologist and the collector of butterflies and insects.

I spent the morning in a hot walk about the scattered thatched town, climbing to jungle-guarded half-ruined old stupas on the rounded hills behind it. Priests of the yellow robe had again appeared, dawdling about their simple monasteries with the leisureliness of men who know that to step on an insect means to be set back that far on the long and difficult road to Nirvana. Speaking of insects, the people of Tran-ninh boast that they are never troubled by mosquitos, because, all their domestic animals being at home under their pole-legged houses, these pests are so busy down there that they never trouble to rise to human height. The custom of living over unconfined stables is further exonerated by the warmth the animals are reputed to give the householders above—for so thin-blooded a race needs its central heating-plant also, during the short tropical "winters."

It was market day, and well fed, almost haughty women, with many brilliant reds and yellows in their dress, were squatted in the shade over their semi-tropical vegetables, and pottering homeward again in long broken files. They had almost nothing in common with the Annamese women, except their sex and the protection of the French. Their lustrous hair piled in great black glossy heaps on the top of the head in an intricate fashion, usually with a saffron, rose-yellow, or red cloth about it, and most of them with stomachers of similar gay colors, they were striking examples of the unrestricted portion of the human race. In complexion they were much like ourselves plus many layers of tan, but were noticeable for bad teeth. The Laosians do not enamel their teeth, but most of them chew betel-nut; and the women seem less unequal socially to the men than their Muong, even their Annamese and Chinese sisters.

In Xieng Khuang there stands a monument to six Frenchmen, five of them killed in France during the war, and one, like the dozen native soldiers whose names also appear on it, *tué par les Méos rebelles.* It seems there was a great Miao uprising in the Laos during the winter of 1918-19, the bloodiest battle of which took place at Nong-het, between the "rebels" and the French, more exactly the native soldiers of the French. It was no surprise to be told that German agents and money had fomented the rebellion, though saner French residents admit that the Miao had long wished to be ruled by their own rather than by Laosian chieftains. That was no unnatural demand, and by the terms of the peace now reigning between them and the French it has been granted. Nor does this change seem to put any great burden upon Miao justice, for in cases involving more than five piastres the contestants may appeal to the French authorities, whom they evidently trust more than they do their own chieftains. The end of the rebellion was typical of these stiff-necked mountaineers. The French issued an ultimatum that the Méo must submit by 9 P.M. on a certain day; and at 8:59 exactly, while the French commanders sat with their watches in their hands, the Miao chieftain strode in and capitulated. The puzzle still remains how a race without clocks managed to time themselves so dramatically. Now they seem quite friendly, though it is not they who put their palms together above their heads and come to the squat when a white man goes by.

It would never do to quote to our own prudish-tongued land all the conversation that passed between perfectly respectable members of the little French colony of Xieng

The origin of the great granite jars on the plateau of Xieng Khuang is
one of the unsolved mysteries of archæology

The Miao of Laos build their homes well above the ground and receive
visitors under a rounded front porch

The chief men of a Laosian village along the Nam khan turn out in honor of my princely companion

Khuang over the *apéritifs* and the Parisian repasts in the *commissaire's* big living-room. For it turned largely on matters of sex, even when, perhaps even more so when, any or all of the three or four French wives of the little official group were present; and those who have lived with them know that the French can bring a blush to the cheek of a New England spinster without having the least notion that they are skirting the precipitous edge of frankness. One wife, I recall, was vehement in her denunciation of the Germans because they have so many children to the family, implying that as the French are unable to compete in that line with their enemies over the Rhine, her beloved native land was sure to be the loser in the end. Yet she and her husband, an officer in the colonial gendarmerie, had been married nearly fifteen years and showed every outward evidence of being able to add to the decreasing population against which she fulminated. But I did not ask the obvious question. It was amusing, when it was not pathetic, to observe how all these groups of French colonials seem to consider it axiomatic that they should not be expected to produce children. Their very manner voiced their conviction that in consenting to "exile" to the colony which they helped to rule they had done enough for *la patrie;* and those who contributed a child or two in addition were rather pitied, and pitied themselves, as the victims of an unkind fate or a deplorable accident. In this community of Xieng Khuang, for instance, the ten or more French residents, most of them married, had one child—that is, legitimate white child—a baby girl.

The huge *commissaire,* now half invalid but still a great force in his province, and beloved apparently by all classes of its residents, was a survival of the earlier colonial days, when a man in his present position was virtually king of all he surveyed. His half-dozen pure-blooded dogs all wore stout canvas pants to assure their offspring against mixture with the local mongrel breed. But some officials had not taken the same precautions with themselves, and had several brown-complexioned children at school in Hanoi, though they were bachelors. I am sure they would not look upon mention of this as unkind criticism, any more than it is meant as such. It is all in the point of view. Neither they nor any of the French wives and husbands composing the official community of Xieng Khuang saw anything wrong in this situation. Had some prudish member of the English-speaking races opened a discussion on the subject with them, he would not have got beyond being assured that it would have been inhumane of the *commissaire* to expect a French wife to share with him the hardships of his productive years, when Tran-ninh was a houseless and an iceless wilderness, and that he was therefore compelled to vent his affections upon the native women.

The *commissaire* could still, with assistance, hoist himself into the back seat of a topless automobile, and that afternoon we drove out to see the archæological puzzle of Xieng Khuang Plain. It did not need the assurance of my immense companion, or of his antithesis, the Midi-tongued vice-commissary, whose Berliet was still the only available vehicle in Tran-ninh, to see that this great plateau should have a great future, in the modern Western sense of the word. Its climate is as delightful as its soil is fertile. One French colonist had already covered a bit of it with splendid fields of wheat and corn, while his pineapples were almost worthy of Hawaii. Yet somehow I caught myself hoping that it would never serve the exploiting portion of the human race as anything more than the excellent airplane landing it was already. Its present pristine glory was too infinitely removed from the horrible picture that sprang up in my mind as I listened half-heartedly to the enthusiasm of the two *commissaires,* of such plains in my own land debauched into cheese-box cities by real-estate "developers." Humanity is scarcely so precious that it must be fed or housed at the loss of such glorious spaces as this one across which we rolled toward *les jarres.*

Far out on the great plain, some miles from Xieng Khuang, are scores of immense stone jars, the mystery of which no man has yet solved. They are made of what the French call *grès,* a natural composite not unlike sandstone, yet quite hard; and they are so large that those I climbed into reached to my armpits and gave me almost room to squat. Many have fallen, some only partly, but the majority are still upright, for all the centuries that have rolled over them. Stone covers, some of them broken, lie on the ground among the jars, many of which are decorated with little clay Buddhas set up on them by the pious modern inhabitants. There are five hundred or more of these jars, in two groups a few miles apart; and the French, after their manner, though there is no money to be made out of them, have built what they call an "automobilable" road to both clusters. But even they have not been able to solve either the origin or the purpose of the jars. Made by some race lost in the prehistoric mists—for recorded history found them already here, much as they are to-day—they are the more puzzling in a region where there is no natural stone of this kind whatever. Amateur archæologists of Tran-ninh contend that they must have been brought on rafts across the lake that probably existed then where the plain is now, and set up on little islands that have become the knolls on which they still stand a bit above the general level. Were they used for storing food, as hiding-places of bootleg liquor, or were they places of burial? So far as appearances go they might have been either coffins or granaries. There are no signs of bones in them, however, no broken bottles or food-remnants either. But then, even bones would have had time completely to disintegrate during the unknown centuries since the stone age in which the jars may have been made, as they certainly were long before the pyramids, and probably before the monuments of Stonehenge. There remains the further mystery of how that prehistoric people, of which there are still found stone hammers, knives, and what seem to have been arrow-heads, fashioned these great hard-stone receptables.

Notwithstanding the time I had lost I decided to go on with the trip as planned, trusting to my own speed and my ability to induce speed in others to bring me through in the time available. So I was off once more before daylight, the *vice-commissaire* doing me the honor not only to lend me his Berliet and his Annamese chauffeur again, but rising to accompany me in person across the plateau and on into magnificent pine-forests. The road, planned to be continued some day across the next province to the borders of Siam, died out about seven in the morning at a hut or two called Muongsuoi. Within an hour the alleged horses that had been sent there days before to wait for me were ready, and I was off on the next stage of the journey. Two Laosian men chosen by the *commissaire* himself did their utmost to accompany me, as I hurried on all day by a trail through abrupt mountains covered with mighty forests along which it would have been a delight to saunter for weeks. Now and again a tropical rain did its best to delay me—first, as a warning, some isolated drops, astonishingly large and heavy, then suddenly a general tambourining on the leaves, quickly followed by torrents of water beating down in mad fury, the light lowering until it seemed to be growing dusk at midday. But I could not afford to be delayed merely to save myself and the men behind me a drenching, and except for the briefest noonday halt for cold fare washed down with red wine I raced incessantly on, into the evening, darkness, the blackest of nights. The little horses had long since lost all ability to carry me at anything like the pace I could make on foot, even had it been possible to ride them in the stumble-footed tunnel beneath the forest where it was impossible to see an obstacle even at the moment of sprawling over it. The last hour or more was down what felt like a great trough in the earth, set at a sharp angle, and in this I slid down to the Nam-khan River at 9:30, establishing a new record; for never before or since, many a French colonial and native ruler has assured me, has any human being gone from Xieng Khuang to Muongyu in a single day. I admit it sadly rather than boastfully, however, for though fate seems always driving me on at top speed, the record I would prefer through such scenery and bucolic delights as lay behind me would be that of the sloth family.

Out in the far outskirts of the earth one who at home is but a mere human insect among our wealthy and political great, our nobility of prize-fighters, football and movie stars, had been mistaken for a real personage, and the king of Luang Prabang himself had sent his own son-in-law to bring me to his capital. He was to be the fourth or fifth king I had ever seen, the second or third with whom I had spoken or exchanged the hand-clasp of greeting, and the only one, perhaps forever, who was so glad to make my acquaintance that he had sent to fetch me. The kindly reader, I am sure, will pardon my emotion. For I suspect that even he would boast of such extraordinary honors, equal in their Oriental way to being commanded to present one's self at court in Windsor—with a foot-note as to Queen Mary's sartorial requirements!

The plain facts of the case were that *Chao* Duong Chan— the "Chao" meaning prince in the language of this region— seemed to look upon me, even in the incredibly mud-bespattered state in which I burst forth from the jungle night, as his social superior. At first, evidently, he refused to believe I was I, not because of the bedraggled rags to which the day had reduced what no longer ago than that morning had been a costume fit to be seen at a *commissaire's* table, but because a telegram had apprised him of my departure, and every one in Laos knew that I could not reach Muongyu that same evening, whatever the evidence of the five senses. But in time the impossible was admitted accomplished, and the rest-house to which I had retired became a place of pilgrimage. We were down in the realm of woven bamboo splints again, and they were used for everything— walls, floors, rafters, granaries, fences, beds—though not for boats, as in Annam. The building to which I had climbed well above the damp and snaky ground was therefore so soft underfoot that there was really no need to open my cot, though nothing in the form of furnishings was to be seen. Gradually a murmur in the night became the sound of muffled voices; torches flashed here and there in the darkness, and at length there crept silently up the very slanting ladder masquerading as a stairway one barefooted smiling Laosian man after another, each bringing me a bouquet of heavy jungle-flowers in a banana-leaf cone, the traditional greeting to honored visitors to the kingdom, as the flower necklace is in Hawaii. Behind these village authorities, after a fitting lapse of time, came the prince himself, manfully erect, who presented a document from the government of Luang Prabang setting forth his rank and explaining the errand on which he had been sent. He was a slender young man of aristocratic features, this *gendre du roi*—son-in-law of the king, to translate one of the two languages on the paper he had laid before me—a prince in his own right many generations before he had married one of the royal daughters. He wore a reddish *sampot*, the adult diaper of Siam, Laos, and Cambodia, and a white jacket of French military cut, starched and spotless, as did also the chief local authority. He spoke excellent French; had in fact, unless my memory fails me, been at school in France, and all in all was a man whom any one might have thanked a king for offering as a companion on such a journey as lay before me.

We were off down the small river about seven next morning. To have started earlier, with a heavy fog filling the whole valley of a stream bristling with rocks and rapids, would have been dangerous. The king's son-in-law and I each had a boat, though I should have liked better to have had him with me, for the sake of information as well as companionship The craft were what the French call *pirogues,* long and narrow, as slim and long in proportion as a lead-pencil, sharpened at both ends, and just about as easily turned over. They were frailly made of boards barely an inch thick, tied together with vines, with a prairie-schooner top of banana-leaves held in shape by a network of bamboo splints, and movable back and forth as sun, wind, rain, or lack thereof suggested; and mine had a raised platform with a mat in honor of my super-princely rank. It was of about the size, and the comfort, or its antithesis, of the mule-litter of northern China, which it strangely resembled in its jerky overbalanced gait, teetering so incessantly that I could not even write rough notes in it. I had four boatmen, two at each of the slightly raised, distant, pencil-like ends of the craft, all wearing tattooed breeches but not much else. Sitting cross-legged and half pretending to paddle, these typical *piroguiers* of Luang Prabang seemed the personification of laziness, until one saw them in the rapids, the rock gorges, the genuine waterfalls they dare to shoot.

The prince in another pirogue always followed me as a sign of my high rank, not, I am sure, because he wished me to risk the countless rapids first. Each time I was certain the frail craft, writhing beneath me like a living being, would be dashed to pieces on the rocks that bristled everywhere and on which it scraped its bottom ominously at every drop. I was astonished, astounded as often as we emerged safely from another of these racing foaming perils. Yet though they worked like demons in the rapids, these boatmen of the Nam-khan, compared with the Chinese, with the Indians of the Amazon when they shovel water, were lazy after all, dabbing their narrow paddles into the stream and pulling them out again like playing children, and most of the time resting completely from that exertion. Again I disclaim any desire to criticize; had theirs been my lot in life I should certainly have worked as they did, rather than at the beast-like pace of labor that prevails in China. It was natural, since they can always pole their way up-stream, that they had never learned to toil like their South American prototypes, except in short spurts in the rapids.

Now and again the prince and I got out and walked ahead, while the boatmen stopped to study a maze of rocks that we were quite satisfied to let them try alone. Every few

Under the projecting porch of a typical house of Luang Prabang the woman weaves the family garments

Ordinary mortals assumed the squat when Prince Duong Chan addressed them

The women of Luang Prabang weave their garments, of ancient patterns, on crude looms, often in the shade of their dwellings on stilts

hours a cluster of jungle houses stood out in a tiny half-clearing on the high bank of the river, and most of these we visited. At each village the chief and the other men of importance, usually including several yellow-robed priests, came to pay their respects. Instead of snatching off hats or head-cloths, and performing an antic between a courtesy and an exaggerated bow, the form of salute in Luang Prabang is to come to a complete squat. Obsequious as this looked, it was evidently merely a gesture of politeness, for even the men of highest rank who had any intercourse with the prince, representative of the king in person, dropped to their haunches, and rose to human stature again only when the interview ended. In making any request of him, or in receiving anything from him, even the boatmen squatted, holding both hands, palms together, above the head. The village notables wore *sampots* of many colors—purple, pink, grass-green—topped by khaki coats of uniform cut, which they evidently donned in our honor. Always they brought us leaf-wrapped cones of flowers, usually on banana-leaf platters. A supply of these bouquets of greeting, one concluded, must be kept on hand for emergencies.

The women were usually the first to see us, for they were constantly bathing themselves and their naked urchins in the stream; and they were clever at getting into or out of their barrel-like single garment without unduly exposing themselves. I saw more bathing on that journey down the Nam-khan than during my two years in China, and less uncleanliness in all Laos than in the smallest Chinese village. The women of Luang Prabang, especially along the rivers, are no burden to their fathers and husbands so far as clothing is concerned. In every village we visited they were naked to the waist, and did not know it; at least they did not seem to be conscious that in other, often less modest lands, such a costume might be frowned upon. They wore a single piece of cloth, spun from cotton grown on the spot, and woven on hand-looms under their long-legged houses. Colored in the thread with dyes made from nuts and vegetable growths of the region, this strip is simply wrapped about the waist. Or, in the case of a few of the youngest, which in that backward land still means the more modest women, the unmarried perhaps, or at least those who had not yet borne a child, it is wrapped about the lower two thirds of the breasts, with correspondingly more of the legs showing. Thus one recognized the girls of flapper age by their shapely brown legs and the matrons by their resemblance in costume to the Venus of Milo. Once a child has arrived, the exposure incident to suckling it seems to overcome virginal modesty; or in the absence of offspring pride no doubt soon joins carelessness in casting out the habits of maidenhood, so that there were displayed the scrawny pendent udders of the sterile as well as the withered rags of old age. The sight of a white man appeared to move some of the women to cover their breasts, a mere matter of deftly raising the garment. Whether this gesture was a recognition of the susceptibility of the French —who surely could not have issued non-exposure decrees!— or a mere matter of politeness, like the male squat, there was no means of knowing.

Though they did not thrust themselves forward, the women of this region were not so retiring as those of most of the Orient. Some of them were distinctly good-looking, well formed, their skin of an almost golden color, enhanced by the frequent bathing of most tropical peoples; and at least one of these village maidens would not have looked at all out of place in a famous Broadway review—

except that she was far too modest both in dress and demeanor for such company. With the conversation at Muongsen still in mind, I took care not to touch these fair damsels in getting photographs of them, though with difficulty, since it has become almost second nature during two decades of wandering among camera-shy peoples to arrange by hand my subjects to the camera's liking. It would have been a sad ending to so officially attested a trip to have been charged with one of the most serious crimes in the Laosian code!

The people of Laos struck me as the most pleasing unspoiled race with which I came in contact in all my Far-Eastern wanderings, though I might have formed a less favorable opinion if I had tried to make my way among them without being sponsored by king and princes. We brought up at the end of the first day at Sop June—at least so it sounded—in time to photograph most of the inhabitants before concocting a dinner from our supplies over a beach fire. There was barely room in my narrow boat at the foot of the village bank to set up my cot, but with China and its crowded, filthy, noisy waterfronts in mind this was a haven of rest indeed. Next morning two big fat otter came out to gaze upon us from the foot of the often precipitous shore, looking in their wet coats, shining in the slanting rays of the rising sun, as large as seals. To my satisfaction, since I have none of the hunter in my soul, they disappeared in the water again before my royal companion could get his rifle ready, much less aimed. Something convinced me that he, too, was just as well pleased, that the Buddhist within him really condemned this aping of ruthless Western ways, with the added Oriental risk of losing face if he had shot without bringing down the quarry. Birds in comic-opera costumes flitted singly and in groups across the faces of the inclosing forest walls, a flock of parrakeets, screeching like a dismissed chorus, sometimes flying clear across the river. Big fish now and then jumped well out of the water, as if to take a look at us or at the scenery. Or they may have been reconnoitering, for curious wigwam-shaped fish-traps, held down by heaps of stones on a platform part way up them, are placed at the heads of rapids on the Nam-khan. Then there were weirs, draining into jug-shaped baskets with small entrances which forked prongs made almost impossible as exits, with a single opening in them just wide enough for the narrow pirogues to slip through; and even these were made impassable to the fish by a row of bamboos, one end of each held down in the river and the upper floating one pointing down-stream.

The villages were as much alike, once one had seen a few of them, as our own stereotyped cities: from half a dozen to a score of woven-bamboo-and-leaf shacks, light as big baskets, raised on posts, in a little clearing overrun with children, curs, pigs, and chickens—four forms of life all but universal the world over—and little else except the surrounding jungle. Chickens of both sexes, perhaps I should have specified, for in this one matter the people seemed to believe in monogamy and to have as many roosters as hens. It was in one of these villages of the upper Nam-khan that I saw the first of still another race, the Kha, which some consider the real aborigines of these forested mountains of the ancient kingdom, as they are indubitably the oldest remaining inhabitants. They were wild but harmless-looking men, wearing earrings, their women adorned with still larger ones. A Kha woman down from the mountains—for like the Miao they are a highland people—had tattooed arms and, at least while the prince and I were

there, was completely clothed from neck to calves, in decided contrast to the river-village women. In another
village several dirty Chinese peddlers, plainly not much
liked by the natives, sat almost insolently on the soft bamboo-splint floor of the clean *sala* maintained for more
cleanly visitors. It was in this same village that our boatmen knelt before the assembled authorities and asked that
new boats, or new boatmen, be provided, as they were tired
or homesick or something. To any one accustomed to
seeing the boatmen of China toil many times harder, often
day after day for weeks at a time, than these tropical fellows had for little more than a day, there was something
childish about them. The petition was promptly refused,
and in due time we took our leave and went on down the
ever wider and gradually less swift rapid-bristling river.

Finally, in the middle of the second day, we were forced
to grant the boatmen's request, for there came a rapid so
Niagara-like that no boats can navigate it. All our baggage
and supplies were turned over to coolies, behind whom we
walked in blazing noonday sunshine and deep sand around
the falls to another pair of pirogues, waiting for us ever
since the prince had passed here on the slow up-stream
trip to meet me, and were off again down an increasing
river until well after dark. The new crew were twin
brothers of the old, and the change of boats had made
little change in the endless series of rapids, for rarely
was there not at least one roaring in our ears—until, toward
evening, they came farther and farther apart as the river
spread out into a wide and almost placid stream. Palisades
and precipices had marked the place of changing boats;
farther down there were rock cliffs again, the ever larger
river cutting circles among them, mighty rocks that seemed

to have tumbled down from them jutting forth from the edge of the stream. The current was still swift, yet after a long afternoon of racing down-stream there was the same jagged heap of mountains just behind us, turning reddish lilac and purple from the setting sun ahead. Bamboo rafts, with little houses on them, made their way more slowly down the stream, so placid now that it mirrored the ever-lower hills densely covered with jungle-forest, networks of lianas, some trees completely shrouded in vines, whole hillsides of huge banana-plumes, flashes of birds across them. Women wearing nothing but skirts were getting water from the river; others, especially at sundown, were bathing themselves and their naked children. Bonzes in dirty yellow robes, loafing, or horse-playing to use up the energy their calling does not permit them to waste in work or domestic happiness, showed themselves here and there along the way. The people seemed darker, burned to an almost Madrasi color.

We landed well after dark, climbing a long flight of steps cut steeply in the earth bank, to find ourselves in a considerable town, as towns go in Laos, with a big, almost a palatial rest-house for distinguished travelers, and a military commander in khaki to greet us. To my astonishment —and to that of many others, it transpired—I found that my boat trip was ended. From just over there in the woods, it seemed, an "automobilable" road ran to the royal capital, and a Ford would come for us in the morning. Royally done indeed! Usually it takes nearly a week for this journey down the Nam-khan, but the high waters of spring had favored us beyond all precedent.

Next morning we strolled a couple of kilometers through splendid forests, to ride twenty-seven more in America's most plebeian conveyance along a fair dirt road that the jungle had already covered with grass in places, through incessant forest. Kapok falling from huge vegetable-cotton trees whitened the ground in large patches. Some of the tribes of Indo-China weave it into cloth. There were trees so covered with white flowers that they looked incongruously like those of our northern clime shrouded with the wet snow of spring.

I reached Luang Prabang town before the sun was high, being delivered at the door of another hospitable *commissaire*, this time still young and energetic and with a French wife equally devoted to her official duties and to their two small children. All the little French colony was still breathless with the news the telegraph had brought them the evening before, that I had accomplished the journey from Xieng Khuang to their very doors, as it were, in three days. There were hints that they credited this partly to American black magic. For in this wilderness land of perfect telegraphic service I had not only exchanged greetings with my family in Hanoï every evening except the one on the river, but the authorities at Xieng Khuang, Luang Prabang, Vientiane, even Hanoï, Paris itself for all I know, had been instantly advised of every step of my journey.

CHAPTER XVI

L UANG PRABANG, venerable capital of the ancient
kingdom of the same name, is a spacious town of a
few wide French streets, softly paved, if at all, with narrow Laosian streets like lovers' lanes between them. It
is well wooded, with roomy yards usually whispering with
palm-trees. In other words it is not a city at all, in the
crowded, noisy, Western sense, but a leisurely congregation of separate dwellings of simple lines, each in its ample
garden-park, or at least with sufficient ground so that its
opinions or doings need not interfere with its neighbors.
In short Luang Prabang town is in many ways what idealists
picture the cities of Utopia to be, whatever insurance com-
panies may think of the fire-risks involved in more thatch
than tile roofs. It sits on a bank of the upper Mekong,
more exactly the Me Nam Khong, that snaky dividing-line
between Siam and at least half of Indo-China, which in
time becomes one of the most important rivers of the
Far East. Just here it happens that it is not the dividing-
line, for a large chunk of Luang Prabang kingdom lies on
the Siamese side of the river. Tiresome persons of statistical
temperament tell us that the capital stands 340 meters, about
1135 feet, above sea-level; but one would hardly know
it from the number of overcoats required. In fact, though
it was still April, my host the *commissaire* knew the futility
of expecting a guest from the temperate zone to sleep until

he had been cooled off with a jaunt by Ford through the tepid after-dinner night.

There were two Fords in Luang Prabang, that which had come for me at Don-mo and one belonging to the king. It would of course have been bad manners for the *commissaire* openly to emphasize his real bosshood by sporting the better car; besides, the garage mechanics of the capital are as inexperienced as filling-stations are rare; hence the transportation that had been placed at my disposal lacked something of the regality of its rival, particularly in the matter of diligent polishing. There were also some horses, a few elephants, several victorias, even three or four rickshaws, though these, except perhaps that of the king inside the palace grounds, might as well not have been imported, for there were no men in this languid Eden both able and willing to pull them. Nearly every one walks in Luang Prabang, barefooted and silent, unless he travels by boat. For the most important conveyances are the long narrow pirogues, some of them surprisingly large, hollowed out of single tree-trunks, which ply the Mekong and the Nam-khan that flows into it above the town. On the bow of each boat there is almost sure to be a bouquet of flowers, a pretty custom, even if it is probably based on a superstition, and one in keeping with this gentle people of a land so kindly treated by nature. Huge fish are caught in the Mekong, weighing a hundred and fifty, two hundred, sometimes even two hundred and fifty—not pounds, but kilograms, fish so big that it takes ten men to carry one of them and one man to carry a severed head. It is easy to understand what the flap of such a fish-tail sometimes means to the fishermen in their frail vine-tied canoes. But it is just the fishing for such a people in such a climate; for every time they catch a fish they can—and usually do—

rest for a week without going hungry. Racing pirogues as much as twenty paces long lie bottom up on bamboo-horses under little thatch roofs here and there upon the high weed-grown river-bank at the edge of the capital, being used only in November during the annual regattas. For rowing—more exactly paddling—is the athletic sport of Luang Prabang.

The main street of the capital, dying out at either end in semi-jungle, is lined by a long market, facing the entrance to the king's palace. But for that matter there is a market just outside the royal palace in Madrid, too, and many beggars also, which here seem to be unknown, unless we count the yellow-clad priests sauntering along with their begging-bowls in the early morning. Even such an Eden as this is not without its serpents, however; and rattling chains on the legs of prisoners working about the town make strange contrast both to its quiet gentle atmosphere and to the regality of its king. The gay garments, especially of the female branch of the population, make doubly picturesque the market and the long lanes of greenery that represent streets. The women of Luang Prabang capital, unlike their country sisters in the rest of the kingdom, usually wear a thin silk or cotton scarf of bright color over their bare breasts, half covering them, and slipping coquettishly off when they wish to make an impression on one of the opposite sex. The Laosian women of the bush think no more of their uncovered breasts than they do of their bare feet; these sophisticated girls of the silken scarf in the capital recognize them as an asset. There was something about their every gesture that recalled our own flappers—with betel-nut taking the place of gum and of lip-stick. Yet their coquetry may be largely innocent, for the French assured me, in some cases rather regretfully, I thought, that in Laos there are few of the *congaïe* facilities so common in Annam.

The king's wives, and the girls of the royal family and of the wealthier class, wear a kind of swimming-vest, usually white, in addition to the brilliant scarf. Perhaps his Majesty does not wish charms meant for his own eyes alone to become even visually common property. Yet the royal wives themselves on the way to market had about them a hint of coquetry, even toward a foreigner, which seemed to be totally lacking among their sisters of the bush. Many of the girls of Luang Prabang wear enormous silver or pewter anklets, some of them weighing twenty piastres or more. Others wore chains of ten-cent pieces. So many French silver piastres have been turned into these anklets, bracelets, the metal collars of the Miao, and other forms of adornment that it is little wonder Indo-China now uses almost exclusively paper money.

Luang Prabang means Kingdom of the Divine Buddha. What more natural then than that there should be many Buddhist temples, shrines, and monasteries in its capital? Indeed there are so many on both sides of the river that the town might easily be mistaken for a holy city, devoted to priests and pilgrims. Some of the temple compounds are bare ground scattered with yellow-roofed buildings of Siamese or Burmese character, with big stupas made of mud bricks and more or less overgrown with vegetation, with mere cells raised on piles, in which languid bonzes meditate. Others are covered with groves of trees, shaded by masses of palm and banana leaves; but in them all great calm and quiet reigns. Just behind the main and market street fronting the royal palace is a rocky ridge called Pagoda Hill, two hundred feet above the plain and half encircled by the Nam-khan by which travelers unworthy of Fords come to the capital from the east or south. It is worth climbing if only for the view it offers of the idyllic city and its surrounding semi-jungle; and along it ramble queer old religious structures, including one built over a gigantic "footprint of Buddha" in the native rock. What feet that far-famed son of India had, and what seven-league boots, to have scattered, so long before the coming of railways and Fords, his bare footprints so far and wide over the Orient!

Some of the old priests of Luang Prabang are honored as demigods by the people of the kingdom. They step forth from their holy dwellings only with a ceremonial para-sol held over them, by one of the surrounding group of youngster attendants in the same bright yellow; and the French *commissaire* himself was almost servile in the re-spectful politeness with which he treated the most holy of them all, whose attitude sometimes suggested that it was he who 'had the upper hand. These bonzes may not even kill a flea, though the provocation must often be almost too strong to be borne; but they may eat beef and the flesh of other animals killed by some one else. Even the cynical French residents say they are real celibates, that they would be expelled from the order if they were caught breaking this particular vow. It might be harder to keep were not all young men expected to be priests for a year or two, as those of European lands become sol-diers, only the ones to whom the monastic life appeals retain-ing the yellow robe, which the great majority soon discard for marriage. Little less sacred than the priests are the dogs that all but overrun the capital, eating the food laid out for gods and bonzes, much as the sacred oxen of India take their toll from pious shopkeepers. Held in a kind of Buddhist reverence by the people and more or less

protected by the priests, these mongrels are not even subjected to muzzle or license, though the French would like
to improve their rules of sanitation to the extent of exter-
minating the harmless but self-confident curs.

But the French do not insist on imposing their religious
beliefs on their wards and colonies. In Luang Prabang they
go so far as to provide for the up-keep of the temples and
monasteries in the annual governmental budget. In a way
this is a means of supporting the educational system, for
the priests act as schoolmasters to their novices. In great
contrast to China, there is not a single Christian missionary in all the Kingdom of the Divine Buddha, not even a
Catholic priest. There was almost a sense of relief in
finally getting completely beyond the reach of missions,
however good an opinion one may form of mission work
in some of its phases. For in certain moods one feels a
species of boastfulness in our insistence that so alien a
race give up its own beliefs in favor of our more or less
generally accepted guess as to the after-world and how to
reach it, in our Western efforts to impose our philosophy of
life upon a people that has a not unworthy one of its own,
and one that seems to make them much happier than we are.

I had come to Luang Prabang, however, on the special invitation of its king, and my chief duty and pleasure was to
pay him my respects. Ignorance is ever embarrassing, so the
natural prelude to such an honor as a royal audience was
to find out something concerning the king and his kingdom, as one skims through the chapter-headings of an
author one is about to meet. That ancient land is hardly
known even to our encyclopedias, to say nothing of our
school-books, but a few basic facts were available in the
jungle-framed French offices of the capital, offices strangely

similar in their atmosphere of *paperasses* and official dignity to those French staff headquarters I had served in during the war. Languid as it is, Luang Prabang's history is not without its exciting moments. For its origin one must go back to that great Nan-chao kingdom, with its capital at Tali-fu in the southwestern corner of China, founded in 629 A.D. and destroyed six centuries later (1234), not by the Chinese but by their Mongol ruler, Kublai Khan. The Kingdom of the Divine Buddha is one of the remnant kingdoms of the great Tai race which, once holding a part of what is now China, was gradually driven west and south, losing or attaining culture until it varied from the high civilization of the Khmer to almost illiterate tribes, according to where its new lot was cast. Best known to the outside world by the Siamese word for man (*lao*), or as *shan*, from a Chinese word used in Burma, this people still prefers to be called Tai.

Laos has eight divisions, of which Luang Prabang is the largest and the only one still boasting a king of its own. A century ago most of it belonged to ethnologically related Siam. I have already mentioned that this greatest division of French Indo-China, about as large and of much the same shape as Italy, has fewer inhabitants than Detroit. This is largely because it was so often sacked, and its people killed by the Chinese, who wanted the land, or carried off by the Siamese to populate her sparsely settled regions along the Menam. A traveler who visited Luang Prabang in 1872 found it the most compactly built city of Siam, with the single exception of Bangkok, which it in some respects resembled. But of several disasters the greatests seems to have been in 1887, when the Black Flags of Taiping days in China burned and almost completely destroyed and depopulated it, so that perhaps it is not by choice of its up-and-coming citizens that it is so roomy, pastoral, and ideal a city to-day.

The same altruism and love of their fellow-man that has given the French the arduous task of protecting the rest of Indo-China led to their present position in the affairs of Laos. About the time the Chinese from Yünnan were pillaging Luang Prabang kingdom a Frenchman named Pavie was sent there on a mission. The father of the present king, born *Tiao* Kham Souk, who lived from 1837 until 1904 and reigned under the name of Ritthithamaronjsac— though he was more popularly known as King Zacharine, and probably not entirely on account of his sweet disposition—was an absolute despot, descended from a long direct line of similar rulers. For the Kingdom of the Divine Buddha has been a kingdom as far back as the memory of its people goes. Zacharine became a great friend of Pavie, at least according to such data as was available in the French government offices of Luang Prabang, and when the Siamese failed to protect him, as they had promised, against the Chinese, he went to Siam under Pavie's wing; and later, in a quarrel with the Siamese, who had burned and looted and carried off most of the people of Vientiane and Xieng Khuang, he made the mistake, like his royal neighbors of Annam and Cambodia, of calling in the French. By 1893 Siam had been compelled to give up all claim to this ancient kingdom and to the magnificent highlands of Tran-ninh, and all Laos became a European dependency under the protection of France.

My host the *commissaire* chose a victoria for our descent upon his royal ward, no doubt feeling that to have used his Ford would be to call unnecessary attention to himself as the only possessor, besides his Majesty, of so regal a conveyance. Besides, the leisurely open carriage was far more in keeping with the calm and woodsy atmosphere of the metropolis of Laos. The king's palace is a building mainly in French style, more like a hotel with a steeple-cupola than the abode of an Oriental potentate. It stands in a fairly spacious yard, not quite large enough to be worthy the name of park, on the eastern bank of the Mekong, at the foot of the hill graced by Buddha's footprint; and it was somewhat in disorder. Chairs were kicking about the foreign-style dining-room, and there were other suggestions of a late party and oversleeping servants. The building was quite new, it seemed; there were few decorations on the walls yet, though a man had come all the way from Paris to cover them with paintings. Evidently he had found the climate not conducive to constant work, particularly work paid for by the day by a protected people; for surely he could not have discovered a means of squandering his time in the social amenities of the king's harem, and there was no other means of accounting for his Oriental leisureliness of execution.

Royal servants went to announce us, though word of our coming had been sent ahead, and while we waited I mentally reviewed the information I had gleaned from the Oriental Almanach de Gotha it had been my privilege to consult at French headquarters on the eve of my royal reception. I make no claim as to its exactness, and still less to that of my memory; but there is a probability that both of them are approximately correct. *Tiao* Sisavang Vong Somdet Prah, present king of Luang Prabang and a direct descendant of an endless line of its kings, was born in 1885, on July 14—no wonder he is a favorite of the French—and succeeded his father Zacharine in 1904. His mother was not his mother, so to speak. For *Tiao* Thong

With a silk scarf worn loosely over a shoulder the women of Luang Prabang capital are more coquettish than their waistless sisters of the country districts

Wind-sieved rice is the principal food of the rural inhabitants of Luang Prabang

The palace of the king of Luang Prabang sits placidly on the bank of the
upper Mekong

The king turned out his chief dancing-girls and masked male entertainers
for my approval

Di, first wife of Zacharine, still known as the Queen Mother, and real ruler of the royal household, bossing even the king himself in domestic matters, according to reliable verbal information from a French and feminine source, had no male children. The second-rank wife, *Tiao* Thong Si, daughter of a high mandarin related to the royal family, gave birth to the present monarch; but in Laos as in China every child is officially the offspring of the first wife. His father Zacharine seems to have been a temperate person, considering his advantages, for the king has only three half-brothers and six half-sisters; though it is possible that Zacharine died with certain secrets buried in his bosom, Occidental fashion. Half-sisters and half-brothers may marry in Luang Prabang, by the way, which is not without its effect on the reigning house. Also *Tiao* Sisavang Vong Somdet Prah has at least this much in common with his English colleague, that he had an older brother who died, leaving him unexpectedly heir to the throne.

The latest calculations were that the present king had fifteen wives and about forty children; on this second point' he did not seem to be very exact himself, no doubt finding it difficult to keep strictly up to date in domestic events within his household. Yet he did not look either worn or dissipated, when presently he came in to shake hands and sit down with us, perhaps because the Queen Mother takes so many of the palace cares off his shoulders. Seven of his sons were studying at the *Lycée* in Hanoï; and the crown prince, Savang Vathama, then sixteen, was nearing his bachelor degree in a similar institution at Montpellier in France, with the avowed intention of studying law afterward. The king himself had a purely Laosian education under Buddhist priests until King Zacharine sent him to a French *collège* at Saïgon. Later he went to the Ecole

Coloniale in the Rue de l'Observatoire in Paris, where French youths prepare for a career in the colonies. He came home once when his father was ill, but upon his recovery was sent back to France to get together a printing establishment with Laosian characters and to learn how to run it, which makes him more or less related to the late kaiser, bookbinder.

The king was plump and pleasant, handsome for his race, by no means betraying his all but forty years. It was easy to imagine the girls of Luang Prabang, if not indeed of France, "just crazy" about him, quite aside from his royal rank. He had a frail Oriental mustache and that beautiful bronze-brown complexion of his race. Unlike most European monarchs he is purely of the blood of those he reigns over. But his Majesty indulges in the chief minor vice of his people, and the only blot on his manly beauty, and not even that of course to the fair ones of his own land, was that his teeth, though they were not enameled, were discolored and his lips somewhat bloody with betel-juice. Even now he seemed to be nursing a quid, though with a regal finesse that it would have done our secret chewers of tobacco good to see.

He wore a white cork helmet, a black bow-tie about a standing white collar on a stiff white shirt with the round cuffs of a decade or more ago, and a snow-white three-button coat which, in so far as my meager knowledge in sartorial matters is trustworthy, was of the latest model. The fact that the middle buttonhole was attached to the upper button may have meant either a dreadful ignorance of Western ways, or merely unseemly haste in leaving his harem; or it may have had no significance whatever. His feet were quite properly incased in low black shoes of faultless last and luster, but—let the spinster reader blushingly turn the page here—he wore no trousers! His rank and calling, it seems, forbade him these final touches to an otherwise perfectly European costume. Instead, his thighs were inclosed in the *pha* or *sampot,* such as is worn by both sexes in Siam and adjoining countries under Siamese influence. It was a kind of short skirt, evidently of silk and of colors verging on the gaudy, drawn between the legs and tucked into the belt at the back, reaching to just below the knees in front and "rather less than 'arf o' that be'ind." Naturally a full-fledged king could not leave the hiatus uncovered and keep his self-respect. Therefore between *sampot* and shoes the royal legs were clad in silk stockings of which the most regal young lady of our own land might have been proud— except that in her case they would no doubt have been of a color to deceive the uninformed observer into thinking she wore no stockings whatever, whereas in backward bar-barian Luang Prabang this would have been bad form. These were jet-black and reached so far up the back as to suggest that they were held by a band about the waist. Indeed, it was immediately evident that the king had missed a splendid chance for extra decoration by not wearing a pair of red garters just below the knees.

A goodly proportion of the royal income must be spent on stockings. For I was assured, not merely by common rumor but by all the Frenchwomen in Luang Prabang—of whom there are three or four—that his Majesty will under no circumstances wear anything but silk about his shapely legs, and that a stocking with the slightest hole in it is im-mediately discarded. It would be easy to imagine his wives, of whom he fortunately has fifteen, scrambling for these discards of the royal wardrobe, and racing for their darning needles, were it not that in Laos even the wives of kings do not wear stockings.

But do not for a moment gather from all this that *Tiao* Sisavang Vong Somdet Prah had the slightest hint of the barbarian in his appearance. Except for the sacred *sampot* in place of trousers, and the proof of a king's income between that and the shoes, his Majesty would have attracted no attention whatever in a Palm Beach crowd, unless it were by his athletic build and his agreeable undissipated smile, and, at close range, the light touch as of fresh blood on his lips beneath the thin well clipped mustache. In fact of all the kings with whom I have hobnobbed he was the most pleasing to look upon, and to all outward appearances a gentleman not even given to bullying his wives. His lapel was adorned with the little red button of a French decoration—the Legion of Honor, I fancy, though I confess to a deplorable ignorance of these important matters—and a gold watch-chain hanging from this drew attention to what was evidently not the thinnest of watches in the outside breast-pocket. A signet-ring not unlike those of our West Point and Annapolis graduates encircled his wedding finger, and he wore a cord of what looked like ordinary string about each wrist.

This cord decoration is something peculiar to Luang Prabang. The *commissaire* wore them also, as did his baby son; possibly his charming lady did too, though I am not sure that mere women are worthy of them. Cords are put about the wrists amid elaborate ceremonies and must be worn for at least seven days if they are to be effective in preserving the wearer from evil. The king himself had come to tie those about the wrists of the *commissaire's* newly born son and heir and thereby assure it constant good luck through all the menaces to health among European infants living in the tropics. The French are good colonists partly because of their wisdom in keeping up and even taking part in such simple and harmless native customs, which the average American and British colonial official would probably scorn as "poppycock," if he did not actually try to uproot them. "Poppycock" it is, to be sure, but the effect which a little sympathy in such matters has on native populations is not.

The king spoke a fair but throaty French, but was not exactly talkative in that tongue, whatever he may be in his own and in the intimacies of his harem. In fact, contrary as it may be to our movie and popular-novel conception of royalty, he was rather bashful, with a schoolboy dread of making a mistake in the foreign tongue he was using, and at the same time evidently fearful of doing or saying anything that might displease the French. His demeanor was a curious mixture of regal old-family pride, a pride reaching so far back that we mere moderns from a barbarian world were not worthy of knowing the secrets of life behind it, and of the anxiety of the star in a royal movie being filmed under the eye of the manager of the great Jewish corporation that is "putting him across." All of which did not remove the first impression that *Tiao* Sisavang Vong Somdet Prah would be a fine fellow to take along for a tramp or a swim, and that it would not be long before one could begin calling him "Prah Old Top."

All hands seemed a little ill at ease. Having exchanged the usual platitudes, we stood about doing nothing much, paused with admiring mien before a new bronze bust of the king, covered with medals and decorations, and a good likeness, though of no better color than his actual complexion, but showing neither the betel-red lips nor the cigarette that drips almost incessantly from them. His Majesty handed out atrocious French tobacco-monopoly cigars worthy of a Chinese *tuchun,* but wisely stuck to cigarettes himself, smoking one after another in rapid succession. We chatted a little on general subjects, the impression growing that the king's French was good enough if only he could have thrown off the feeling that it would be an intolerable disgrace for a king to make an error in speech. Can it be this that makes modern monarchs and presidents so taciturn? Among the thoughts that passed between us I gathered that he wished to visit the emperor of Annam when Khaidinh celebrated his birthday the following year. I have never heard whether he was able to do so, but if he and his fellow-protégé, whom he so far had never met, were allowed to get together out of hearing of the French they must have had a great chat—provided of course that they had a language in common.

At a mere suggestion from my companion, and as if it were a relief from a tense situation, his Majesty graciously stepped to the main doorway of the palace, an excellent jet-black background for a blazing tropical sunshine that outdid anything Hollywood can devise in lighting-effects, and posed for his photograph. Another merest hint from the *commissaire* and *Tiao* Sisavang Vong Somdet Prah went off at once like a small boy to dress up for his picture, and came back in a surprisingly short time in his most regal robes, a radiant royal costume quite beyond my power to describe. All the medals on the breast of bronze near-by were now in place on the living model; he was again in women's silk stockings, quite evidently brand new, and this time held up by round-the-leg garters of brilliant hue. A green and saffron flowered-silk *sampot*—but how foolish for a man who cannot even describe a ball-dress well enough to give his wife any conception of it to attempt so impossible a job as this!

Never have I found a king more docile in meeting my

every suggestion. Barely a whisper from me and he ordered his throne-room decked out in its coronation best, had his royal attendants summoned. Cringing flunkies brought in swords of state, big golden bowls, a marvelous hat of half cowboy half women-of-the-plume-days style, studded with jewels, and with a Burmese-pagoda top. Ascending his throne, the king assumed his most regal aspect, his white gloves flashing like those of a traffic policeman during a Catholic procession. The master of ceremonies of the palace himself brought tables and other regal paraphernalia to off-set my lack of a tripod; two men in green, each holding a great sword, knelt fearfully at the foot of the throne, and—and I muffed the picture. No doubt the nervous tension of photographing kings on their thrones in their coronation-robes would be enough to cause an even calmer and more experienced photographer to misjudge tropical light conditions; at any rate I so under-exposed that strip of film that only those with keen eyesight can make out more than the general lay-out of the throne, and the king's white-gloved hands on his richly sampotted knees.

Lesser catastrophes have left broken hearts, but it did not so much matter about that throne-room picture after all, for, again at the merest suggestion of the *commissaire* and as promptly as a circus seal obeys its trainer, the king once more stepped to the spotlighted doorway of the palace, hat, robes, medals, and all, to give my camera another trial, finally posing with his French boss at his side. The *commissaire* was also in all his glory. Three great medals that proved he had done this, that, or some other brave deed—for he was not a man to have successfully bootlicked this, that, or the other high authority—blazed over his heart. His white uniform coat and black trousers had fancy neck, waist, wrist, and trouser-seam bands; he wore a sword, with rich belt-tassels, and carried white gloves, though the white *casque* on his head and the black shoes on the blistering pavement had nothing unusual about them. In short his dress was as out of keeping with his plebeian name of Mill— were names translated—as it was with the simple backwoods life about us. Finally his Majesty, of his own volition unless my eyes were momentarily off their guard, was graciously moved to insist that I also stand beside him in the doorway spotlight and let the camera again do its worst. In vain did I plead my unworthiness to be thus immortalized, like one of the boon companions of his Majesty, particularly in my vagabondish incongruities of rumpled semi-whites, once-tan shoes still half decided to be black, a necktie that insisted on the right to be temperamental in a tropical climate, a pocket bulging full of—how should I know what? The king, I long afterward noticed, wore quite a different face in these pictures in true royal garb than that of the genial boulevardier he presented in mufti, something like his own elder brother, with all the cares of state upon his shoulders.

But all this was only the beginning of the honors that were heaped upon me before that epoch-making day was done! Immediately after the signal distinction of being photographed by the resplendent *commissaire* at the side of the even more luminiferous king I was knocked breathless —or at least I might have been if the *commissaire* had not that morning whispered to me the possibility of what was to happen next, probably before the king himself had thought of it; in fact there had been subtle hints to that effect as far back as Xieng Khuang, if not in Hanoï itself— by the announcement that his Majesty was about to confer upon me his most regal decoration, the most prominent of the many medals on the breasts of the *commissaire* and of

The king met us at the door of his palace

In his royal garb the king was a resplendent being, even beside the French commissioner in his full-dress costume

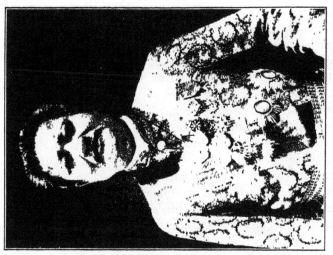

Tiao Sisavang Vong Somdet Prah, king of the ancient kingdom of Luang Prabang

His Majesty insisted that the day would not be complete unless I posed beside him

the king himself, both in bronze and in the flesh, the highest honor of which this protected Oriental potentate is capable, something corresponding in Luang Prabang to the order of the Rising Sun in Japan, to wit · the order of the Million Elephants and the White Parasol! For you must know that Luang Prabang is not only the Kingdom of the Divine Buddha but even more officially the Kingdom of the Million Elephants and the White Parasol, just as King Sisavang Vong Somdet Prah's real title is Master of Heaven and of Life. I do not know whether it is actually claimed that there are so many pachyderms in the kingdom at the same time, but a little exaggeration is always admissible in the tropics; or it may be that the souls of departed elephants are also included in the reckoning.

The king announced his magnificent intention by a little speech in French, with a manner strangely like that of a school-boy sentenced to make the class presentation speech to a favorite teacher, and from it I gathered that I was to be decorated because I was the only American—and the word he used made it mean of either North or South America—who had ever done his humble capital the honor of visiting it. The only one of whom there is any official record, no doubt he meant, if indeed he was not indulging in a bit of royal spoofing; for it is known by many, if not by the king himself, that at least one Protestant missionary once came through the kingdom on a scouting expedition, and the chances are that he was American. But naturally he had not announced himself to the constituted authorities of a country that does not allow Christian mission work, and it may be that he did not enter the capital.

I had hitherto always been under the delusion that the bestowal of an order meant the pinning on of the corresponding medal by the bestower's own fair or sun-burned

hands, and with war days in France in mind I knew not
what moment I might get a betel-juicy royal kiss on either
cheek. But this dreadful misgiving was but another evidence of my appalling ignorance. On the contrary, to be
decorated evidently meant merely being given permission to
decorate myself. It is true that there was handed me later
in the day an engraved diploma, in Siamese and French,
bearing here and there three elephant-heads surmounted by
a white parasol, and with my name written on the dotted
line by a master penman who certainly had not learned his
calling in a Buddhist-monk school. It was neatly rolled inside a section of bamboo to protect it from the rainy season
that was almost certain to break upon me before I reached
modern forms of transportation again. In fact I am not
sure that the king did not personally bring me this diploma,
though I do know that it was prepared in the French-
staff-like government offices far from the royal palace. But
the medal itself, the visible public proof that I have been
honored beyond any of my fellow-countrymen, any of my
fellow-hemispherites for that matter, I should have to spend
many francs for in a department-store at Hanoï, if ever
I reached there again. Being as Scotch of disposition as
I am abhorrent of the red tape incident to making a pur-
chase in a French department-store, I should certainly never
have squandered that hard-earned money, even with the
franc at one of its lowest ebbs, had not the family tyrant
absolutely insisted, refusing even to discuss the matter.
She won of course, and the gaudy elephantine-parasol trinket
and the ribbon in Spanish colors that goes with it has been
tucked away somewhere among my rarely-unpacked belongings ever since. Ah, those happy bachelor days when a
man could do exactly as his whims or his conscience
prompted!

I might wear that medal now, or at least the modest lapel-ribbon that stands for it, if I did not realize the injustice that would be to those of my veteran friends who, having risked their eyesight and digestion at Paris and Chaumont over maps of the western front, are entitled to display similar adornments to an envious, disappointed world, or if I were not fearful of being mistaken for a visiting Elk or Moose or some other fraternal wild animal and dragged into the gilded cages provided for those creatures. My resentment at being forced after all to decorate myself, by way of the pocketbook, has subsided, for it seems the same rule is true of Phi Beta Kappa pins and class numerals; but I shall never entirely forgive Luang Prabang for bringing me as near as I ever expect to come to the divorce courts. For when everything was over, and I had broken the great news to my son at Hanoi in the telegrams we exchanged on that most auspicious occasion, which chanced also to be his fourth birthday, I discovered to my domestic dismay and perpetual regret that the order of the Million Elephants and the White Parasol is also conferred upon women—at least of France and allied countries—and that if the king had suspected that I had a wife—queer I did not show it after nearly five years of married life !—he would have—but what is the use of bewailing what is past and done with and irreparable?

The decoration speech over, the king ordered out his dancing-girls, deathly pale with hastily floured faces, and his male entertainers, in masks meant to be terrifying, the gaudy colors of their festive garments contrasting with the scarcity of soap discernible through the crevices of their costumes. They posed rather fearfully. Some of the girls were as young as ten, I am sure, and certainly none of them were over twenty, for the king has a Broadway taste in these matters. Dancing-girls and masked male figures alike wore an elaborate headdress in the form of a pagoda—the Rangoon style of pagoda, not those of China—which suggested a close cultural relationship between Luang Prabang and Cambodia. As to the welter of colors that flashed forth from them in the blazing tropical sunshine I shall not even attempt to say anything; just let the bootlegged imagination run riot, so long as you do not forget the reddish teeth and the swollen lips driveling with betel-nut that gave them the look of ghouls that had just eaten a warm corpse, or of harmless childish-faced trolls that had been caught in the act of gorging themselves with currant jelly in the royal jam closet.

Neither the dancers nor their king gave any sign that I had outstayed my welcome; nor was I expected to back away from his Majesty when at last I voluntarily took my leave. But I have a suspicion that there was more frankness in the attitude of the baby elephant that was cavorting about the royal lawn in the wake of its chained and mahout-ridden mother. For when I tried to coax it into a proper filial position for a photograph the little beast set out after me in a manner entirely out of keeping with its status as the property of a tame king. So graphically could I still describe this experience when I reached Hanoï again that to this day my son regards the time when the elephant "switched its trunk" about me as the height of my intrepid career.

The king of Luang Prabang keeps a number of royal elephants; and he is no nonentity as a business man either, by the way. Supplementing his salary, if the word suits a monarch, of forty-six thousand piastres a year, and thereby offsetting his consumption of silk stockings, he has much private property, including great forests and sawmills, in which many of his elephants work for him. For a time some of the royal elephants were assigned the task of dragging rollers used in the making of roads about the capital; but they are a tender beast, for all their size and reputed longevity, and even with only four or five hours of labor a day, at their two-mile-an-hour gait, with the privilege of resting every third day, two of them died from this unwonted exertion. The king, evidently no figurehead in his capacity as business manager of his personal estates and property, protested, and from four to six water-buffaloes to each roller now take the place of an elephant.

In theory the many wild elephants in the Kingdom of the Divine Buddha also belong to the king. When new recruits are needed in the royal stables, some of the wild beasts are caught by digging pits. Then a tame and a wild one are chained together, leaving the wild elephant to tug furiously at a collar with sharp iron points in it. The most bellicose are fastened to a tree by a lasso about a hind leg until they are worn out with struggle and hunger, when the two largest *éléphants de chasse* available take the captive between them and shake and roll him until he decides, like the man who foresees the lawyer fees involved in an action for divorce, that after all he will be happier in the domestic state. Most of those captured do not wait for this third degree, but, suddenly resigned to their new fate, give in to the barbed collar and stroll homeward with their false brother, pulling up tufts of good grass as they go and calmly tapping each mouthful on a front foot to shake the earth off the roots before transferring it to their dainty mouths.

Whatever the baby elephant may have meant by accelerating my exit from the palace grounds, the king himself evidently had no intention of dismissing me so cavalierly. For

within an hour of our arrival home, that is, at the rambling
one-story soft-brick house of the *commissaire,* with its crow-
ing roosters—if I could rule a king I should at least banish
roosters from the back yard on which the windows of my
honored guests opened—his Majesty came alone in his Ford
to return my call and stay to lunch. He had changed back
into civilian garb—not the same garments of course in which
he had first received me—perfectly European again except
for another gay silk *sampot* and black silk stockings out of
a newly opened box. Were kings relieved of the task of dress-
ing and undressing, what duties would there be left for most
of them anyway? He was received like any other invited
luncheon guest, though he was always addressed as *Majesté*
by the *commissaire* and his well chosen wife, and the half-
dozen French functionaries they had been able to scrape
together in the kingdom. In lieu of a box of chocolates his
Majesty had sent ahead some Laosian food that is served
as dessert at the royal table. One dish was a kind of custard
cooked in small cocoanuts, the base of the husk cut down to
resemble the shank of a goblet, and preserving the cocoanut
taste. Another was a kind of vermicelli covered with nut
dust, not unlike a similar dish in China. The ordinary people
do not indulge in such delicacies, which are reserved for the
royal palace. Even there, according to my hostess, there
are few changes of menu. The king was well versed in
Western table manners, though he did not take a very active
part in the conversation, which of course was in French.
He showed up best as a sympathetic listener, and was easily
amused. In so far as my own almost unknown country
was concerned, he seemed to be particularly interested in the
Mormons and in what the French call the *régime sec.* He
laughed for some time in his merry yet kingly way when
told that Brigham Young had forty wives and a correspond-

ing number of children, apparently without seeing any connection between this and his own fifteen and forty respectively. Or it may be that he was laughing at the plight of Brigham from the vantage-point of his own experience. The *régime sec*, in other words, prohibition, he plainly did not understand at all, any more than does the average Frenchman, and there was nothing to be gained in trying to make clear the American point of view on the subject. He would of course have been horrified to learn that there are persons in that benighted wineless land from which I came who have never heard of his ancient kingdom; nor did I feel it quite safe to pad out the conversation by bringing up the question of silk stockings in its relation to our national economic problem, for one can never be sure just how sensitive kings may be on these very personal matters.

It became more and more evident, however, that *Tiao* Sisavang Vong Somdet Prah was not born anybody's fool, even if circumstances and the foolishness of his father Zacharine had left him and his kingdom in an embarrassing position. There was something behind his Oriental-Gallic courtesy and his almost perpetual smile. Nor did he seem to take himself or his regality or his white elephants or any of the rest of his royal trappings too seriously. On this subject of white elephants, by the way, he mentioned that one was now supposed to be on its way to him, some Laosian merchants among his loyal subjects having captured or purchased such an animal that had been seen in a distant part of his kingdom. He thought Bangkok used to have one but that his Siamese peer was now forced to do without this adornment to their respective kinghoods. They were not white anyway, he went on, but rather a pinkish light-gray, like the albino water-buffalo; and his manner implied that whatever his royal cousin of Siam might think about it, a white elephant to him would be merely an interesting addition to his menagerie. "May you live as long as an elephant!" is a common form of greeting in some parts of the East; but quite aside from the doubtful kindness involved, it is based on one of those many mistaken beliefs of mankind, according to the king, corroborated by all the French present, who asserted that no elephant ever lives longer than have many men and women. As monarch of what may be the most elephant-infested corner of the globe he should be a credible witness on the subject.

All through the luncheon the punka over our heads had moved in fitful spurts, for the coolie squatting on the cool *dalles* of the veranda outside fell asleep even in the presence of royalty. His Majesty was as hard to get rid of as an awkward country cousin, and the hostess grew visibly fidgety before he finally remounted his Ford, for her other guests included the doctor who should long since have been back at the government hospital, and other functionaries eager to take up their protective duties again, yet who could not of course show any desire to leave so long as their monarch and master remained. One somehow had the feeling that a king would wish to get back to his affairs of state, or at least to his harem, as soon as possible, but this one gave evidence of so greatly enjoying his luncheon party that he seemed capable of sitting there forever listening and smiling.

There are really four kings in the Kingdom of the Divine Buddha, or were until one of them recently died. None of them are to be replaced, however, as they pass on toward Nirvana, except this real one with the title of *Majesté*. The others are merely *Excellences*. Twice a year all the chiefs of Luang Prabang, which is a province of Laos as well as a kingdom, come to the capital for a conference under the

A Miao woman on her travels carries bed and food

Two royal elephants saw me off from the palace, the youngster showing a desire to make me depart on the run

French *commissaire*. It is a leisurely conference, one fancies, for the people of Luang Prabang, high or low, do not include the word "hurry" in their active vocabulary. Not long before, the king had gone to Hanoi, whether for praise or a scolding no one but the governor-general seemed to know. Nine of his suite missed the return train to Vinh, and one old mandarin wept like a child because he could not believe that anything, six-o'clock trains particularly, started at the very moment these strange white people said it would. He had ·been barely half an hour late, yet the conveyance had left without him! From Vinh, by the way, all but the most important members of the party had to walk home with the coolies, while the king proceeded by automobile over the route by which I had come. Even the prince who had been sent to meet me at Muongyu had made this long tramp. Evidently the position of prince has its drawbacks in an ostensibly absolute Oriental monarchy—for that Luang Prabang still purports to be, with the French merely advisers to the hereditary despot. You may marry a king's daughter, but that does not mean that you may ride in the king's Ford. But the travelers by automobile gained nothing in time, for the whole outfit had to wait a couple of weeks at Xieng Khuang until the baggage caught up with it, while the undressed monarch remained officially incognito until his trunks arrived. On another occasion a French aviator took him to his forest-girdled capital in a single day.

There are ceremonial occasions when the king comes to the home of the *commissaire*, not by Ford but on an elephant, and is carried up the steps seated on his throne, white parasols over him and a great retinue about him. The French residents condoled with me particularly because I had not reached Luang Prabang *quinze jours*—a fortnight—earlier. For in the Kingdom of the Divine Buddha New Year's had fallen on April 12 that year, and with it comes the ceremony of the *petit serment,* as distinguished from the *grand serment* in November; that is, the swearing of fealty to the French and to the king—please note the order. Then the king rides on several elephants, I gathered, though probably only one at a time, and is carried through the town on his throne, followed by long processions of notables and mandarins in white jackets and *sampots* of every color of the rainbow, if not indeed several which it lacks. The common people, all the inhabitants of the capital except the Annamese and the French, kneel and bow their heads to the earth, for then they must not look upon their king, though it is said a few of the least reverent sometimes do get a glimpse *à la dérobée.* To judge by the pictures French residents had taken of the recent ceremony it was a sight worth coming two weeks earlier to see. In them all the inevitable cigarette was dangling from the king's lips; no ceremony is so solemn, no place so sacred, that *Tiao* Sisavang Vong Somdet Prah will go without his smoke. As many a photograph of the few remaining European monarchs and their possible successors shows, he has good precedent for thus openly indulging. Perhaps it is a sign of increasing democracy; or such informal and plebeian habits may always have been shared by kings, though our expurgated histories do not mention them. Cigarette or Ford, however, the people of Luang Prabang take their king very seriously, more seriously than he does himself. The native doctor at the government hospital, educated in Hanoï and outwardly entirely French except in complexion, kneels and touches his forehead to the floor before he gives medicine to one of the king's sons in the palace nursery.

CHAPTER XVII

FROM the capital of Luang Prabang I again broke all existing records by making the trip overland to Vientiane, the French capital of Laos, in five days. Normally this takes twelve, or at the very least ten, and every articulate person in the metropolis of the upper Mekong insisted that it would, or at any rate should, be quite impossible to accomplish this journey within the time I chanced to have at my disposal. Fortunately my ideal host of Luang Prabang, and a few others who had also seen our army in France, though neither he nor they had ever been in the Western Hemisphere, admitted that perhaps an American could do it, especially an American who had made the trip from Xieng Khuang to Luang Prabang capital in three days and a couple of hours. At any rate the *commissaire* and the king he served offered to do all they could to help in what they considered a very dubious undertaking.

Once again I loudly disclaim any desire to hurry; there is nothing I dislike more. Yet as between the misery of rushing and that of missing some important part of a country through which I am permitted to pass once in an existence I prefer to hurry. If only I had been born believing in the delightful doctrine of the transmigration of souls, with the assurance that there would be plenty of other lives after this one in which to roam through every corner of this interesting if often disillusioning old footstool of ours, no doubt I could be as phlegmatic and time-impervious as any Oriental back-woodsman.

This time I had to hurry because the fortnightly steamer from Vientiane was to leave on the following Thursday morning, the first day of May, and it was already midnight on Friday when I finished my packing, got my bamboo-protected diploma of decoration safely tucked away and a few supplies bought, and turned from a final social evening with the *commissaire* family into the last soft wide bed in some days to come. It was doubly too bad that I had not arrived *quinze jours plus tôt*—a fortnight earlier, for then I should not only have seen the ceremony of the *petit serment* but I might have avoided the hardships both of hurrying and of the overland trip. Perhaps I am getting lazy in my old age, or it may have been the climate, and the recent exertions of swift travel and royal excitement; at any rate I should have preferred to go down the Mekong with a floating village that had been prepared for a party of Frenchmen, and women, who had left just before I arrived. But for the automobile disaster on the way to Xieng Khuang I might have joined them; though I might not have reached Vientiane in time for the steamer, for with the water as low as it was then those floating villages sometimes take two weeks for the trip.

More exactly they are floating furnished houses, a combination of raft and boats surmounted by three or four rooms and servant quarters, two small windows on each side of the superstructure, and all those refinements one expects among such a comfort-loving people as the French. At high water these house-rafts can go down the Mekong in fewer days than are required for the overland trip through the jungle, though by no means so fast as I proposed to make it; and at all times this way of leaving Luang Prabang is so usual

that rarely does a Frenchman in the colonial service go by
land. In fact most of those bound for the capital come up
the river also, though that is a hard and tedious job—for the
native boatmen. An official salary continues unabated irrespective of speed. Upon due reflection, no doubt, an income
forever dragging at the heels of my personal exertions has
much more to do with my weakness for hurrying than have
any impressions on the transmigration of souls. This trip
down the river is not only comfortable, but interesting and
sometimes exciting, if not dangerous. The *piroguiers* say
prayers and throw food into the air, or place it, as well as
flowers, on the bow of the boat before passing bad rapids,
that the unseen spirits may be propitiated. But on board, all
the amenities of French civilization prevail, from whist to
the three-cornered drama, and romance has culminated and
domestic disaster befallen during these long and too restful
journeys.

By trail Luang Prabang is 347 kilometers from Vientiane,
nearly 225 miles, which was quite a distance to be divided
among five days, even with a slope of several hundred meters
in my favor. Luckily those twenty-seven kilometers of
"automobilable" road at the Luang Prabang end would again
be useful, and there were about a hundred, with a growing
tendency, stretching northward from Vientiane, leaving me
something like a hundred miles of mountainous trail to cover
on foot and horseback. To make matters worse it rained
most of that Friday night, so that when I set off before the
crack of dawn in the *commissaire's* Ford, the Annamese
chauffeur did not promise to make record speed. This soft
dirt road gets very slimy on the least provocation, and there
were slopes enough during that mildly up-and-down ride
through the forest to provide many a skidding place. By
seven, however, we were back at the village of Don-mo, and

if the local Frenchman had not been so slow in breaking away
from his *congaie*-shared breakfast in his thatched hut I should
have been off again at once instead of half an hour later.
Here I found three good horses, the *commissaire's* own
mounts, with comfortable French cavalry-saddles. One was
bestridden by a Laosian sergeant who had won two decorations in France, and one by another prince, *Chao* Thong Souk.
Related to the king and to my former emissary, *Chao* Duong
Chan, he was an equally delightful and helpful companion,
a bit younger and, I gathered, unmarried, a youth of most
pleasant manners and disposition, speaking excellent French.
He had left the capital the morning before, with the horses,
the sergeant, and half a dozen coolies carrying some supplies
and all but the nightly indispensable portion of my modest
baggage; now he and the coolies sped on ahead, leaving the
sergeant with me as guide and body-guard, while I passed
the unavoidable courtesies with the Frenchman in native
garb.

That over, we were off by a trail that had been cut more
or less directly through the jungle-choked forest, first across
the flat, then up a hill so steep that sweat ran even on horseback. Up this we had quite a job coaxing along the Laosian,
or Pwun, coolies, who wished to stop and eat even before we
overtook the prince and the others. When we did join them,
it carried me back to my old care-free vagabond days to hear
again the cry of "Kin kow!"—the Siamese equivalent to the
"Come and get it!" of our army cooks—like the voice of a
friend of long ago and far away. For the language of Luang
Prabang is almost that of Siam, the writing quite the same.
We ate and drank and pushed on again; one secret of breaking cross-country records is to give less than French attention
to the delights of the table. It looked strange to see men

wearing only a loin-cloth, and a dagger in a scabbard woven like a basket and held by a fiber band across the chest, putting up telegraph-poles; but the French insist on being able to talk to one another anywhere in Indo-China, and government ownership of telegraph lines has at least one advantage over the high-cost private system of the United States and China.

No wonder the Chinese drove out the Tai! Two Laosian carriers bore between them about half the load of one Chinese coolie; they made much less speed, not to mention their many complaints along the way, and at that they had to be relieved every few hours, or at least at the end of a day. For a load I had often seen one Chinese jog along under day after day of from ninety to a hundred *li* we had eight men; the cot or the valise that a Chinese coolie would carry at one end of his shoulder-pole, with as much at the other, and any odds and ends on top, these tropical fellows put in the middle of two long bamboos between two men.

Do not misunderstand me as blaming them; as between the two I should act like the Laosians. But the difference indicated how great is the adaptability of the human frame, for these men were if anything larger, sturdier, certainly more visibly muscular than Chinese carriers. They were like those muscle marvels one sees in gymnasiums and in physical culture magazines, no good at all beside the wiry little shrimp when it comes to real sustained hardships. Unless hunger or the white man drives them, the Laosians do little work; they are so happy-go-lucky in their tropical fairy-land that their rulers even have trouble making them keep their communal granaries filled against possible famines. For that matter, neither do the Chinese work unless driven, of course; but they have been incessantly just one jump ahead of starvation for so many centuries that they do not remember, cannot imagine, anything else, until their frames have grown to endure, on far less food, what would kill a plump muscular Laosian.

Up and down we went, through cool forests and over red-hot mountain ridges where too much good shade had been cut away for the telegraph line, with one hard river to cross. In this I lost the precious army canteen that had served me all through China, the sergeant having tied it to my saddle with a piece of vine. I might have known that there was no real string in such a land and been less careless about seeing my orders carried out. It was the most serious mishap of the trip, for without water always within reach even riding becomes a hardship in tropical jungle where streams are often hours apart.

While prince, sergeant, and I looked in vain for the rushing stream to cast up the canteen, the coolies went bathing. They were all of the "black paunch" tribe, as distinguished from the "white paunch," or untattooed ones, though it is not really the paunch that is decorated. The man of this branch of the Laosian or Tai race is never without his pants, even when he is stark naked. Nearly all of them are solidly tattooed in blue—invisible alas to the ordinary camera— from the waist to the knees, a wide tattooed belt with lacy ends about the floating ribs and a lacy effect like ruffles just below the bend of the knees. The design of this hip and thigh covering is always "lions" within squares with rounded corners, all touching one another, either as a protection against or to give the wearer the bravery of the lion. With the figures are mingled sacred texts, said to be Pali in Laosian or Siamese script. The priests especially are covered with these sacred writings, it is said, but one can never really know what is under the yellow robe. Women seldom if ever wear these tattooed substitutes for the Scotchman's kilt, say those who should know, perhaps because they are in no danger from evil spirits, or cannot be saved anyway. Some of the men also had red tattooing on the upper part of the body, red squares on the chest, all sorts of things on the back, though none of them obscene nor as crude as the tattooing on some of our sailors. One of my men was overrun with red lizards; some were whole picture-books or comic supplements or intricate signs of the zodiac. There was one fellow whose whole back was covered with a lesson in arithmetic or geometry, even trigonometry for all I know, as if a small brother or a schoolmaster had used him as a slate. Others had only one leg tattooed, generally the left, or both of them only on the buttocks, or simply the fronts of the thighs, or merely spots here and there, all according to personal caprice, taste, swank, or an attack of cowardliness before the job was finished. Unlike most tribal decorations of the sort this tattooing may be put on at any age, whenever courage is ripe.

I thought several times that afternoon that the men were going to give up entirely. They lay down in the road as if completely exhausted, something I had never seen a Chinese carrier do in all my two years of wandering in China; but finally we coaxed them at dark into a scattered little thatched town in the jungle on the edge of the clear rushing river that had made off with my canteen. The place was named Ban-long, with a waterfall to lull me to sleep in the basket-weave *sala* where I soon stretched out on my cot, for we had to start very early again. There was difficulty in getting men in time, and without the prince I should not have been able to get them at all. But he, working most of the night through the obsequious village head-man, collected twelve substitutes for our eight lazy Pwun or Nuong carriers, and we were off in the soft, black tropical night between two and three in the morning.

Two of the new men had gathered some sections of dried bamboo six or eight feet long to be used as torches, which made it to some extent harder than ever to see the way through the steep gullies cut deeply into the soil of the densest possible jungle and forest. Particularly was it hard going after the torches had gone out, much worse than if we had never had them, and for more than an hour we struggled in utter darkness over a devilish trail. It was one of those damnable trails that are always wading a stream, always the same stream at that, like a chatterer who can think of nothing original to say, and now and again climbing steeply up and down the bank of it. Daylight showed the dense vegetation deeply green, a land as far from China as if we were on another continent, and disclosed our dozen carriers to be Kha wild from the mountains, picturesque figures even in a land as out of the ordinary as Laos.

Instead of tattooed pants or cloth *sampots* these primitive fellows wore short cloth breeches like running-pants, and some of them had more or less of an upper garment also. They showed no tattooing, or at least very little, but rattled with bracelets of glass and other cheap materials, and had large earrings of all shapes, preferably not mates and if possible utterly unlike on the two sides of the same head. The few who did not have earrings put flowers or vine strings or leaves in the holes in their ears to keep them ready for more prosperous times. They had the eyes and the ways of the real wild man; yet, being former slaves, they were more docile than the Laosians or Pwun.

Of the aboriginal tribes driven into the mountains by the Tai invasion of nearly two thousand years ago, it is estimated that there are still a hundred thousand of these Kha and other more or less indigenous stock. Thus there is a great mixture of races under King Sisavang Vong Somdet Prah, besides the "black paunch" and "white paunch" Laosians of his own race. At Muongsing, chief town of the military territory, administered by Luang Prabang, in a far corner of Laos, a French official counted thirty-two races, each in its own costumes and with its own customs, at the weekly market day. The Kha are a hill people who made complete submission to the former rulers of Luang Prabang, admitting themselves slaves, and now they accept the present monarch as king and are loyal to him, lending help of this kind upon royal demand, though one could not hire them as carriers in the ordinary way. These fellows carried a slim ration of glutinous rice in little round baskets with a telescope cover, and some uncooked rice in a cloth at the back of the waist, just as do some South American Indians. At their sides hung a kind of machete, in a sheath made of half a bamboo with wooden strips across it, much the sort of thing a Boy Scout turned loose in the woods might contrive. They were as small as upper grammar-school boys, and though they looked hardier than almost any tame people, they were really even less useful as carriers than the Pwun. They prefer to carry by a band across the forehead, but as my baggage was not arranged for that method most of them were forced to endure one end of the stiff whole-bamboo that takes the place of the wiser springy split-bamboo or hickory carrying-poles of the Chinese—because one of them alone cannot carry a real load. Yet on the whole the long file of silent, rather anemic fellows made better time, thanks perhaps to their lighter loads, than those of the day before.

Unlike the talkative Laosians and in great contrast to the chattering Chinese these aboriginal mountaineers made hardly a sound as they plodded along. The language of Laos or

Luang Prabang is less noisy than the guttural up-and-down Annamese. The men of the first day had spoken with an almost English intonation; Kha speech seemed a bit more Chinese, with much rolling of the *r*. Some of them spoke Laosian, but with what my prince called a "malabar" accent.

In the mountains of Luang Prabang kingdom, high over several of which I passed on my overland trip, especially on this Sunday, one of the longest days of my life, the Kha live in as primitive conditions as in the days of Alexander the Great. The Kha villages I saw were the lowest type of human dwelling; filth and stupidity seemed to be the prevailing characteristics. All our romantic yarns about the simple life of savages leave us with the false impression that they are hardier than civilized people, and the writers rarely mention the dirty, the truly animal conditions in which they live. The Kha are as innocent of any idea of cleanliness as the lowest class of Chinese, in great contrast to the Tai about them, and it is not strange that they have more smallpox than the rest of the population. Some were so timid that I had to drive them out of their reed and grass huts into the light necessary for photography, just as one might drive some wild animal out of its warm but dirty lair, so timid that I had to manhandle a group of both sexes that came along the trail one day, before they gave up their temptation to run away without posing for my dreaded camera. In most of the huts grandmother and even skinnier grandfather were tending the third generation while the intermediate one was out in the hills in quest of a livelihood. Some of the villages had their basket-like thatched-top huts raised above the ground, like those of the other people of Laos; the commoner custom was to squat on the ground itself in a thatch structure like a flat wigwam. The women, and for that matter the men, were all naked to the waist, a disgusting custom in the case of the old women, whose breasts were as shrunken as if they were about to dry up and drop off. They gave one an unhappy reminder of how brief is the span of human existence. Old men and women alike had holes in their ears large enough to hold a cigar.

All day we climbed over great hills, one veritable mountain range. Most of these were densely wooded; yet in places there was little real forest, but mainly *brousse,* especially the swift-growing bamboo, because they had so often been burned off. Here and there patches of hillsides, even of mountain-sides, were being or had recently been cleared in this primitive way and were now more or less velvety-brown and strewn with fallen charred trees. For like the Miao the Kha still burn a new strip of forest whenever they wish to plant, cutting down mammoth trees just to clear the way, and leaving them to rot. What the coffin-makers of China would not have given for some of them! But I saw nothing planted, perhaps because the end of April is too early in these highlands, as in the grass-grown rice-fields we came upon lower down. Every now and then a tiny hut as bright as if it had been made of new straw stood forth in the middle of a recent clearing, the sleeping-place evidently of a pioneer husbandman too far from home to commute. Upland rice, needing no flooding, and other jungle products are grown by the Kha and the other hill people, and sometimes carried to Luang Prabang itself, though most of them merely grow enough to feed themselves.

The little clusters of very simple huts of the Kha were not near even this rarely traveled trail, but in places half inaccessible—and for many people wholly so—beyond valleys or great gullies across which they can look and see in miniature the very thin trickle of traffic and consider themselves in the world but not of it. One fancied they would not enjoy an apartment at the corner of Broadway and Forty-second Street. These hardly accessible places were often so far apart that it would take hours of climbing to call on the nearest neighbor. No wonder, when the cluster of huts of the nearest girl is across three chasms and two ridges, that the swain knocks her on the head and brings her home without further formality, to save himself the labor of courting under such onerous conditions.

In contrast to China, the only visible evidences of religious belief in these wilder parts of Luang Prabang kingdom are bamboo arrows and bits of woven wicker squares and the like, beside the trail here and there. These, the prince told me, were warnings, either that a trap of arrows had been set for wild animals somewhere on the path leading off into the *brousse,* or that a Kha village was engaged in formalities to which strangers were not invited. Docile as they are, the Kha have been known to kill even Frenchmen who have overlooked or persisted in disobeying these warnings. Hence little is known of the religion of this primitive tribe, except that it acknowledges innumerable genii, good and bad, and that there are many things the visitor must not do, many things taboo not only for the Kha themselves but for any one who enters their villages, because to do them would be to stir up the evil spirits to wreak vengeance on the villagers themselves.

Now and again there was a mighty granite mountain with the sheer sides of the sky-scrapers it dwarfed in size, clothed with as much vegetation as can get foothold, vegetation made wilder and more hardy by the struggles of its ancestors in such places. But for long distances there were no signs of man, except the twelve carriers snaking along through the tall grass, touches of red in their old and often ragged and

always weather-faded garments contrasting with their brown
bodies and their black heads bobbing above the vegetation.
We went for hours along a mountain ridge in a path all but
obliterated by a wild grass often horseman high, with many
splendid tiger-lairs. Great bamboos or trees had here and
there fallen across it, so that there was sometimes just room
for a horse to pass without its rider. These ridges opened
out great green vistas of scrub and forest on either hand,
and of the striking peaks of the long range over which we
climbed most of that arduous Sunday, to end in rain and
slippery going through ever hotter jungle. For at the end
we went down miles of trail steeper than any stairway, into
shaded jungle lanes, with rivers to cross incessantly, the
raging rivers of another watershed. Down, down, down to
what in season would again be flat rice-fields with earth
borders set like trays one above the other. On the swift
slope we passed an old man and a boy with a crossbow and
some pencil-like arrows, who were evidently stalking birds,
for all the rain. One of the pleasant things about simple
"wild" people is the companionship between old men and
boys—and, I suppose, between old women and girls when
they are off by themselves—so much closer and more congenial than among civilized people, where the old have usually
been educated entirely out of the naïve childhood point of
view and cannot forget how much more they fancy they
know than the child knows.

Unlike the Chinese the Kha coolies were not afraid of the
rain—or at least they were less afraid of it than of the prince.
They slashed down banana-leaves as umbrellas and kept right
on going. Yet a little rain makes a jungle journey quite different. The slopes become toboggans, the trails impetuous
streams or quagmires, rivers rise until they cannot be forded,
all vegetation wets whom and whatever it touches, leeches

sally forth to seek whom they may devour—so that we were glad indeed when the rain let up a little and insects began again to chirp and birds to whistle rather than sing their gladness.

We came down at length into the valley of Ban-napha, with a splendid sky-line of mountains behind it, and finally brought up, rather weary, at a *sala,* just long enough before dark so that we could hope to make preparations for another early start in the morning. Village chiefs bent low before the emissary of the king, putting their hands on their knees, for evidently this prince was not close enough to royalty to be worthy of the complete squat; or the people here may have been more independent. In turn the head-man of a village is a real boss—provided he has a very commanding way. This one of Ban-namon, otherwise known as Muong Kassy—*ban* seems to mean town, and a *muong* is a division something like the commune of France—did not have much head-man personality, or he had less respect or fear for princely orders than his attitude suggested; so that when I went for my daily conversation with my family I had also to wire back to the *commissaire* and insist on fresh horses, for none had been provided, the strict orders of the king and the French notwithstanding. I did not wish to abuse the stout animals of my good host of Luang Prabang, and two days over such trails was a good week's work for any horse, though I walked as much as I rode. But the threat to go on with them served excellently as a lever to move the prince to force the head-man to have other horses available in the morning. We knew they could be had, for we had seen not a few well fed ones in the fat wet fields of the little valley, along with water-buffaloes taking their ease in their beloved mud-holes.

I found my way back from the telegraph hut through the

A Kha home in the mountains of Luang Prabang

Grandfather and grandmother of the primitive Khas tend the children
while the intermediate generation seeks the family livelihood in the hills

Wherever his habitat, the water-buffalo is happiest when immersed to the
nostrils in a mud-hole

One group of the many Laosian carriers who bore my few belongings
across Luang Prabang

densely dark and humid night to a two-room *sala* with the usual springy floor of woven-bamboo splints, set in a wide grassy yard beside the trail. The sergeant, for whom this forced march was hard work, since he seemed to have brought back tuberculosis as well as a decoration or two from his war days in France, was worn out; and even the prince admitted that he was tired, though at his age one never really is. The Kha should have been most weary of us all, but they crawled obsequiously in on their hands and knees to bring me water in a section of bamboo or to hand me anything I asked or the prince sent them for. They ate jungle food that had very little in common with ours, out on the soft floor of the raised porch on which they slept. Somehow I was sorry to lose these simple picturesque fellows when we left Ban-namon.

We were off again at daylight, with poor native horses, as if the head-man had picked, or had imposed upon him, the leanest in town, and with somewhat less "wild" coolies. We had marched in the rain for barely two hours when the cavalcade all halted at another town, with an humble *sala*, for a lunch all around and to change coolies again, though those from Ban-namon had hardly gone five miles. Probably that was all the weak head-man could get them to agree to do; or it may be that certain towns are definitely stations on this overland trail. The prince had only to order the village chief, or the inhabitants themselves, to furnish new carriers, however, and they were soon there, though from then on we changed as often as we came to a village, sometimes two or three times a day. The coolies still seemed to be Kha, but they were men who had come into more contact with the outside world than those who had been with me all that strenuous Sunday, and they had lost some of the ornaments, simplicity, and politeness. Perhaps they were not Kha at all, for they had all sorts of tattooing, and some of them had raised welts, like the bush negroes of Dutch Guiana. Each man according to his fancy wore a kind of kilt that was really a mere strip of cloth wound about him from waist to knees. Now and then we passed a woman on a journey, in a costume in which she would not have been unnoticed on Broadway, wearing earrings, neck-rings, two bracelets on each arm, and a barrel-shaped strip of cloth from nipples to knees, and carrying her bed and belongings, consisting of a sack hanging down from her forehead and on her back a rolled-up grass or reed mat on which to spend her virtuous nights.

By this time I had fourteen coolies for what one Chinese would have, and often had, carried—except that the prince and the sergeant had a few things. With every change we seemed to get more carriers, as if they were bent on dividing the task until no one had anything much to carry; and at that they dawdled along, using every possible excuse to halt. Fancy me traveling with three horses and fourteen men, and most of my things in Hanoï at that! It was almost like a *safari* in central Africa, such as my wealthy fellow-wanderers can afford. Certainly the passive resistance of which we have been hearing so much of late is no new doctrine in the East; your Oriental carriers or servants were past masters at it long before Gandhi was born.

Or perhaps the fellows were spreading out my baggage as much as possible in order to give me more honor; for in Laos the importance of a traveler depends upon the amount of baggage he carries, the amount of trouble he puts the country to in getting him through it, even as in many other lands. The king never travels without an enormous retinue and tons of baggage, whether he needs it or not; and if he gets separated from it he withdraws into incognito. One reason the coolies of Laos cannot carry more is that each of them has a *musette* containing his personal belongings and food, a knife in a wooden scabbard, and increasing odds and ends, until by this time they had nearly as much baggage as we, in sharp contrast to the Chinese, who, in a land of strong and constant competition, carry almost nothing of their own. On this third afternoon two men carried nothing but the loads of the others, and they seemed to be getting weaker as their own loads grew ever bigger. If this kept up I should have to have two men for every one who was actually carrying for me and my escort.

Rocky mountain scenery increased, with great sheer cliffs, filtered sunshine on wet vegetation and brown. Here banana blossoms were a beautiful pink instead of the usual beautiful purple; there were giant ferns in great clusters, one leaf easily twenty feet long, a tree so covered with vines that it looked like an old ruined pagoda, cathedral aisles of damp and deeply shaded path. We crossed many streams; and— who says "wild" men do not know enough to invent speedy measures?—found on either side of them several of the two or three section pieces of bamboo which the people of this region use as water-pails. The men caught them up on one side of the stream, scooped them full of water as they crossed, drank as they walked, and threw them away again, to be picked up once more by the next comer from the opposite direction. All that third afternoon we went down with a small river through a narrow corridor of magnificent cliffs, everywhere wooded except on the sheerest faces—spires, turrets, pinnacles, stalactites and stalagmites, whole Milan cathedrals of jagged rocky peaks, scenery which, were it within two hundred miles of New York, would have a hundred thousand visitors every Sunday; yet here no one but a rare roving foreigner ever gives it a passing glance. Lost in the *brousse* and unnoticed, it was like many an unknown thing, deed, person, in the self-styled civilized world—far greater than others many times better known because they happen to have won publicity.

This region is noted for its leeches, especially during the rainy season that was now descending upon us. On that rainy Sunday afternoon the feet of my Kha were all bleeding, and were covered with the scars of what were evidently old leech-bites. These pests snatch upon the passer-by from the bushes overhanging the narrow trails, particularly after a shower; they get in somehow, even though one is not barefooted, soak the traveler's legs and socks in blood before he knows they are there, and he may be all day or all night in getting the flow stopped. In the middle of this third afternoon, chancing to pass a hand over an ankle, I felt a disgustingly soft lump under one of my high socks. Suddenly feeling the other leg with misgiving, I found it had two such unwelcome guests. Not far beyond we halted at a lonely little rest-house in the bush, and while the men rested and washed their feet, some of them put lumps of tobacco, such as they used in their long slim pipes, and other jungle leaves, on the three wounds; but at least one of them did not entirely stop bleeding until the next day. In the shade of the rest-house sat an aged priest in trail-worn yellow robe, who was making his way slowly northward, though he was old enough to be done with earthly traveling, at least in his present body. If that lasted, he hoped—or perhaps we should say expected, for he looked like too true a disciple of Gautama to be still burdened with the earthy desire we call hope—to reach Luang Prabang toward the end of the next month.

The last half of that day was bright with sunshine, through

A stream came down in strands of silver, flowed beneath the French highway, and dropped in a reunited river far below

The main street of Luang Prabang, with its covered market facing the king's palace and backed by the hill of Buddha's incredible foot-print

Perhaps there is really nothing incongruous about a saffron-clad Buddhist priest riding a bicycle

Influenced by their sisters across the river, the women of Vientiane cut their hair in the ugly Siamese fashion

ever lower jungle between mountain ridges, until we put up on the broad springy floor of a *bonzerie* in a place called Banphatang. The sergeant and his helpers from among the carrier coolies did our cooking out on the covered porch, some of the village round about languidly looking on; but the priests who occupied with us the building and porch showed little curiosity indeed. I had time for a shave, to the surprise of the beardless natives, then for a bath in the clear little river that raced past the town. Down this shot now and then a man with only a loin-cloth over his tattooed thighs, riding a little green bamboo raft, the only part of the craft above water being a raised place for a bundle of a few clothes and other belongings, and a jackfruit for possible hunger. Simple travel indeed! It made one long to be a care-free youth on the road again. Women were bathing children and themselves here also, especially now toward sunset, but no one came to stare at me, though in China there would have been a regular circus audience. Nor was this for lack of energy, for on the whole these were a well built, muscular, and very healthy-looking people, with few if any signs of a social disease so common in Annam and China and with almost none of the filth diseases. Though the women all showed their breasts and thought nothing of it, one never saw even a bathing man completely naked. So-called barbarian peoples, though they commonly wear only a loin-cloth or its feminine equivalent, are usually as exacting about having that in place as we are with our own clothing.

The uncrowded, simple, but commodious houses of these Laosian villages are always set well apart and high above the ground, back among palm-trees, banana-plants, and the like. They do not have to crowd together and save all the arable land for rice to feed too numerous mouths, for here a gentle Buddhism takes the place of an ancestor-worship so ardent that offspring must be had at any effort and cost. Most families have round or square granaries like huge covered baskets made of wide woven splints and covered by a big thatch roof, all raised off the ground out of reach of rats. The simple houses themselves were of similar materials, a ladder of half a dozen bamboo or pole rungs leading up to the big porch at one end, and close to the floor, a tiny window or two that can be pushed open to one side. Such a village is a thousand per cent more pleasant than a Chinese town, even when there is no public stopping-place except in the same room with slightly supercilious priests who sometimes break sound sleep with their devotions. There is an incredible amount of bathing and great quiet compared to densely packed Chinese existence. Such a village is like a country home in its atmosphere, while those of China resemble tenement-living on the worst of East Sides.

The half-naked women had little objection to posing for their pictures, though they were fully as modest as their sisters anywhere else. Some of them would not have commanded princessly salaries in a New York extravaganza, unless they could have worn masks; others were distinctly attractive even in features. Yet all this South Sea talk about the ease of life in such tropical Edens is largely nonsense. They take life more tranquilly, it is true, but they have a lot of hard work to do for all that, much more hard work than do the citified people of our own land who rave about this idyllic life on the sweat-band of Mother Earth, many things which they would in fact be quite unable to do; and there seems to be just as much force of public opinion, the same politicians and similar nuisances to make life miserable. If there are no coal strikes or gasoline despots, on the other hand there are leeches in a more literal form; though there are no trolley or motor cars, in compensation spring chickens sell at a nickel and really fresh eggs at two or three cents a dozen. A gentle unspoiled people, too obsequious by our standards, on the whole they lead a visibly happier life than do our own serious and hurried people of the West.

These Laosian villagers grow their own cotton, and the women spin this and the kapok of their great tropical trees on a crude wheel without a felly, then weave it on hand-looms into the garment they wear as skirt or wrapper. Beneath many a house, or under the projecting porch roof at the end of it, may be seen the lady of the family, in the usual comfortable and economical upper garment of nothing at all, leisurely engaged at her household tasks, while others, some of them far from ugly, sit in the shade beneath their pile-raised dwellings weaving their simple wardrobes, in rather striking patterns and of excellent wearing qualities, on the crudest of looms, with a stick shuttle that is thrown back and forth by hand. They hull their rice as it is needed, by stepping on the end of a long pole ending in a big wooden pestle, which falls monotonously into a wooden mortar, a hollowed section of large tree-trunk. These seem to be the chief occupations, but there are many others, as the traveler with time to watch their goings and comings during a few evenings will discover. As in southern China, the pan-basket in which rice is screened and prepared for cooking is made of bamboo splints, but they use clean water rather than any filth in which to wash it. The most hurried Laosian journey is a great relief from the putrescence, the crowding curiosity, the debauching superstitions of China. I thought I liked the Chinese, but I was less sure of it after this trip among the Laosians of gentle Buddhist faith.

The smallest village has a few Buddhist priests, the support of whom by giving them food seems to be almost the only religious practice of the lay inhabitants. The younger bonzes make the rounds each morning with their begging-bowls before the sun is high, and now and then a man or woman kneels on the ground as a priest pauses to perform for a moment or two some hocus-pocus in reward for the charity, and then turns abruptly away, as if to imply that the giver has had his money's worth. Begging is not looked upon as in the West, but as something perfectly natural, so that neither giver nor receiver seems to feel he is doing anything out of the ordinary. If I may judge by my two princely companions, all Laosian Buddhists say their prayers before going to bed as religiously as any Christian, nay, as any true Mohammedan. But they were more like people thanking a kindly benefactor with unforced gratitude than like men praying out of dread of a punishing God, and the true Laosians at least showed little if any of the fear of demonology rampant among the super-superstitious Chinese. No doubt nature is so gentle with them that the religion of fear, the dread and consequent attempts at propitiation of innumerable evil forces always waiting to do them harm, does not grow up within them.

On the other hand these naïve jungle-dwellers do not lack physical fear. They crouched at the trail-side raising palmed hands to me; in the more settled districts farther south long rows of them crowded against the wall of the mountain road, even turning their faces away, as if fearing a blow, which seemed to speak badly for their rulers, whether the old ones or the present French—or were they merely dazzled by my magnificence? When our pace grew too slow to be borne, I could always drive the coolies on by galloping after them shouting, whereupon they actually ran. But soon they settled down to an almost lazy stroll again, covering hardly half the ground of the incessant dog-trot of the indefatigable Chinese; nor were there by any means as many smiles and childish pleasantries as among those far harder workers and sufferers of many times greater hardships.

There were good horses at Ban-phatang, and no difficulty, at least so far as I was concerned, in getting three excellent ones for another daylight start. We rode on down a fertile but narrow valley, closely walled on either side by high mountain ridges that gave us the sensation of descending a corridor of mountains all that fourth day. But as in China there was no place purposely provided for a road; we were constantly climbing rice-field dikes and making our way haphazard across what would soon again be flooded trays of pale-green paddy. There was one very striking wooded precipice— which would have been still more striking if some of the myriad rocks that seemed ready to fall at any moment had done so just as we were passing beneath them. Little huts on stilts everywhere awaited the coming of laborers to the fields, lying fallow in grass now, but planted in July and harvested in November. There is no water for flooding at other times, because it does not rain enough, though with the industry and ingenuity of the Chinese they could easily harness the rivers that run away toil-less to the distant sea. But there is no need to do so, because there is no such crowding and consequent hunger as in China and its slender little offspring, Annam. In many parts of those ardently ancestor-worshiping lands, particularly in Annam, there are three harvests a year, as there might be here if this people went in as strongly for children.

On that fourth day I was riding well ahead of my party when I passed near a great jungle fire far up on a high hillside, probably set to clear off ground for new planting. Great masses of red flames, and brown, almost reddish swirls and columns of smoke, licked at the sky, and there was a great roaring miles off. At a mile it was like a battle on the Western Front, a constant irregular musketry that was evidently the bursting of the chambers of the bamboo and louder cannon-shots that were probably great trees falling.

Had it been in China or South America, this important trail between the two principal capitals of Laos would be impassable, in spots at least, which is the same thing so far as an overland trip is concerned, during the rainy season that was now upon us. Thanks to the few French overlords, however, mile after mile was welded together by many woven-bamboo bridges that sagged like bed-springs under our weight. Birds sang; a gentle air and people made the trip a constant delight in spite of the perpetual necessity of forever hurrying on. The French hope to colonize the Laos, but I hope that they fail; it would be a pity not to have any such virgin lands and simple peoples left for our children and our children's children to see.

Then the country grew tamer, the people more independent, perhaps because we were now outside Luang Prabang kingdom, where the prince, having only French backing to his commands, was recognized as the servant of an alien king. We lunched at Vang-vieng, where a lone Frenchman in jungle-torn sun-scorched garb, who was doing some sort of work there with a band of coolies, probably in connection with the telegraph lines, insisted on loading me down with a bottle of wine. The little I had brought had given out, and he was sure I could never complete my hurried journey alive without that prime necessity. We changed coolies there, and again, with more trouble and a longer wait than we had ever had before, at another village well outside the old kingdom, and brought up by sunset at a jungle *sala* in the wilderness, kept by a family sent there for that purpose by the French rulers.

CHAPTER XVIII

VIENTIANE AND BACK TO HANOÏ

WE were off again soon after dawn, by a road instead of a trail, a wide road that is by this time no doubt "automobilable," though a car could hardly have gone over it then even if one could have reached it, an execrable new road of five hours of incessant *montagnes russes,* constant ups and downs, and sadly in need of the shading tree-tops of the narrow trail. The prince and I left the coolies far behind before this torture was ended. The French are gradually pushing a highway from Vientiane to Luang Prabang, and the last few miles of this unfinished portion still had high earth pillars left in the cuttings to show how much was due the contractors whose coolies had excavated them with hand-baskets. I lunched with the Frenchman in charge of the road-building, whose Annamese companion had recently given him another hostage to fortune, in a house on a hilltop overlooking a great vista, that in some ways resembled a South American hacienda. Here I took leave of the prince, who had changed his mind and decided not to go on to Vientiane. It was plain that he would have given much to do so, but evidently either the French or the king, or both, had him under strict discipline. A miserable Ford, that had been waiting for me since the day before in order that my hurried trip should be crowned with success, cranked up, and at two we chugged away in great heat over the last 106 kilometers to Vientiane.

347

There was nothing of interest to me on this last ride, though there would have been for one who had not made the delightful overland trip. The people were much less attractive nearer what we are pleased to call civilization, especially the road-gangs. Half-way in we met the big automobile of the chief ruler of Laos, sent to find what had become of me, thanks to a strong but unwarranted suspicion that the Ford had broken down. Thereafter the view of the surrounding landscape was as from an airplane, and I reached Vientiane in time for a glimpse of it before dark, and dinner with the cream of the large French colony—with children as scarce as elsewhere.

Vieng-chan, which under the French has become Vientiane, is a place of former glory and power of the Tai race, capital of another of those kingdoms of earlier days. Its last great period of prosperity was between 1628 and 1652, after which civil wars dispersed its power and Luang Prabang declared its independence, though even in the eighteenth century it was still powerful. Then, in 1828, the Siamese destroyed the city, carried off and dispersed the people, and it has never been rebuilt. In 1893, when a treaty with Siam gave all Laos, all the land east of the Mekong and some west of it, to France, Vieng-chan became the French capital of Laos, as Luang Prabang is the chief native center.

Formerly Vientiane had a hundred and twenty magnificent temples, so well built that, in addition to many ruins lost in the bush, some still remain symmetrical and perfect in general form, though their beams have rotted away and the masonry has been exposed to tropical sun and rain for a century. There are some striking doors giving entrance to roofless ruins; within the falling shell of a temple near the *Résidence*, in which I was lord of all I surveyed because of the absence of the "résuper," two big Buddhas sit in the infinitely

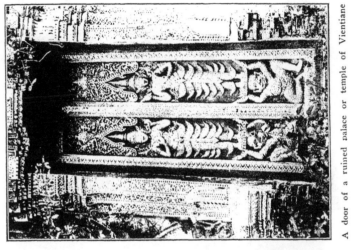

A door of a ruined palace or temple of Vientiane

This ancient monument in Vientiane, French capital of Laos, is the most curious remnant of its regal days

Within the ruined temple the Buddhas sit, in the infinitely patient
attitude of the East, crumbling away under the rains and disappearing
beneath the encroaching jungle

Though the French have brought automobiles to Vientiane, this ancient
form of conveyance still predominates

patient attitude of the East, though the rains fall and the sun beats down upon their coiled-serpent-covered heads, while the vegetation piously strives to clothe and hold them together as the mud and stone of which they are made crumble bit by bit away.

Perhaps there is really nothing incongruous about Buddhist priests in bright-yellow robes riding the latest style of bicycle, or even about women who, wearing only a kind of skirt, with at most a thin gay scarf thrown hastily over the breasts, indulge in the same frivolous form of locomotion. But these things are likely to catch the attention of the visitor to Vientiane, at least during his first day there. Though the French have brought a few automobiles, the humped-ox cart —a curious cart with a movable axle and huge wheels higher than a man—is still the more common type of conveyance. Vientiane has an avenue of flamboyants of which it is justly proud, and a lot of good French residences, with a pleasant woodsy atmosphere out of keeping with the solemn air of French officialdom.

Siam lies just across the river, and here the same race lives on both sides of the Mekong, though the Laosians on the other bank rarely come over to work for the French. From Muongyu onward all the men had worn their hair pompadour; at about the place the last Ford picked me up even the women, no doubt influenced by their Siamese sisters across the river, rather than by any world-wide movement to do away with the chief glory of the sex, took to cutting their hair man-fashion. At Vientiane the women on both sides of the Mekong have these absurd Siamese hair-cuts, each hair standing on end as if the eyes beneath it had seen a whole flock of ghosts, and as they also chew betel-nut to make themselves still more repulsive it does not matter that one can rarely tell the two sexes apart.

The steamer of the Messageries Fluviales got stuck on a sand-bank just as its picturesque Corsican captain was moving up to take on his passengers, so that I not only had the residence of the chief ruler of Laos entirely to myself for nearly twenty-four hours, but was able to take in all the sights and meet nearly all the hospitable French residents. The boat got away at 2:30 and was off down the river, leaving me behind after all my strenuous exertion to overtake it. But that did not matter, for the thoughtful French had planned it that way, so that their distinguished guest might finish his siesta and spend no more time than necessary on the uncomfortable craft. About four some of them leisurely set out with me by automobile and put me on board at a stop made for my especial benefit as far down-stream as the road then reached beyond Vientiane.

That afternoon we touched Siam and finally tied up at a place called Ban-along, where I slept well only because there happened to be room to set up my cot on deck, until we pushed off again at three in the morning. All day we steamed down the Mekong between Indo-China and Siamese jungles, now and then stopping at the French or at the farther bank. After the manner of the aggressive West, the French claim all the Mekong and allow no Siamese steamers on it. For centuries the Siamese and Chinese had most of the trade with Laos, which came and went by way of Siam; now the French are gradually diverting it, illustrating another of the advantages of protecting backward countries. No small amount of smuggling still goes on, especially in opium, and mainly engineered by the wily Chinese. Once some Laosian opium-smugglers who had tied up for the night at the Siamese bank were arrested by the Siamese police. The French, in keeping with their claim to the entire stream, made this a serious "diplomatic incident," and to-day the

Siamese can do nothing against smugglers and similar law-breakers until they actually step ashore with their loot.

A fierce storm at dark on the second day drove us up against the Siamese bank again, at a place that seemed to be called Ban-naqué, but we were off once more at daylight and pulled into Thakek while it was sitting down to its midday meal. There an automobile that had been sent over the mountains from Vinh was ready to carry me off at once, but there was time to spare and interest enough in this frontier post so that I decided to stay out the day. The chief French official was languid with fever and bored with life. The head of the police, on the other hand, with a still larger native family, seemed to enjoy this placid tropical existence, and when the sun began to show an appreciable decline he called a queer-looking official craft and took me across the river to Lakhone in Siam, the first time I had actually set foot in that progressive land in nearly twenty years. As far at least as this frontier village was concerned there did not seem to be any great change. The natives were of the same race and similar customs as those of Thakek, but had an air about them of saying inwardly, "Well, at least we are not subject to French nagging." The difference between them and their cousins across the river must be much like that between a bachelor and a henpecked husband—and their communal housekeeping bore out the same analogy. Leg-irons seemed to be no detriment to prisoners who wished to run after us and beg money to buy opium, neither of which things would be permitted their fellows in French territory, at least within sight of Europeans. On the other hand there is less active unkindness to prisoners on the French side.

There were a few games of tennis in Thakek when the sun was low, with even two or three white women among the players, and next morning comfortably after six I was

off for Annam. A native secretary of the ruler-in-chief of
Laos diffidently shared the back seat of the big open car with
me, and the Annamese chauffeur of course had his assistant,
confidant, and water-boy, for your Oriental driver will not
go without company, be it only to have some one as a re-
ceptacle for his conversation. It had rained and there was
much skidding between Thakek and Nakai; in fact at that
time of year automobiles usually cannot get through, and
ours was the last one that did before that season's rains settled down in earnest. I had never been sure of getting back
to Annam by this route—until I got there. Had it become
impassable as early as usual I might have gone on down the
Mekong by the incommodious Messageries Fluviales clear
to Pnom Penh in Cambodia, with a bit of railway about some
falls, and made all the journey from Saïgon to Hanoï over
again, unless I could have crossed the mountains from
Savannakhet, by a road still less likely to be "automobilable"
in the rainy season.

We turned up in time for lunch at a mountain shack in
dense forest in which the "résuper" of Laos and his wife,
about the most delightful people I met in Indo-China, were
roughing it for a few days with their small son. I trust that
the reader has not confounded Laos with Luang Prabang,
which is merely the largest and most western division of it,
its lone king decidedly subordinate to this lean and com-
petent Frenchman whose palatial *Résidence* I had occupied
in Vientiane. Besides Luang Prabang and the 5ᵐᵉ Territoire
that goes with it, and spacious Tran-ninh of Xieng Khuang,
there are half a dozen other divisions in this sparsely settled
territory ruled over by my *déjeuner* host across the plain
board camp-table.

The secretary and even the extra chauffeur remained at
the camp, as I should have done for the rest of that Sunday

myself had I suspected how good the road still was from there on. Besides, an elephant-hunt was at its height near-by, an unusually large herd having been discovered almost within shouting-distance of where we sat. In Siam it is forbidden to kill elephants, because they all belong to the king. So they do in theory also in Laos, or at least in Luang Prabang, but with the French ruling over it and the Chinese ready to pay high prices for tusks, the sacredness of the king's protégés is limited. In Canton we wondered where the carvers of myriad ornaments got all their ivory, rather suspecting them of relations with the local slaughter-house; in Laos one wonders where the hunters find sale for so many tusks. I heard much concerning the life of this region during that convivial *déjeuner*. Elands abound, and there are great herds of gaur, that wild cattle-like survivor from an earlier age which seems to be found nowhere else, a red-brown beast weighing on the average two thousand kilograms. There were at the camp half a dozen heads of this animal, shot within the past day or two, the foreheads unnaturally high, the female horns closer together than those of the male. The birds of these parts build no nests in the trees, because the monkeys, especially the black long-armed gibbons, steal their eggs. On the other hand partridge and quail, after building their nests in holes in the ground, roost in the trees as a protection against serpents

I thought often of that *résident* of a Cambodian province who broke five ribs by running into a deer, as we raced on eastward by a forest-walled road as unpeopled as if it had been built for my especial use, bounding every little while over bridges held by vine and woven-bamboo cables, the bridges themselves merely a larger form of wickerwork or basketry. To my astonishment and, I am sure, to that of the chauffeur also, we had no difficulty in making the entire run from Thakek to Vinh in a single day, though it had not been certain that we could even make it in two, and a day later we might not have been able to make it at all. But even nature seemed to take an interest in my record-breaking trip, and we were agreeably surprised to find astonishingly dry parts of the road which should have been sloughs of despondency. It was still only a little after noon when we halted at the village *sala* that had been officially chosen as my night's stopping-place, just long enough to tell the servants that their guest was flying onward.

Soon afterward we picked up a Chinese merchant from Yunnanfu, whose mandarin was nearly enough like that of Peking so that I astonished him by managing a meager conversation in his own tongue. He had two bullock-carts loaded with tigers—everything except the flesh—and many deer-horns, all valuable in the medicine-shops of his native land, especially the tiger-claws, to be powdered and drunk in wine by the faint-hearted, if I fully understood him. At the pace his native Jehus were making he would have been from ten days to a fortnight in reaching Vinh. I am notably soft-hearted, so when he and the chauffeur joined in coaxing me to let the Celestial go along with us, it seemed so much like making a man a present of ten days of life, more precious than money, that I succumbed—and for my pains was cramped for the rest of the trip into the off front seat, the left of course, usually occupied by the assistant chauffeur. The Chinese showed all signs of glee, even though he was of a race to whom ten days is no more than five hours, and paying off his simple Laosian bullock-drivers, he began loading his moth-eaten trophies into the car. I had miscalculated the loads, or fancied he would throw most of the worthless stuff away in order to ride with us; but no, indeed—I began to wonder whether he was even going to try to tuck the bullock-carts away in our maltreated conveyance. Of course the chauffeur got a nice little thing out of it—in fact he as much as said so in his hybrid Annamese-French, with a subtle hint that for this favor he did not expect me to tip him at the end of the run—and I have no doubt that all this had been cooked up between them when bullock-carts and automobile met two days before a few miles farther west. That would explain the extraordinary occurrence of leaving the assistant chauffeur behind; probably he eventually got his share of the grateful Yünnanese's gratuity, for walking back to Vinh during the rainy season.

There were some coffee plantations, among corn and rubber-trees, that afternoon, the largest of them belonging to the man whom I had met at Cuarao on the outward trip; but he was not at home—this home, at least. We had already begun dropping down out of the great Annamese chain, the road in places a serpentine succession of descending curves magnificently framed in vine-clothed forest and precipices, and by three we were back in Annam again, another world, with its groves of slender *aréquiers* climbed by betel-vines, its many villages surrounded by high thick bamboo hedges, its water-buffaloes of elephant and albino colors, its tombs and grave-mounds, its *bacs* and rice-fields, its joss-houses and red-saliva-splotched roads, its myriad people in parasol-hats, diamond-shaped breast-covers, necklaces of grains of gold, black cheese-cloth overcoats, gowns of the color of tobacco-juice, its endless files of pole-carrying coolies of both sexes and all ages; in thinly populated Laos the battle with hunger is not so keen that children need to begin their labors so early.

The Chinese and his tigers got off in the outskirts of Vinh, lest the government hear of the misuse of its official transportation, and the air was still more reminiscent of afternoon than of evening when I entered the same room of the French-Spanish hotel I had occupied when I first came northward along the Mandarin Road three months before. The chauffeur had protested that his orders were to drive me to the *Résidence,* but I felt that I had been overdoing French colonial hospitality, now that it was possible to provide for myself. Yet I was forced to dine with the *résident* who had driven me away toward Xieng Khuang twenty days back, and he and his wife succeeded in convincing me that they were really disappointed because I had not come to occupy the palatial room they had once more prepared for me. For one can have no secrets in Indo-China. The incessant telegraph keeps one's doings more in the public, or at least the official, eye than does the most flagrant of our yellow journals, and barely had I passed the village *sala* that had been officially chosen as my stopping-place that night than a telegram had warned the *résident* that the wild American was again breaking records.

In early May the Vinh-to-Hanoï landscape is a sea of ripening rice from which those great black-gray rock hills of strange form and varied strata stand forth like fantastic islands. I cannot remember ever having endured a hotter day than that train-ride. This was the hottest time of the year, just before the summer rains, utterly cloudless and often without the slightest breeze. With June come torrential downpours and cooler weather. There was a wind that day, but it happened to be blowing in the same direction in which I was traveling. Going south would probably have been pleasant riding; going north was intermittent torture. When we stopped, as fortunately we did often and sometimes for fairly long periods, the breeze from the south made life quite agreeable; but as long as the train was moving, sweat poured forth as from a fountain. Even when it blew to advantage the wind was as if it came off a red-hot stove, and all day long there was not a fleck of cloud in the sky to temper the wicked sunshine. Cattle lolled in groups under the trees; water-buffaloes, if they were to be seen at all, squatted in their mud-holes; but though "citadels" were waffle-irons and the highway a burning strand, men and women in their broad hats and coppery-brown garments still trotted in endless files along it and the by-roads that were mere thin lines drawn in a vast expanse of greenery; for rice must be had for hungry mouths no matter what the weather.